PEACE DRUMS
JESUS WAS A HIPPIE

Note: This picture is about higher consciousness, NOT Flat Earth Theory.

Built to Last

By Joan Rivard

Disclaimers:

Poems about governments or religions are listed in bold, with respect for those who would rather avoid those topics. Suggestions with poems are not meant to be guilt trips. They're intended for those who have time and would enjoy that kind of activism, and who often ask, "What can we do?"

Inserts about what Jesus didn't teach are placed below multiple poems, not to be repetitious, but so that this information can be included if poems are copied individually. Poems may be copied and shared for non-commercial purposes. Street people using them to get donations they keep is not a commercial purpose.

Religious material (or sacrilegious, depending on your point of view,) is not meant to make people believe or worship anything. It highlights the Golden Rule and the Bill of Rights and the goodness of ordinary people as solutions.

Situations on Haight Street changed dramatically in two years during the writing of this book, which is revealed as the story unfolds. The decision was made to present the earlier material as it was written, instead of putting it in past tense. The intention is that it should not be seen only as a history book, but as an urgent message about current events.

Joan Rivard

Sold on Amazon.com

Cover design by Haight street artist jessicabechtelart.com.

ISBN: 978-1-7353419-0-3   Copyright 2019   TXu 2-161-272

Peace Drums Publishing   peacedrums.org

TABLE OF CONTENTS

Busloads of tourists   1

The Haight   2

God's Eyes   3

Generation X   5

Lilies of the Field   7

Constellations   9

The Closest Thing to Coming Home   11

The Drum Circle   13

The Nomads   14

The Log   16

Freedom So Close   19

Love on Haight   20

Wendy Whimsey   23

Between Structure and Chaos   24

Making Friends on Haight St.   25

A Hippie Van   28

An Honored Tradition   30

Hope America   31

Another Love-Sick Hippie for God   34

Haight Hospitality   38

Rainbow's Porch   40

A True Love Story   42

Customers Only   44

Poisonous Laws   46

No Music Allowed   48

Kaneh: Free the Holy Oil   52

Hemp   54

A Precious Record   59

Stella the Hella   61

Pancake Breakfast   62

Putting Ourselves Back Together   65

Hidden Treasure   67

The Stoned the Builders Rejected   70

Tibetan Gift   73

Another Time   76

To Embody Christ Consciousness   79

What Jesus Didn't Teach   81

The Deluge   84

Gearless and Fearless   85

Homeless   86

Unlawful Laws   90

An Unforgettable Vacation   92

Blessed Beyond Belief   93

He that Is Not Against Us Is for Us   95

Heaven   97

He'd Have to Kill Him to Get the Dog   99

The Beast   101

The Right Spark   104

How to Train Your Dog   108

I Saw Where Jesus Was Hiding   109

On Hippie Hill   111

Jesus Clones   113

Puritans I   115

Breakfast at McDonald's   117

Married in Tie-Dye   119

A Happy Family   120

Puritans II   121

Big Red Hearts   126

Big Skulls   127

Branding Us   131

CIA Mind Control on Haight Street   135

The Mando Saved Him   138

Leftovers   140

Blessed Are the Peacemakers   142

Ducky's Mandolin   144

Lit Up Like a Saint   146

Other Visions   148

Cops at the Log   150

What's in a Name?   152

Riding the Bus with Two Dreamers   154

Mutiny Radio   156

Diamond Dave – "Defender of the Poor"   158

Peace In the Park   161

The Great Escape   162

Diamond Dave's 80th   163

A Case of Mistaken Identity   166

Things Jesus Said   168

A Fight Avoided   170

Too Far Out   172

Street Justice   174

Stay Awesome   176

The Pirate Queen   179

Pig Ears from Heaven   180

Dumped and Stranded   183

Flashes of Light   185

Machines   186

Haight Street at Night   190

Amal's Deli   193

The Red Victorian   194

When God Is In the Picture   196

A Different Level of Existence   198

If You Sow Love   200

Puritans III   202

Delicious Corndogs   204

Becoming Jesus   207

A Ten-Wheeler   208

Steel-Jawed Liability Laws   209

You Can't Beat Hate with Hate   212

Lambs Among Wolves   213

Grateful Dead Jesus Freaks   215

Love Thy Neighbor   216

Unstoppable   219

Street Love for Everybody   220

$1500. To Get Her Dog Back   221

Nightmare   223

Corporations   225

Can't Help Being Good   229

Hazardous Condiments   230

A Nudge from God   232

Puritans IV   234

The Poor   237

To Be Human, Be Humane   238

A State of Suspended Hope   242

Not Bored with Bliss   243

The Haight Street Pumpkin   245

The Light in Their Eyes   246

Trainhoppers and Gutterpunks   249

Resonating with the Holy   251

Witch Hunts   253

Our Two-Spirit Brothers and Sisters 2

America II: Spacious Minds   259

Nobody's A Bad Person   263

Fencing Off Heaven   264

Christmas Eve   267

The Fire Dancer   269

Joshua Tree   271

A Renaissance Man   273

The Return   276

No Loitering   278

Missing McDonald's   280

The Eye   282

History's Wonders   285

A Dream-Like Feeling   286

Bulldog and Shortstack   289

The Rainbow Way   291

Fresh and New   293

Painted Brown   295

An Outpouring of the Spirit   296

Love on Our Side   297

Something Different   302

Love Without Limits   304

They're Not Letting Us Be Good   306

A Terrible Loss   309

Microaggressions   310

Cages   313

Liability Gods   316

Old Sidewalks   318

Jackhammers   319

No McDonald's   322

The Only Elegant Solution   324

St. Patrick's Day   327

Chain Saws In the Morning   329

Dream On   331

The Spirit Is Willing   333

Bill of Rights Day   335

Bill of Rights   341

Police Sweeps   347

A Vortex   344

Business Improvement Districts   347

Approaching God   350

Shot Twice in the Chest   352

Liability Laws   356

Hit and Run at Haight and Ashbury   358

If the World Hate You   360

Orange Plastic Barriers   363

Looking for Something to Believe In   364

Bold Outlines   368

A Living Saint   370

Living the Dream   373

They Can't Erase Us   375

Seeds of Hope   377

"We Love You!"   379

Greater Works   382

A Renaissance Is Rumbling   384

Holding On   385

Connection with God   387

We're Still Here!   388

Peace Drums   389

We Will Survive!   392

The Peace Sign   392

List of Names   395

Author Bio and Photo Gallery   400

BUSLOADS OF TOURISTS

The hippies have been chased away from sitting on the front steps of the McDonald's on the corner of Haight Street and Stanyan in San Francisco, in the hippie capital of the world. It's too bad because their gathering there was a major tourist attraction, giving people a taste of what they were looking for in coming to this historic place. The tourists craned their necks and aimed their cell phone cameras from the tops of the double-decker buses.

These tie-dyed, scruffy-looking gypsies are some of what remains of the great vision of universal brotherly love ignited here in "the Sixties." Some of the older ones never left, having lived in and around this place for half a century. Since that time rents have skyrocketed, making this Bohemian paradise out of reach for most of the artists and thinkers who made it. They refuse to leave, some actually camping in the park if they have to in order to stay. About fifty to a hundred people live on the east side of Golden Gate Park, next to the Haight-Ashbury district.

The vibrant rainbow colors of their exotic accessories and decorations catch the eyes of the tourists as they peer down from the tour buses. Many of them wear some kind of costume, or just something to identify who they are and what they believe in. Their sparkly jewelry and bright feathers and ribbons contrast with the drab survival gear they must wear to attain this kind of liberty. The dream of brotherhood is very much alive on Haight Street and in the park, but life can be hard for the remnants of that magnificent time. These people are not owned by anyone, pay no rent, but most of them live outside.

There's a "No Sit and Lie Law." Along the sidewalks of the Haight where so many used to congregate and talk about saving the world, now there is mostly only concrete. An occasional panhandling musician, and the brightly-decorated stores and merchandize, are often the only outward clue that something extraordinary happened here. Still the tourists come and they gawk, straining to catch even a whiff of incense or the flash of a strobe light, or the sound of peace drums. They buy over-priced rainbow tie-dyed T-shirts and bring them back to their loved ones in various parts of the country and the world. This place represents for them something that dreams are made of.

THE HAIGHT

You can tell it's not an ordinary place. The ornate Victorian row houses in the neighborhoods around the Haight are incredibly beautiful, like jewelry boxes or elaborate cakes in pastel colors. Their curved balconies with rounded windows, their rich decorations of gold medallions and intricate carved edgings, are works of art. They have towers and turrets like a castle, arched bay windows, and round pillars like you would see on a temple but on a smaller scale. These houses were not slapped together like track houses. A lot of thought went into every detail of each magnificent creation.

The people who live here also have many dimensions, many bright and pleasing colors in who they are and what they believe in. Billy Preston and George Harrison lived here. The Grateful Dead lived at the "Grateful Dead House" at 710 Ashbury, and there's "The Red House" storefront above which Jimi Hendrix lived. We've often walked among giants on these streets. There are many reasons why this is a special place. It feels like home not only to those who live here but to countless millions, in their imaginations, as a spawning ground for the biggest peace movement the world has ever seen.

The colorful businesses on Haight Street express a multi-dimensional approach to life. Stores offer exotic wares with spiritual meaning, with names like "The Tibetan Gift Corner" and "Love of Ganesha."

A tiny tattoo parlor has an amazing storefront, done all in mosaic with gold and red mirror tiles. The designs on it look like flames, with wrought iron work on the windows in a shape like a radiating sun. Along the side streets there are big wall murals of icons like the Beatles, Jerry Garcia, Janis Joplin and Jimmy Hendrix, surrounded by swirls of rainbows and stars. The Burger Urge has a giant plastic burger over the door, red white and blue neons, and a decoration around the edge of the roof that says "PEACE" in foot-high letters, and "1967," the year of the Summer of Love. ☼ 🌈

It's not that rare for people to get together in a spirit of good will, but here in this historic place, it has deep meaning. This has survived from the wondrous renaissance called "the Sixties," when a whole generation of young people decided that the Golden Rule was the best strategy. Most of them did not worship the Prince of Peace, something he never asked for. Instead they went around saying the same things he'd said, often without even realizing it. Their obsession with brotherly love and peace, and treating people with respect, is something the violent world has hoped for. ⋛ 🖊 ⋚

A Volkswagen bus goes by, hand-painted purple with fluorescent rainbows and flowers all over it. The double-decker buses sway around the corner where the park meets the business district, looking like a ride at Disneyland. The tourists look at the "house-free" hippies with their dogs. The young people smile at the tourists and make peace signs. Often the tourists smile back and make peace signs too. ✌ ♡

GOD'S EYES

I first noticed them at the next bench over from the drummers' bench, a separate group of homeless youth who often congregate there. They wear different clothes than the rest of the people. Their clothes are darker and somewhat dusty, but serviceable for survival. Next to the bench there is often a large carpenter's cart loaded with sleeping bags, tents, and backpacks. Everything has to be watched all day so that it won't be confiscated by authorities or stolen (by outsiders). Most of these people have to carry all their stuff with them everywhere they go. This particular group has a communal arrangement going, in which their belongings can be placed in the cart and watched together by one person.

I've also seen them walking across the meadow to their camps in the evening, their many dogs trotting behind. They have a special silhouette and a special gait as they lumber by, each harnessed with a backpack loaded taller than their head. Some have a cat perched right on top of the swaying backpack, riding it as if riding a camel. There are dogs on leashes and dogs running free, and often there's someone playing a guitar as they go.

The way they walk is very strong, in sturdy hiking boots meant to negotiate the forest paths. At night they make their camps in the woods, sleep on the ground inside their tents. It's a way of life they're used to. Some have been doing it for years. The routine of putting up and taking down their small dome tent is the closest thing they have to a household. Their dogs make it seem like a family. Those who live alone treat their animals like partners. Couples treat them like their children.

Their clothes are not the pastel polyesters of the picnickers, but they have flashes of color. Tie-dyed t-shirts are a uniform, though some are faded and worn. Hand-made jewelry of natural materials, political and religious emblems, are their decorations. There are brightly colored fabrics of paisley or rainbow designs, feathers, bells, ornate pouches and belts. Their clothes are so much a part of who they are that they seem molded to their bodies.

They really dress like gypsies, wearing their valued items on their person where they can't be confiscated or ripped off. Someone who barely has enough to eat will invest in a very expensive and ornate coat made of rich materials, because it says something about who they are. They will wear that coat on the street and in the park, sleep in it every night on the ground. The edges will become worn and some buttons might be lost, but the coat will still make the wearer look and feel like a prince. A dark brocade can mask any stains.

A beautiful young girl with pink and lavender hair walks by with a powerful stride, easily carrying a tall backpack with a lovely black and white cat perched on top. 🐈 She's dressed like a fashion model in an ornate short skirt and bright multicolored tights. Her attractive boyfriend walks beside her, also with a backpack, his long loose hair blowing in the wind, both hands holding the leashes of their two dogs. She has tattoos on her arms of butterflies, which symbolize metamorphosis, and of peacock feathers, which are supposed to be God's eyes.

GENERATION X

Like plants pushing through cracks in the sidewalk they have grown,

    so strong that hopeful dreams still stir within them like great seeds.

They came from broken homes and broken dreams

       and a sick nation that had also lost its way.

The advertisers called them "Generation X" or "Y" or "Cybergeeks,"

     and "mooks n' midriffs, iGens," and used tricks to sell them lies.

They made them clothes of black covered with skulls that made people afraid,

    or baggy pants which gang members allegedly employ to hide big guns.

These kids have been exposed to TV brainwashing totalitarians made
to twist their minds to give up hope and think that other people are no good.
They saw dead things on every channel all their lives since they could talk,
and twisted, sneering cartoon characters designed to make them hate or fear.
They ate fake foods with dyes and chemicals that made them sick.

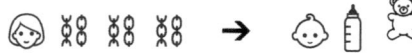

They played with video games that could be used to teach them how to kill.
When they were born, they got an artificial substitute for mother's milk
and hugged stuffed animals instead of moms at their three jobs.

They didn't have advantages like those a generation past.3
Their college dreams vanished because economists made shady deals.
They can't travel the world by hitch hiking the way others have done
because it has been made into a crime.
The small apartment that they crave is out of reach,
a thousand bucks for each small room.
A job no longer pays a living wage; three are required to survive.
You can get jailed for downloading a song or 1000 other phony crimes.

Built to Last

Libraries close, jobs go overseas, and insurance makes driving out of reach.

The icebergs melt and media brainwashing becomes more weird.
Despite all that these young people play peace drums in their tiny
                                        rented rooms,
    as quietly as they are able, so neighbors won't call landlords or cops.
Christ's dream of peace still stirs in them, though most don't call it that.
      Respect for all the world, not lies and greed, is what they want.
That spark of hope on each bright face, the brotherly love that Jesus taught,
    could be what's needed to ignite again the torch of Liberty.

LILIES OF THE FIELD

People look at them sideways as they pass by along their way toward the drum circle. 🤔   These street kids are the dustiest, wildest-looking bunch. They look as if they've lived outside for years, and they have. They share a rugged existence in the forests of Golden Gate Park. Many of them have small tents which they put up each evening and have to take down early in the morning, or else rangers might come and, according to legal guidelines, confiscate everything. Diaries, artwork, precious family photos, gone.

If someone leaves their tent even for a few minutes, they're liable to come back and find all their stuff gone. Most rangers are pretty nice about this, but some are not. The loss of tent and sleeping bag and warm clothes in this cold, foggy place can be devastating, but most of them are strangely calm when it happens. Many say it's happened to them several times before. It's a very rough way to live, but in the middle of unbelievable challenges and occasional really hard times, something spiritual happens here, though some might not call it that.

Many of the homeless youth and others who camp in Golden Gate Park are real nomads, living a very hard life but a very free one. They do all the things that the old hobos used to do, have the same skills and knowledge and some of the same social traditions. Many of them "ride the rails" all over the country, since hitch hiking has been made illegal in many places. They do this with their dogs and heavy camping gear, some of them in wheelchairs. They have incredible grit. They are as wise as serpents and most are as harmless as doves.

They live in the moment and close to the bone. They experience cold and heat and sometimes even hunger and a thousand other hazards out there on the road or in the park. They can lose everything at any time, through confiscation by authorities or theft or even by something as silly as forgetting their stuff. They can lose their dog for inability to pay fees and fines. As they move from state to state, they can be arrested for warrants or tickets they didn't know they had, since they often don't get their mail. They live on the razor's edge, but they live a lot like the lilies of the field, like Jesus suggested. Many of them don't call themselves homeless, but "house-free."

There's something uniquely satisfying about the hippie culture, whether here at this epicenter or in individual lives around the country and the world. It's full of invigorating dreams, bright colors and bright thoughts. A certain solidarity, an unspoken understanding, has existed from the beginning among the long-haired Pacifists. Here at the Haight more than anywhere else, it's expected that people take care each other, love each other. That's what "the Sixties" was really all about.

CONSTELLATIONS

It was some of the most beautiful tie-dye being sold on the Haight. The colors vibrated with rainbow lights. The rich, heavy cloth had complex patterns of starbursts, and areas that looked like constellations in the universe. The cloth seemed alive and to flash and vibrate. It was hard to imagine how such amazing effects could be made with simple tie-dyeing, and it turned out that it wasn't the only method used. Some of it had actually been painted on by hand.

The most gorgeous items in the Haight Street Bazaar were on a deep turquoise background (Zeyma Collection). There was something uplifting about the blue cloth and the electric rainbow patterns. There was something in it that spoke about liberty, maybe ecstasy. There were even political statements in it. Only someone who believes in freedom would wear these clothes. Only someone who has a positive view of mankind, and a hope for the future, would dress in rainbows.

I tried on a skirt, a top, a sort of long vest, and an intricately-made long-sleeved jacket, all of the same material. The hems of each were uneven and fell in graceful layers one over the other. The skirt hung down in points, some parts shorter than others, so that I still wore a full dark blue skirt underneath that reached the ground. These clothes were made to make an ordinary woman feel and look like a queen, not a drone or a peon. That's another thing that's real political about them.

Looking in the mirror I felt transformed. These clothes were not only comfortable but also very flattering. They hid all the flaws in a woman's figure and directed attention toward her face. There was no forced display of sexuality in them. At the same time, they were deeply feminine. The cloth was heavy and seemed to embrace me. I could feel the weight of the rich layers flowing over me. This is what I wanted to be when I grew up. Looking back at me from the mirror was a person who was living what she believed in with confidence. As bright as tie-dye, as loud as peace drums, the ideals these clothes stand for are powerful. They're the same concepts Jesus talked about when he said to love your neighbor as yourself. 🕊

I had no choice but to put down a large sum of money. It was an investment in what I like to call "the Movement," that push for peace and civility and kindness that ignites millions around the globe. The Golden Rule screams out from the beautiful colors and images the Peacemakers like to adorn themselves with. The Bill of rights is evident in the loose, flowing styles that don't constrict like the Establishment's manufactured clothing.

AMERICA HAS A GREAT RESOURCE AND A GREAT GIFT THAT IT'S NOT USING. The long-haired Pacifists and their culture are uniquely American. Much of the beautiful rock music about saving the world came from our own garage bands. The same concepts Jesus taught about love and forgiveness and cooperation fill up the travel-worn journals in the backpacks of the "house-free" youth, more than most people would ever imagine. The desire to make just laws and treat people with respect is at the heart of what could be called the Consciousness Movement. The notion that people should be free and not always hemmed in by artificial things, is the same belief in the pursuit of happiness which the nation's founders embraced.

🎒 🗒 ⚖️ 📕 🗽 📓 ♡ ⌛ ‼️

How often have so many of the rich and poor, all races and different kinds of people, gotten together the way they do when it comes to this? We should be proud that this rare historical phenomena is happening so powerfully in our country, in our own people. The lurid media images put out to demonize them, the sleaze, are not them. The weird bands with mean faces, the emphasis on sex and things that most of people aren't comfortable with, were added by others. The Golden Rule, plain and simple, is what these people are into. Negative propaganda about them is as different from who they are as Paul the Apostle's violent doctrines are different from what the Bible says Jesus taught.

It was those raised on the American Dream at the time, with mostly secure families and homes, who'd had the confidence to advance such vital concepts. They were proposing that mankind should finally free itself from the kind of dominance imposed by alpha apes in the jungle. They were actually saying that people were made for better things than to go after each other's throats and scrape by just to survive. What Jesus taught, when looked at separately from what other Bible writers added to it, is merely the way civilized people behave.

Dressed in all this I walked out into Haight Street amid the tourists and the "house-free." I had not wanted to change out of the new clothes and had instead placed the ones I'd been wearing in the bag. Down the crowded sidewalk I moved, layers of rainbow cloth billowing like sails as I walked. The reaction to my clothes was instantaneous. Everyone smiled or flashed a peace sign as I went by. The tourists took pictures. These bright colors, the free flowing of the rich folds of cloth, meant something to them that moved them deeply.

THE CLOSEST THING TO COMING HOME

Many of the street kids haven't seen their families in a long time. In most cases it's just because their families are too poor to take them in or don't have room. Many were foster kids. Their "brothers of the road" have become their family. I want to make the point that when I write "kids" in this book, I'm not referring to anyone under-age. Most of the people who refer to themselves and others like them as "kids" are in their twenties or thirties or older. When writing about "youth" or "young people," I include any elderly among us, who tend to be very young at heart.

Though nomadic, their informal networks stretch nation-wide. They have their gatherings at music festivals and rock concerts, where most congregate in the parking lots and don't even buy a ticket to go into the show. Some of those events, which mostly include concert goers who are not nomads but believe the same way, have a lot of the feel of the

religious revivals of the 19th century. ☆✦ 🕊 ✝ ☆✦ 🎷

Golden Gate Park is one of their favorite stopping places, because of the sweet feeling of community that exists there. This happens of course in other places, and in fact it often happens almost any place where people gather in a friendly way. But there's something special about the way it happens here in the city that spawned the Sixties peace movement. For some of these rootless nomads, coming here can be the closest thing to coming home. These are our own homeless children who ended up here when they had nowhere else to go. In getting to know them I found that economic conditions, broken families, job loss and high rents are the

cause, not anything wrong with them.

Sitting on a log next to the tunnel can be for them almost like sitting on the couch in a familiar living room. 🛋 Sunbathing on the grassy area below the Haight Street entrance to the park, called "the Horseshoe," can feel like being in their old backyard if they close their eyes. The sound of the fountain at the pond can be reassuring and familiar. This is where old friends are reunited, or are heard about from others who've seen them on their travels. On these accustomed paths, where music, pot and stories are shared openly, friendships and romances are rekindled.

THE DRUM CIRCLE

Walking into Golden Gate Park I could already hear the drums. The rhythmic sound echoed all across the meadow, where so much happened in the Sixties and is still happening. Spectators watched as a motley group of about two dozen drummers, some of them strangers who'd never made music together before, performed in perfect synchrony. They picked up on each other's signals like trained musicians, with some inner unexplained communication. The people listening also seemed tuned into the same force that moved the drummers' hands. They too swayed and moved to the heartbeat sound.

It was more than entertainment, more than art. The drummers were swept up by inner visions. Half a dozen congas gleamed in the sun with their smooth fiberglass sides, and as many Djembes, carved wooden drums. A man kept a strong rhythm on his gorgeous drum, its smooth white top tied to its base with strings of heaven blue. Another had a large beige drum that made a powerful sound. There was a double-headed drum placed on its side, struck with sticks on either end. Its ancient African design was held together with gleaming modern metal clasps. There were two snare drums on a stand that a Native American played with drumsticks. A homeless man played a white plastic bucket.

A beautiful stately woman played an amazing drum that was painted rose and gold with swirls and butterflies and suns. She wore a dress with musical notes on it, silk flowers in her hair, and a small rhinestone tiara. Comfortably installed on the park bench that was the focal point of the circle, it was obvious that she was an important member of the group. She closed her eyes, her strong drumbeats setting the rhythm of the circle

A young man struck with passion a drum he'd brought on a bicycle, carrying it on his back. Another beat furiously on a drum that was a work of art, made of dark wood. It had cobalt blue strings and brass studs around the base, and a ring of what looked like carving around the bottom but was actually a strip of recycled tire tread. It stood enthroned on a gleaming chrome stand, where he played it standing up all day. His hands were so damaged from drumming that he wrapped them with white adhesive tape around palms, thumbs and fingers, on both hands.

Other instruments were brought, an electric keyboard that made the place sound like a church. 🎹 There was a cowbell hit with a drumstick, and also two long horns, about six feet long, which were actually didgeridoos, but which were fluted at one end so that they looked like the kind of long horns ancient religions used to call people to prayer. Two men sitting on chairs blew into them with all their might, making an eerie, vibrant sound that was amplified with a portable amp. One horn of ebony wood was decorated with semi-precious stones. The other was made of what looked like horn, wrapped with gold bands around the base.

The drummers played all day, until their hands were raw, taking short breaks. They played into the sunset when it started to get really cold, their fingers numb. ❄ The young man packed up all his stuff and his big drum on the bicycle and started off across the field. But then, hearing some irresistible beat and unable to pull himself away, he came back. He unpacked everything that he'd just carefully arranged, the drum, the drum case, basket and backpack and his folding stool, and set them up again, and joined the circle like before.

THE NOMADS

Ducky was one of the first real nomads I met. The first time I saw her she was panhandling on Haight Street, a beautiful young woman in a wheelchair, with cancer. She was accompanied by a couple of her "brothers of the road," acting as her helpers. Her large brown dog lay curled up under the wheelchair on the sidewalk. Her stuff lay in a large pile against a light pole. Her radiant smile drew me as I walked along the sidewalk lined with whimsical shops and restaurants.

Her dark curls and dark brown eyes contrasted with her light skin. There was benevolence in her face, and what actually looked like a kind of peace. There was something very appealing about her. She asked for nothing, but I gave her a dollar. She was happy to start a conversation. Not much was shared there on the street where it was so loud, but I saw her later sitting on the ground with a group of about six people and as many dogs, in a shady dirt area just inside the park entrance. I walked up to them and they invited me to sit with them, probably because of the way I was dressed in tie-dye. 👋

That patch of ground is supposed to be planted with grass, but it's so popular with people and dogs that there's nothing there but finely-ground dirt. I sat down there with that same road-worn group which tourists avoid when they choose what to take pictures of. It made me proud to be invited to sit with them. I sat right on the powdery dirt, on the lining of my skirt. A beer and a joint were offered. Taking a swig and a hit felt like a holy communion. A silent connection was made. 🍾 ♣ 🚬

It was a beautiful afternoon and it was pleasant to sit in the shade and share stories. Ducky didn't explain why she'd chosen that nickname, or when someone had given it to her. Out on the road most people use "street names." It's an easier way to remember who somebody is and to identify them to someone else who might ask if they've seen them. The nicknames tend to describe something about a person or to refer to some event or trait they're known for. Plus, some of these people might be running away from one thing or another. They might prefer not to be identified by the tag assigned to them by the world. Like Native Americans they like to choose their names or to have the names come to them in a spiritual way.

Ducky was estranged from her family and spoke wistfully of a little sister. They have all lost ties to their loved ones in one way or another. Most of them just don't want to be a burden on their families, who are also struggling financially. Their only family now is the amorphous group of people who periodically live in the park as they travel around the country. This gritty patch of dirt under this tree is the closest thing they have to a home. Amid their neat backpacks and rolled-up sleeping bags and dogs on leashes they look like they're just travelling through. It takes a while to realize that they actually live here much of the time.

My bright tie dyes contrasted with their olive drab road clothes. Sitting there with them, I felt honored to be allowed access into this very special space. There were no walls, but this was their living room. Like hippies did all over the country in other living rooms, they were talking and arguing about how to fix the world. It didn't take long before they started telling me about the love they have for each other and for the other people in the park and on the Haight, how they all help one another. The common greeting among them is "Bro."

THE LOG

The east side of Golden Gate Park is where most of the people camp, because of its proximity to stores and McDonald's, Whole Foods, and other facilities. At night they find hidden places to sleep in the bushes, in the hollows of the hills in the forest. During the day they hang out near a grassy area called "the Horseshoe" that's at the east entrance of the park. A little further in there is a beautiful man-made pond, next to a paved walkway that passes through an ornate stone tunnel. If you look carefully through bushes and trees, you can see cars and traffic rushing by on the road on top of the tunnel.

Right next to the artful doorway of the tunnel, beside the walkway and across from the pond, there's "The Log." It's where groups of people always gather, the rough equivalent of the old village green. There are actually many logs there that people sit on, lining the side of the road for over a hundred feet. There are other logs strategically placed all around the park to sit on. But when people say, "We'll meet you at the log," this place is what they mean.

The artificial pond across from the log is spectacular. It seems to evoke every dreamscape with its towering trees, rock-lined miniature inlets and bays amid sparkling waters and exotic plants, some of which look prehistoric. Individuals like to sit on parts of land that jut out into the water and play instruments or draw or write. A line of people sitting on the logs across from it enjoy an inspiring view, and the sound of a little fountain from the mouth of a small concrete frog on an outcropping, next to a miniature pagoda. You can smell the water in the oxygen-laden air. Someone might be playing a mandolin, and someone else a guitar.

A graceful young woman in a bright red flowered scarf and a long full skirt looked like a real gypsy with her black curls and the rings in her lip and nose. The vision of her against the embankment amid sun-dappled oak branches was reminiscent of a Romantic-era painting. A man sat on a log stroking two dogs. He told me he's called "the Dog Whisperer" because dogs like his nails. The two dogs were zoning out under his very rough hands and claw-like hands.

The friend with him talked about riding the trains. He said the gondolas were nice because you could be hidden there, but it was good to have a tarp because there was no shade. You could get "windburn, sunburn, every kind of burn." He said the boxcars were ok, but they could be hot and humid and full of mosquitos.

He and some others discussed how to stay alive on a "suicide porch," a sort of steel balcony at the back of a train where you and a dog could sit, but you had to be real careful not to fall through the big hole in the floor that went right over the tracks, and not to let your dog fall through. He said he tried not to look like a scumbag train rider, but one time he came off a coal train covered in grease. He said he looked real bad but had been able to hitch a ride anyway, because he had good energy. 🚂🚃🚃🚃💨

A youth was trying to corral an orange kitten. He had to watch it constantly because it had no leash. 🐱 He told a story: He was at a pancake breakfast of a men's club and they wouldn't give him a pancake. But he ended up getting more than anyone, out of the trash can.

😊 🗑 🍽 He had beautiful eyes, was worried that he was not educated enough. He called people "Bro." He said he was hoping the Movement would re-start. He didn't have to name it because we all knew what "the Movement" is. It's a deep connection between people that you don't have to join or send money to.   ✌ 🎩 ⋛ ❤ ⋚ COOL 💨

The long-haired young man was carving a heart out of a piece of soapstone, using an ancient method of rubbing it with bamboo and horsehair. He told another story: He went to a restaurant in Colorado and ordered a large pan of lasagna because he was real hungry. All they served him was a tiny portion with leaves on it from a tree outside, and it had spit on it on top. He said that he'd paid for it anyway and that he ate it without saying anything (after taking the spit off.) Afterwards he made sure to thank the cook, because as they say, "what would Jesus do?"

FREEDOM SO CLOSE

    A curved wall of rough stonework culminating at the log opens to a short tunnel that goes under a road where people drive back and forth to work. There are fancy wrought-iron gates on each side, and on the embankment are giant trees, with pink flowers at their base with big flat round leaves. Inside the tunnel on the ceiling there are fake concrete stalagmites and stalactites like in a cave, like they make at theme parks. When it rains, sometimes the drummers set up in there and make their music in its echo chamber.

    On the other side of the tunnel from the log there is another sitting area, and other logs, under some trees. There I joined a group of people enjoying the morning. A Native American there said he was a member of all tribes. He greeted me with, "Hi Angel." He had on a glass turtle necklace and said the whole of North America used to be called "Turtle Island."   His gorgeous shirt of bright light blue tie-dye had a big rainbow heart on the chest, and a rainbow design on the sleeves that looked like rays. He said he had a whole collection of tie-dyes and showed me a phone picture of some rainbow pants. He said someone had just given him a skateboard.

    There was a retired man named "Avatar." He said the name means "God in Spirit" in different manifestations.   He carries in his backpack five books about five different religions.   There are beautiful Celtic designs tattooed on his arms. He said he likes to go on spiritual journeys, is celibate and uses no alcohol, though he smokes a little pot. There was a boy named "Holiday Chris" because "every day's a holiday." There was a woman named "Change" who wears dreadlocks and also the wisdom of the ages on her face. She told me that she feels caged in a house and prefers to be "house-free."

A dog started to chase a cat and we talked about whether the dogs are dangerous, a lot of them Pit Bulls. Everyone agreed that they could be sweethearts. Change told a story about how they were camped in the Northwest with some people and somebody's dog caught a deer and broke its neck. She said they all cooked it and ate it for a week. No sense wasting it, although I'm sure a lot of them were vegetarians.

A girl with pink braids and a purple hat petted her dog named "Static," a majestic beige and cream Husky with amber eyes and huge, thick fur. A guy named "Empty," wearing a rubber chicken hat, had a golden-brown brindle bulldog wearing a sea-green bandana. He said it takes more muscles to frown than to smile. A young man proudly wore a long coat of many colors that his mother had knitted for him from multicolored pastel rainbow yarn. I'm sure there isn't another one like it in the park and probably in the world. His fashion statement was completed with a black top hat.

The log and everything around it is an end-to-end tableau with animated, laughing people, maybe a glimpse of what Paradise would look like. Cars go by over the bridge, including rush-hour traffic in gridlock, employees hurrying home trying to get a little bit of free time in what's left of their day. Little do a lot of them realize that freedom is just a few feet below them under the bridge, so close.

LOVE ON HAIGHT

The rounded pillars of the tie-dye store "Love on the Haight," look like something out of a Disney fairy tale cartoon, with painted pink, yellow and blue diamond shapes that seem to glow. Between each big arched window, on top of each pillar, there is an amazing geometric blue flower design that also seems to glow. Along the edges of the arches there are painted three-dimensional borders, one turquoise and one orange, adorned with green or pink diamond shapes. A thin black outline makes the borders look like stained glass. The centerpiece is the word "LOVE" in big letters under the main arch, with a red and blue heart with a lightning bolt through the middle. On the sidewalk on the Masonic side are two dozen of Haight Street's big red painted hearts.

♥ ✧ ❋❋ LOVE ❋❋ ✧ ♥

Inside the store there is an explosion of color, from the floor with a brilliant floral pattern to the ceiling with an amazing display of light. This is where you can buy a rainbow tie-dyed t-shirt  with "Love Is the Answer" on it, or a clown nose, 🐼 or a tie-dyed top hat. 🎩 The hand-made psychedelic fashions they sell are wearable art. The fabrics are so bright you might need sunglasses but that's no problem, because you can also buy heart-shaped rose-colored glasses on Haight Street.

The store is part of an effort to "revitalize Haight Street by bringing back the color, creativity, and consciousness that this street is historically known for." Their website says, "WHAT HAPPENED ON THESE MAGICAL STREETS SHAPED WHO WE ARE AS A SOCIETY TODAY." It says people are "unique entities of unlimited potential that are one with all."

🕊 🗽 🎩 ☮ [COOL]

It says the staff want to be "Rainbow ambassadors to the Haight-Ashbury to spread "Rainbows, Sparkles, Peace, Love and Kindness." Everyone who comes into the store gets free glitter. There is a sign that says, "Never be afraid to sparkle." The beautifully-dressed staff like to greet people out on the sidewalk, often sharing thoughts about what the Haight represents. Two brown dogs live at the store, one big and one little. The little one is called "Dr. Dave," named after the beloved founder of the Haight-Ashbury Free Clinic, Doctor David Smith.

The store owner looks like a Celtic goddess or fairy queen, gold and copper curls framing her luminous glittered face. She is as youthful and thin as the young women working in her shop. Sunshine "Sunny" Powers, known as "The Queen of Haight Street," wears the most gorgeous kaleidoscope prints and tie-dyes I've ever seen, feathers, and glitter eyeshadow. She renamed the store "Love on Haight" in honor of the 50th anniversary of the Summer of Love, and "because we need more love on Haight Street."

The most amazing thing about the store is that it's done so much to help the homeless kids living on Haight Street. A few years ago, Sunshine got money from a private investor to buy out her partner. Instead of being paid back, the investor agreed that profits for ten years would be donated to "Taking It to the Streets," a nonprofit youth organization that provides food, shelter, and job training.

It has already gotten 250 homeless youth off the street and plans to get 300 more. Taking It to the Streets hires street kids to clean the streets and storefronts, and the public toilets and showers they brought in. They just got the largest grant in the history of San Francisco for homelessness, and also the Supervisor Award for changing the way San Francisco views homelessness.

On the web site there's a quote by Ghandi: "Be the change you want to see in the world." There's also one from John Lennon: "I am he as you are he as you are me and we are all together." There's a picture of Sunshine wearing an amazing 18th-century velveteen coat, rainbow tie-dyed with big turned-back cuffs and pewter buttons. She's giving two thumbs up. A comment on the web site says, "When you walk into Love on Haight you will feel the love emanating off the walls and hopefully you will take that love and encourage more."

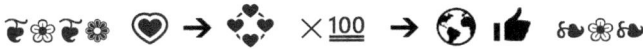

WENDY WHIMSEY

She says she's Wendy from Peter Pan, who rescues the lost boys. She dresses in many different eras all in the same costume, with jewelry, pouches and tattoos and wire-rimmed glasses, one lens pink, the other purple. Most of what she wears is purple, including an intricate purple and black long patch skirt with a large appliqued rabbit with a lightning bolt on each side. She has an Elizabethan fitted bodice of dark purple corduroy with ornate, heavy pewter clasps, over a black gypsy blouse with delicate tucks at the shoulders and down the long sleeves. Her clothes have many emblems and buttons expressing political beliefs and spiritual symbols, and a sheriff's badge.

From an ancient style of leather belt that closes in the back with lacing and eyelets, there hang chains, keys, two small flashlights, a brass bell, and a purple bandana. Peacock feather earrings move in the breeze against her honey-colored braids and a bowler hat. The hat, adorned with a short peacock feather and lots of Bernie buttons, is not the cheap kind you get for Halloween. You can tell it was bought at the fancy hattery on Haight Street, where it certainly cost at least a Benjamin Franklin. Its rich felt is strong and weather-resistant, not likely to crumple like on cheaper hats. It's an exact vintage reproduction of the ones they made a hundred years ago. Sometimes she says she's embodying an Edwardian gentleman.

Aside from the amazing way she dresses, there's something magical and wise about her. There's depth and goodness in her face as she listens attentively to people who come to her and gives them whatever comfort or help she can. For me she's kind of a centerpiece at the log in her flowing long skirts and striking jewelry and all the spiritual and political statements she wears.

Her many colorful tattoos represent every spiritual path that we as a people have been on. Her colorful clothes are lady-like and evoke respect, unlike the skanky, skimpy wear sold to us by corporations. Most are hand-made by local artisans, not cranked out by slave labor. Each thing she's adorned herself with means something. She is wearing who we are.

It turns out she has a van she can sleep in, but still takes along with her a suitcase on rollers and a backpack, and a skateboard. She often prefers to stay in the park and sleep outside. She has her own small business, sells pins and patches, mostly to "family." She wants to start an internet business but has no laptop and recently lost her phone.

To sell pins she sets up on a log under an oak branch leaning over the path, with a purple scarf tied to the branch like a sign, and her wares displayed on velvet display boards on the ground. I bought an intricate turquoise and gold pin from her. She said it represents the universe, the two opposite forces that exist in all things, positive and negative, like the Mayan butterfly of transformation.

BETWEEN STRUCTURE AND CHAOS

Wendy was wearing great steam punk type goggles with metallic purple decorations. As usual making her own fashion statement, she had a skirt tucked into her belt on one side, a lovely purple brocade with a wide gold band edging, over another skirt and colorful tights. In this warmer weather she was wearing the purple bodice without the long-sleeved gypsy blouse, so that I got a chance to see her many tattoos. On her ches3t she has something that represents the heart chakra. At the back of her neck at the throat chakra there is a two-triangle star with a pyramid in the center (with no Masonic eye in the middle.)

She has a rose tattooed on each shoulder, one red and one black, and at her neck another rose. Under the red rose there's Hebrew writing that says, "Strength, Mercy, Knowledge." On one leg there are stars inside of stars and a lotus, and on the other leg there's the mystical configuration of the Tree of Life. On one arm is a Shri Mantra of intersecting triangles. The other arm has a meditation labyrinth like a maze, and an upside-down torch that means death. She said she is planning to have another one done on the other arm that means life, as soon as she can afford it.

She'd just bought some expensive supplements at Whole Foods across the street and was mixing them together at the log. Carefully she blended and stirred the powders in a jar. She said she has seizures and panic attacks. "I can't afford to not be healthy with all the things that are wrong with me," she said. "Better to live to fight another day. I have to be careful. It's like chasing a train. Sometimes it's better to let it go."

Then surprisingly she said she's happier now than she's ever been. "I get all that oxygen!" she said. "I used to have back trouble and I don't have it any more since I've been sleeping on the ground. The sand here is like a Posturepedic!" She said she tries to hold onto hope for a change in society. She said: "Between the light and the darkness, the structure and the chaos, we exist somewhere in the middle."

MAKING FRIENDS ON HAIGHT STREET

It's hard to just walk down Haight Street if I'm in a hurry, because there are just too many things to see and people to meet. The beautiful buildings and exotic shops, the art murals covering so many of the walls, are enough to slow you down. But more than anything it's the people who are irresistible, many of them unusually friendly because of what this place represents. The "house-free" are always willing to start a conversation, whether you give them any money or not. Without being plugged into electronics, meeting people is their form of free entertainment.

   The benches in front of the Haight Street Grocery are a good place to sit, where tourists and the house-free can interact in a meeting of worlds. There's often a knot of people blocking the sidewalk there, and two or three leashed road dogs lying down in the planters next to the benches, where well-groomed paying customers sit next to untamed wild nomads and enjoy conversations.

   The nice thing about the organic grocery store is that it lets people sit there in a "parklet" without buying anything. I sat down in the sun and watched a conservative-looking man having a good time giving away chocolate to the nomadic young people. His hat had a rainbow on it, and he seemed so excited about the encounter. You could tell he was going to tell the folks back home about it.

   I met the group blocking the sidewalk, a girl and two guys going to Pennsylvania with two bikes and five dogs, probably going to the Pennsylvania Rainbow Gathering. The boy had a small dog riding on his shoulders and another slung into his shirt. Two leashed big brown dogs rested in the planter and a smaller dog, the mother of the two littlest dogs. We had a rousing discussion about religion and politics, which is permitted on the Haight, unlike at family gatherings. We all agreed with everything each other said. We exchanged poetry.

   I'd like to point out that just because young people travel together doesn't mean they are romantically involved or intimate. There are so many reasons why it's better to travel with someone, rather than travelling alone. A young woman on the road is certainly much safer with a male escort and a couple of dogs, than she would be alone. A travelling partner can watch your stuff or watch your dog when you need to go somewhere or go into a store. They can tell your family or friends if something happens to you or you need help. In so many ways, travelling with a partner can help with the work of survival, as well as providing the companionship which human tribes are designed for. Most of us feel scared alone in the forest.

Then they and their dogs left to go to Pennsylvania and I continued on up the street, until I stood in front of the amazing tie-dye emporium at Haight and Masonic called Love on Haight. All around are unique buildings and decorations, but this one stands out with its big rounded pillars painted in rainbow colors. The store sells nothing but tie-dye. Walking into it is an experience, surrounded by the brightest colors and designs imaginable and stuff hanging from the ceiling. I met a smiling white-haired woman in the back who said Jesus was a feminist and told me about an epiphany she had about a synchronized time in life. I bought a blue tie-dyed top hat for a princely sum.　🎩 💰🦋 [OK]

Out on the street there was a young man wheeling an old man in a wheelchair, near the bus stop next to Whole Foods. He had a beautiful Christ-like look on his face, framed by medium-length thin dark blond hair. He was very thin. They were not related, but the younger man was taking care of him tenderly. It was easy to start a conversation and soon I was reading something I wrote to them and the old man was pulling out of his backpack something he wrote that he wanted to show me. Then he timidly asked if I could help them get something to eat. I could tell they really needed it and gave them five dollars, hoping it would buy them something at McDonald's.　🐕 🏃 ♿

At McDonald's I met a girl with nine alien tattoos. 👽   A guy walked in, immediately started talking about God, energy, and aliens. He knew a lot. He said laughing that he likes his independence and would tell a girl "I may not be Mr. Right but I'm Mr. Right Now." Then I met two girls, one with turquoise hair. We read poems and had a good talk about Haight

Street magic. You could see they were homeless but like so many others they said they were happy.

Then I joined a group of youths sitting on the curb of the planter next to Whole Foods. We discussed life and shared poems, shouting to overcome the noise of traffic going by.

A HIPPIE VAN

At night when the parking meters stop and most tourists have left, you can park right on Haight Street for free, and there are sometimes open vans there and sidewalk get-togethers. People make friends with people walking by, even after dark. A friendly group invited me to stop, offered me refreshment and started conversations. They were in a nice camper van, the kind you can almost stand up in.

A pretty girl in a long skirt and with beads in her hair sat in the front seat with the window open, and two young men lounged inside the back of the van with the side door open. We talked about how beautiful Haight Street can be at night all lit up with the colored lights on the big trees, with lots of people going by and gathering in groups, some playing music, and music coming out of clubs. They let me read some of my writing. It turned out one boy is an internet wiz, something I really need. He likes what I'm writing and said he would help me with my website for free. I felt the love. Any spiritual thing I need, I find on Haight Street.

There's free parking on Sunday too and when I walked by the next day the van was still there. The girl was there, doing housekeeping in the little home. I got to look inside. It was thoughtfully decorated inside, surprisingly home-like. There were dream catchers, necklaces, Tibetan prayer flags, and an Indian bedspread on the ceiling. Everything had a meaning. Rich draperies around a comfortable-looking bed in the back made that area look like a shrine.

On the wide dashboard of the van there was a whole magic world, with antlers, rocks, religious statues including Jesus and Mary, and containers full of crystals. On the passenger side of the dashboard there was even a tall narrow cut-open hollow rock where the inside is coated with crystals, like those displayed at "Love of Ganesha." Missing in the van was anything plastic. In a cooking area there was a carved wooden cabinet like in a gypsy wagon. Hand-painted on it were the words: "What the caterpillar calls the end of the world is a butterfly."

As I walked on there was a young man making and selling beautiful art made from only re-used cardboard from the trash and a felt pen. With his single black felt pen he was drawing intricate mandalas, round geometric designs, on squares of discarded cardboard. I only gave him the dollar that I had as a courtesy, not expecting to buy with it something that must've taken a long time to make. But he insisted I take my pick, though I had no money. I chose the smallest one but then was glad I did.

Getting it home I noticed how beautiful and powerful it was and realized that I'd chosen it not only because it was the smallest and the guy might be able to sell the others for more. I had been drawn to it. Holding it in my hands I could feel in it the young man's energy, picture him making all the careful marks on it in a contemplative state. He had seemed like a fine person.

The edges of the art piece were slightly ragged, as if they'd been carefully torn by hand along folded edges. The guy didn't even own a pair of scissors. I took my scissors and trimmed it neatly in honor of what it was, then displayed it proudly in my room.

AN HONORED TRADITION

The circle of about twenty peace drums is often on the pavement right in the middle of the main thoroughfare through the meadow next to Hippie Hill. That means that people usually go around, so much that there's a big bare area on the grass encircling the lower half of the drum circle. The other side of the walkway is bordered by the long park bench the drummers sit on, on the uphill side of the road, so most people don't walk through that way behind the bench.

A few people go through the middle of the drummers if it's not too crowded. Some even stop and dance or linger to stand on the sidelines. Sometimes a baby carriage or wagon lumbers through, for which the drums open up. During the busy part of weekends, the drummers try to leave an open spot on either end so that people can walk through, but soon someone starts to stand there and play an instrument. Then the people have to walk around again.

No one complains among all the thousands who walk by. The park rangers don't tell the drummers to get out of the road. The drum circle seems to be an honored tradition, something that even some officials are kind of proud of, something tourists come to see.   There's also the basic principle of respect in Pacifist society. Even the strangers walking by don't want to interrupt the rhythm of the drums or disturb the musicians in their trances.

While surfing the net I found the most astonishing thing. This guy recorded the creakings and other sounds trees make and then sped it up. He discovered with amazement that trees actually make a rhythm with each other, a kind of heartbeat of life. When I listened to the recording, it sounded like the drum circle.

HOPE AMERICA

Hope America, lift yourself up like some phoenix in some new day.

    It's not too late to reclaim a good name as Land of Liberty.

All of mankind has hoped in your great dream,

    based as it was on higher impulses that human beings can have

to make a world where none need grovel at the feet of bullies any more

    or suffer needless want because of artificial economic means.

There's a connection between people, a holy bond,

    which scientists have failed to measure with their graphs and charts.

"The pursuit of happiness!"

    What a grandiose goal: to save the little from the big.

Wasn't this just what Jesus meant

    when he said, "love your neighbor as yourself?"

There's no doubt this country's Founders had this in mind

    as in candlelight they penned great charters to set us free

from all the ills that had beset the world since men had learned

    to dig metal out of the ground to fashion money, chains, and swords.

It didn't come out the way they'd hoped

but there've been times when it's come close.

The New Deal and the War on Poverty

    can make us proud.

Lawmakers braved assassins' bullets trying to free the poor

    including two sons of the rich who tried to stop a war.

Even today dangers abound

    as heroes pray for courage in the legislative halls.

Built to Last

   Bill of Rights 📜 Use It or Lose It

We must stand up against the ones

    who'd like to turn this country into one vast prison camp,

with cameras everywhere and giant penalties for everything,

    so that we're caught, whether by poverty or prison doors.

The unjust laws they've made, contrived by greed and not diplomacy,

    should be removed from our law books the way a cancer is removed.

The Patriot Act should be allowed to lapse.

    Some "justices" should go home now before doing any more harm.

UNDO! UNDO! the larcenous laws that corporations and railroads made,

    the lies that lying liars told.

UNDO the complex scams of insurance companies

    that keep tightening their noose around our necks.

REPEAL! REPEAL! Mandatory sentencing, three strikes, forfeiture,

    which have made us into something we didn't intend.

We are too good for laws like this to soil our name,

    our vision of free men with compassionate hearts.

Let's be as great as all the songs and all the hymns say that we are.

    Let's do something for history books to make our children proud.

It's not too late to set things right

    if we will use the potent tools right in our hands:

the Bill of Rights, the Golden Rule, the handshake of our neighbor too

    can save us from the monster's jaw

if we believe the thing that Jesus taught

    when he said we could do all that he did and even greater things.

LET'S TAKE ONE STEP TOGETHER: At the giant Rainbow Gatherings in the wilderness people yell "WE LOVE YOU!" repeatedly on one side of the camp and others answer back, "WE LOVE YOU TOO!" Let's do the same thing out our windows at sunset on Saturdays, so that the Voice of the People can be heard! We could also play drums for half an hour at sunset on Saturdays at a window. Visit with or meet neighbors! WE NEED ALL OF US! (right + left)

Poems may be reprinted and shared by homeless for donations they can keep.
TELL TEN TO TELL TEN TO VOTE DEMOCRAT!   REGISTER 100 DEMOCRATS!
(https://www.usa.gov/register-to-vote) (vote.gov) (rockthevote.org)
Democrats against forced mandates and other oppressive liability laws.
BILL OF RIGHTS   GOLDEN RULE   peacedrums.org   UNITE!

"If not us, who? If not now, when? John F. Kennedy

"Injustice anywhere is a threat to justice everywhere." Martin Luther King

RAINBOW: "ANOTHER LOVE-SICK HIPPIE FOR GOD"

There's an art store on Haight Street, right on the main drag amid the exotic storefronts, wild murals and ornate row houses. There are few retail businesses on that tourist stretch besides restaurants and head shops, but there is an art store. Maybe it's a remnant of when more artists lived here, before they got priced out. Or maybe it's still in business because when people come here to the Haight, they might start to feel artistic or creative themselves. Maybe the rich assortment of beautiful things they see, the swirls of color and light, make them want to add color and light and beauty to their own lives. If tie-dyed T-shirts and trinkets from Tibet aren't their style, art supplies might be a worthy souvenir from this place for them or their kids.

Before I met Rainbow, I saw him at the art store. He was trying to decide which color of paint to buy with the only five dollars he had, which would only buy one color. I wanted to offer to buy him another color, but he quickly paid for the one and was gone in a flash, off on some errand. I could tell he was a real artist who really lived here. I watched his colorful form hurry down the street, in a faded tie-dyed t-shirt and a vest from India and paint-marked pants, his curly grey and brown hair and bushy white beard marking him as a genuine Hippiesaurus.

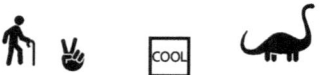

A week or so later I was brought to his studio by drummer Jubah, a tall African American elder with a kingly presence and a trim white beard.

Some of the young people idolize him, both at the drum circle and on Haight Street. By introducing me to Rainbow he's done so much to bring special people into my life like Rainbow, Diamond Dave, Mr. Natural, Global Val, and Mona Lisa.

Rainbow's third-floor room is in an ancient row house just a block from Haight Street. The building has multiple narrow pillars on the front, painted green with a flat paint that makes the Victorian look less fancy than it really is. The thick time-worn doors to the several flats are also painted a dull green. But right across the street there are some of the most gorgeous row houses I've ever seen, painted in pastels with gold accents. Above his door there's a sign that says, "PEACE." He lives not far from where the Grateful Dead used to live at 710 Ashbury. 🌷 🎶 ✨

As soon as I met Rainbow, I knew we were going to be great friends. He talked about God in an unreserved way, like someone who's really experienced something. In hushed tones, with wonder in his voice, he spoke immediately about the sublime. Seeing him up close I noticed what a beautiful smile he has, what a kind face. There's something about him that's the personification of goodness. His profound humility has innocence and genuineness. His sense of wonder is at the same time childlike and deeply intelligent. 😇 + 🧠

Walking into his third-floor walk-up studio I was startled by all the brilliant colors. Every wall and surface of the small room is covered with paintings. Most of them have mystical themes but some are portraits of rock stars, icons of the Sixties and seventies. I turned around and tried to take in the brilliant images of Jesus and Mary Magdalene, Krishna and his consort, Buddha, and of the Beatles in their Sgt. Pepper pastel satin band uniforms. Some of the paintings are small but most are large, several feet across. Most are on canvases, but many are on very thick and heavy pieces of particle board, scavenged from the trash, the only thing he can afford. 🖼🖼🖼 🖼🖼 🖼🖼🖼 🖼🖼🖼

More paintings are stacked up along the walls and against the art tables, several deep. The tables are packed with bottles and tubes of paint, many of them old and dried up. The only evidence that someone sleeps there is a folded foam mat which, when it's laid out, covers most of what's left of the floor. It's a very small and Spartan room but a very pretty one, and very antique. These wooden floorboards have seen the sweep of long skirts.

It has curved ceilings edged with decorative plaster moldings, a plaster medallion around the light fixture, and a cute archway over the built-in dresser and mirror, with a plaster decoration that's painted gold. The dresser and mirror are both inaccessible, covered with paintings. That's all right because he only owns about two suits of clothes. "My whole wardrobe is worth about ten dollars." he said. I noticed that there was nothing to eat in the room. Either poverty is one of his spiritual practices, or the San Francisco rental market has taken its cut.

The south side of his room is at the front of the house, which has two round towers like a castle. The tower makes up one whole side of his room, with three beautiful large windows like they used to make, in which the glass is curved to make a curved window. As I looked at the paintings, the windows with their southern exposure let in a wall of light that washed over the tiny art studio. The paintings shimmered and glowed, made with bright primary colors, with vibrant highlights and pulsating halos on each of the saints and deities he'd painted.

Rainbow stood by while I studied and admired each of his wonderful paintings. Here is a real artist, not someone who does finger painting. He knows how to draw, how to get the special effects he wants. More than that he captures something in his paintings, a warmth and a depth of feeling. His subjects all look intelligent and serious and kind. The rock stars have the same calm, wise expression as the deities and saints.

It turns out he does do finger painting and also uses brushes. One day when visiting him I was astonished to find that while we were talking, he'd put a canvas on his lap and was dabbing it with paint with his finger, straight out of the tube. That's how he makes the leaves of the trees and those amazing golden highlights, with bright primary colors. He said that sometimes he uses his thumb. Looking at the vibrant halos and light fields, I could see the outlines of his thumb.

He asked me if I wanted some tea, the only thing he had to offer, and went into the communal kitchen to boil water.  The rest of the apartment, which takes up one whole floor, has a long hallway and three or more other roommates living there. Meditation music rings out through the hallway from the door of Bruce, who meditates for hours every day, and rock music comes from another door, plus incense. I wouldn't be surprised to find someone levitating in that place. The hallway is full of paintings, and there are gorgeous big ones in the kitchen with groups of avatars, Jesus and Mary Magdalene, the lion lying down with the lamb.

The house was built in the early days of plumbing and it has a separate washroom and toilet, each with paintings. The walls of the toilet room are plastered with many other posters, post cards, poems, and decorations of a spiritual nature. Just one visit to this hippie bathroom could maybe get someone enlightened.

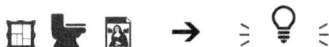

Rainbow has a name for the mass movement that has uplifted so many. He just calls it "the Renaissance." Playing guitar in a kind of trance he sang one of his poems: "Your life itself becomes like a dance, knowledge is a gift 💖 I must further learn to expand, I feel a strong urge to grow, to understand and to know… Heaven is inside of me."

He said, "I need to be a soul searcher, riding the waves of consciousness, becoming purified, becoming kind." One of my favorite things in his room is a big painting that says, "Are You Kind?" Rainbow said, "I'm just another love-sick hippie for God."

HAIGHT HOSPITALITY

When I needed to be in town an extra day and didn't want to drive back to where I was staying twenty miles away, Rainbow was my gracious host. I climbed up the two steep flights of stairs to the long dark hallway of his ancient Victorian building, where music and incense emanated from several of the rooms. Entering his crowded space, I was surrounded by color and light and the pleasant scent of the paints he uses to make his art. It looks like a place where a lot is going on. Rainbow said that some people call it "The Magic Theatre." ☆✦ 🎭 ☆✦

At night it was dark in there because his one lightbulb had broken, and he had to wait for his Social Security check to buy another one. 💡 The only way to get light was to turn on the TV, where we watched "Yellow Submarine" on a video. I slept on the floor of his tiny art studio, which was also his living room and bedroom. Because of frequent homeless guests during cold weather, he had a spare foam mat like the one he slept on. When it was laid out between some paintings under the windows it took up all the remaining floor space on that side of the room. I slept there alone, comfortable, often staring at the bright colors of the paintings, inches from my face.

In the morning we went to a hippie coffee shop near Haight Street. In a room done up in dark wood to make it look rustic and organic, we sipped strong coffee with honey and ate wholesome pastries. He used vintage hippie expressions like "Groovy" and "like" and "dig" and "do your own thing." He said, "groovy is like record grooves. Like the Earth also has a groove. In the groove. Like in the flow."

He said, "I want to turn the world to beauty instead of ugliness. This world's attitudes are like a shoe that doesn't fit. Maybe there's enough sanity in this world to keep it from going over the edge." Rainbow's room, in addition to being the Magic Theatre, seems to me like a womb incubating the kind of powerful thoughts that could help humanity.

In the evening I figured he would enjoy being fed and took him out for pizza, vegetarian of course, clean of violence. 🍕🍕 He told me about how one time he saw cows being loaded onto trucks to go to the slaughterhouse, how frightened they looked. He said "I saw terror on those cows' faces. All life is a reflection of us."

🚚 🐄🐄🐄

Afterwards we walked several blocks on Cole Street to a coffee house named "Sacred Grounds" that has a weekly broadcast poetry reading. The room is rather cavernous, with a side area where you have to step down. The walls are a rich dark color, with posters and some of Rainbow's paintings. There's an area next to the storefront windows that serves as a stage with a microphone, though there's no raised platform. There's the scent of strong coffee and sweet pastries. The place looks just like what a Beatnik coffee house must have looked like. It serves exactly the same purpose, and it probably was one. 📻 🍩 🥞 ☕ 🕶️ 🎷 COOL

I could see "Mr. Natural," who'd created this scene, sitting at a table in front of the stage area. He was busy at a computer sorting out something about the internet feed. His long white beard, balding head and heavy frame made him look exactly like R. Crumb's cartoon "Mr.

Natural." That's not his real name but he's called that as a local celebrity.

The Sacred Grounds Poetry Hour, which would be recorded and broadcast online, began as various persons started streaming in, some carrying instruments. One after the other went up to the microphone for about fifteen or twenty minutes, each sharing their vision or their poetry or music. I got to read my poetry and Rainbow got to play his guitar and sing a few songs. After the event was over and the place was closing there was a lively discussion outdoors, about the finite universe vs. the infinite universe.

RAINBOW'S PORCH

Rainbow had the same thing on his front porch that Jesus would've had: a homeless person sleeping there. They didn't even have a sleeping bag but had spent the cold foggy night with only their jacket draped over them. Their boots stood neatly near their head where they wouldn't be ripped off, and their backpack was used as a pillow. I stepped over him carefully as I left Rainbow's art studio early in the morning, where I had slept on a foam pad on the floor. I managed to walk over the guy without waking him up, and to reach over him and pull the green door shut. It turned out that this was another friend who sometimes crashed at Rainbow's. I realized later that it was probably because I was there that he'd had to sleep outside on the porch.

I started walking from Page Street toward the Haight a block away. Like I said before it's hard to ever go directly from one place to another on the Haight and in the park. The distractions there are too spiritually enticing. It wasn't long before I met Scott, wearing a gorgeous blue and black thick brocade 1700's reproduction coat. It had large lapels and cuffs made with close-cut brown velvet, and amazing pewter buttons with lions' heads on them. Under that he wore a beautiful purple and black silk paisley brocade fitted vest, very finely made. The shirt underneath was also paisley, and the silken handkerchief he used. He was clean-shaven. His long, beautiful hair with salt and pepper curls to the shoulders, and his archaic-style top hat, also made him look like he was a time-traveller. 🎩

He said his mother was named Rainbow and was close friends with Joan Baez. He didn't seem concerned that he'd slept on the sidewalk in the freezing cold without even a blanket. He admitted with a laugh that he had no possessions except for the extraordinary clothes on his back. He said matter-of-factly that he's sometimes had to camp out in very extreme weather conditions. ☾ ☂ 🌧 ❄ zzz

A guy walked up with a green fluorescent star on his shirt, a top hat with an orange Ostrich feather, and fluorescent green sunglasses. He was friendly and open with strangers in the tradition of the Haight. He offered us some of the plant whose leaves are for the healing of the nations.

☆ 🕶 🎩 ☮ 🚬

Walking on down Haight Street I met Dan sitting in his wheelchair on a windy corner. Though "house-free" he was neatly dressed and well groomed, with a short beard and medium-short reddish greying hair. Even in clothes from Goodwill he looked like a lawyer or a professor. He said society needs to change. He'd written an E-book, "The American Homeless Companion," about "baseline economics" and a new way of looking at homelessness.

Many of the people out here have projects to heal the world. For some it's a private thing they don't tell anyone about. For others it's something that consumes them, which they spend their lifetime trying to promote and achieve, even if they live on the street. We talked a long time in the cold wind, my very full bright pink long skirt and turquoise tie-dyed shift blowing around madly. My beige suit jacket didn't keep me very warm, but still I lingered.

He said it was less stressful for people to "move around in a state of dense now." He talked about "natural providership," saying "anything I need just appears!" Much of what he said sounded a lot like things Jesus had also said. Later I went away on a road trip. When I came back, I found out he had died. 🪦 💔

A TRUE LOVE STORY

On another morning walk I ran into a somewhat disheveled twenty-something young man with blond dreadlocks and we sat on a stairway of one of the row houses and talked. The lady who lived there was nice when she came out to go to work, greeting us with a smile as she stepped over my satchel and sleeping bag that were in the way on the stairs. She declined my offer to move them.
You could tell this was San Francisco.

He started telling me how much he was in love with his wife. They were high school sweethearts named "Darian and Adrian." He said, "I don't know what she sees in me to choose to stay out here with me." He said they had two children who lived with his mom. He said the state took their first baby at delivery though there was no pot in his system, only some in the mom. Then they took the second one even though there was no pot found in either the baby or the mother. He said his wife was really upset about it.

He talked openly and without embarrassment about his relationship with God. Echoing something the "house-free" have expressed to me before, he said, "I love this life. I met God out here." He said "I'm doing the work for Him. He takes care of me. All He asks is that I spread love and respect." It was amazing that he still felt that way, because I found out they'd just had all their stuff confiscated.

They'd slept on the ground in the park last night, without their tent and sleeping bags. The thing he was saddest about was his guitar. With that he'd been able to make a little money as a street musician. They'd found an old shag rug to sleep in and had spent a very cold night. He said that when their stuff was taken yesterday, they hadn't even left their camp but were sitting just a few yards away, their view of it blocked by a bush. When they came back everything was gone. The rangers must've been very quiet.

He said, "Attachment leads to suffering." He said it was ok to lose things because someone else might need them. But he admitted that since sleeping on the ground he felt a pain in his left side. He asked for nothing and seemed to minimize his many challenges. I gave him a packaged dinner I happened to have in my satchel, which had been given away by a charity group at the Horseshoe the evening before.

We went to Goodwill to buy him a blanket or sleeping bag, but they didn't have any. We had to settle for a curtain panel and a bright red Christmas tablecloth, which might be better than nothing.   He wondered again why his wife stayed with him out here. Then he told me that when they got married the minister seemed in a hurry and rushed through the ceremony. He said he wished it had lasted longer.

Then we went to Whole Foods where I used my card to get him a little cash, which he tried to refuse. Sitting on the benches outside Whole Foods we shared the gentrified cookies I had to buy to use the card. A well-groomed couple walked by, obviously not of the same class as the

"Dirty Kids" panhandling nearby with their dogs. My friend said to the man, "I like your jacket." I laughed at the thought of this grubby slightly overweight young fellow with dreadlocks telling this elite-looking guy that he liked his fashion sense. He said, "I like to give people compliments. It makes their day." ☺

He told about how one day he'd asked God for just one cigarette, and within minutes he'd found a whole pack lying on the ground. He said, "Why would He care about just me?" He said "You have to learn to live with joy in your heart. I know from my conversations with Him that it pains Him to see us in pain." He said that he'd seen God. It was easy for me to see what his wife saw in him.

FOR CUSTOMERS ONLY

The bathrooms at McDonald's are for customers only. Every morning people arrive there from a main gathering area across the street at the east entrance to the park. Each is hoping to find a little water to wash in or a place to do their business out of the freezing cold. ❄ A security guard stands near the entrance to the bathrooms, requesting a customer receipt for entry. Sometimes the guards break the rules and let people in anyway.

In my heated bedroom I thought about them, sleeping on the ground with only the thin fabric of a tent between them and the Bay Area's frequent Arctic winds. Soon after dawn they have to hurriedly pack up their stuff and take down their tent and then trek to a distant, unheated park bathroom. ❄ This must be very hard for those who are old or sick. One woman confided to me that she had stomach issues and terrible headaches. She said that the other day she hadn't even taken down her tent all day, she was so sick. Luckily, no rangers had come by her remote campsite.

For many people, especially seniors, managing their stomach in the morning can be a lengthy challenge or ordeal. It must be daunting to have to hurry from their tent site to a far-away unheated park bathroom, or to the frigid public bathroom pod on Stanyan Street that has no seat but only cold stainless steel or porcelain. ❄ At every use, when the door shuts after the previous person leaves, it automatically showers the whole interior including the floor to disinfect it. The seat is not only cold, but it's wet so you can't sit on it. Or the person can try waiting in line to buy a coffee at McDonald's so they can use the bathroom. 🚶

What about girls on their period? What about when it rains? Where do they go during the hours when those bathrooms are closed? They also have to bathe in places like the McDonald's bathroom, or take sponge baths in the freezing cold public restrooms at the park, which are open to the elements without any heat whatsoever. Yet I've seldom noticed any odor on these people. Contrary to what many housies might think, each traveler is as clean as anyone could be under the circumstances. I'd like to see how those who judge them would make out trying to stay clean while living on the streets.

I won the Whole Foods toilet lottery: they weren't locked and there was only one person in line when I got there. The health food store lets the house-free use the toilets without a receipt. The downside is that they are often out of order or have long lines. Once inside one of the two private bathrooms, you are surrounded by luxury and beauty.

The upper walls and ceiling are done up in reflective stainless-steel panels, which mirror the bright tilework on the lower walls, cobalt blue in one bathroom and bright green in the other. This effect is enhanced by lighting designed to make it hard for drug addicts to find veins to shoot up, though I've never seen a needle on Haight Street or heard anyone talking about hard drugs except to say they don't want them.

The door is also covered with the mirror-like stainless steel, as well as the paper towel dispensers and the frames of the baby changing table and the mirror. The shining metal reflects the purplish cobalt blue or vibrant green under the special lighting. It feels like you've entered another dimension. You can tell it's a hippie bathroom. Even the waiting area is painted bright blue with rainbow spirals on it.

POISONOUS LAWS

The corporate Beast conjures up poisonous laws

    and places them inside the legal codes that rule our lives.

With stealth and cunning and a thousand lies it leads us to believe

  that we must fear each other, not the things we really need to watch.

How vigilant it's made us be against intruders, terrorists and gangs,

    none of which most of us have ever seen.

At the same time, it makes us look the other way

    while bureaucrats sign papers saying they can take our homes and cars.

Our children too may be required by the Beast,

    whether by courts or Children's Services or by draft or recruit.

"Equal!" it shouts as it applies its tyranny to all of us in the same way.

    "Safety!" it croons, as nets of liability entangle everything we do.

The Beast wants to be in our homes and survey all our days

    in order to protect the kids, the elderly and cats and dogs.

It wants to put sensing devices on the airport gates

    that can detect if we smoked anything a month ago.

Built to Last

All that we do or say or feel can become designated as a crime

    by teams of lawyers somewhere down the line.

Cash registers ding while innocents are put away,

    or crushed with fines or fees that put their families on the street.

Like hunted animals we scurry underneath the cameras' gaze,

    another thing we would've never voted for.

A wrong move in a diamond lane might bring a giant fine.

    Breaking a law nobody knew was there can ruin your life.

The Bill of Rights was there to shield us from shenanigans like this,

    but black-robed "justices" appear illiterate of its fine words. 🙈 📜

The advice of the Prince of Peace is also totally ignored 🙉

    by lawmakers who spend all day in church and won't leave tips. 👛

The bullies and the takers of this world have run roughshod

    over the people of the land that was once free.

Christ's dream of hope and love and peace has been violently raped, transformed into what's on the faces of some televangelists.

NO MUSIC ALLOWED

Next to Whole Foods along a flat wall are, there was a guy playing a guitar, making nice music. His friends greeted me with hugs. He said he wanted to play a song for me. He told me that he too was a red-letter Christian like I am, someone who focuses on the things the Bible claims Jesus said in the four gospels, in red letters. These things are way different from things others wrote about Jesus in the rest of the New Testament. That's because many of them came from a different document called "Gospel Q," which is lost but which evidently the gospel writers had and included in three of the gospels. Also, the deceptive red letters in the book of Revelation refer to a guy's visions while "in the spirit," not to anything the gospels claim Jesus said.

Also suspect is the last chapter of the Gospel of Mark, which doesn't match Jesus' teachings and which reputable theologians believe was added over a hundred years later. It's the only place where they've got him saying you have to believe and be baptized or be damned. Right next to that it tells people they can pick up poisonous snakes and drink poisonous liquids, and speak in tongues and prophesy.

I was carrying a lightweight drum and passed it over to one of his friends, and I brought out my tambourine. We were making music, people starting to dance on the sidewalk. Then I saw two big police officers in dark uniforms coming toward us. They looked even bigger than they really were, in all their gear and the bullet-proof vests they wore under their shirts. I decided to leave. Too many hippies.

From a distance I watched as the officers talked to the guy with the guitar and his friends and told them to move on. There was no ticket issued but it was a warning. According to new "security" guidelines and criminal laws resulting from Nine Eleven, MORE THAN THREE PEOPLE GATHERED TOGETHER IS DEFINED AS A CONSPIRACY. I wonder what the nation's founders would think about that. The law says: "**A conspiracy exists when two or more people form an agreement to violate the law, then act on that agreement**." It's the theory of "vicarious liability."

Many of the police are surprisingly sympathetic to the kids. These usually get transferred to other locations. There was a blond police woman that everybody liked. She's gone now. Most of these cops chose this career because they wanted to help people and protect them from real crimes. Some resent being enlisted in a war on the poor and our constitutional right to peacefully assemble. They are not our enemies; toxic corporations are. One police officer I met said he cried every night because he felt sorry for people he was forced to arrest. They are in debt and worried about paying high rents and being poisoned by chemicals, just like the rest of us. Real law reform can't happen without their support.

That there were police everywhere is understandable because there'd been a stabbing (by someone not from around here) at the Horseshoe a few days before. The open grassy area behind the Horseshoe, where people normally come and sit to get warm or to dry their belongings from the rain, was empty on a sunny day.

To shake off what had just happened I walked toward the pond. But instead of going to the left like I usually did I went to the right, toward where a different group of hippies often gathers on a small hill above the pond. There's a log and a concrete ledge there that they sit on, enjoying morning gossip and refreshments, and the sights and sounds of the forest. Different groups of people in the park have different areas where they like to gather, like neighborhoods.

Trying to be unobtrusive though dressed in blinding tie-dye, I approached the edge of their gathering. Across the sparkling pond I could see other people on the logs that were next to the tunnel. It's important to be considerate with people and not barge right in. After all, this is their living room. 🛋 It's good to be able to read people's signals and to avoid interrupting anything. Usually if I walk by a group and if nobody looks up and smiles at me to invite me in, I figure they're not in the mood for company. This time they were all smiles and many of them already knew me.

A rousing conversation was taking place about God and man, history, and the meaning of life. From different positions on the log and the ledge, road-polished nomads shared differing opinions, but they mostly agreed with each other. They looked like gypsies sitting there, not the kind you see on Halloween but the real thing. The open air of the road seemed to cling to them. If you were to ask them where they were from, some might answer, "Everywhere." 🚂🚃🚃🚃💨

The dappled morning sun filtered through some tall pines and shone on their faces and on the clothes and other things they wore, each item of which was either practical or rich with meaning. Each individual had a backpack nearby, and one or more dogs. Three of the dogs had their leashes tied together so they wouldn't go far. Even this isn't legal. All dogs have to be on a leash with their owners at all times, under penalty of a huge fine. Even tying them to your backpack a few feet away isn't good enough. 🐕🎒❌   🐕‍🎒❌ → 🐕🐕

There was a guy there with very long hair and a neat beard and beautiful eyes. He was surprised and laughed when I told him I thought he looked like Jesus, and then I realized that he looked exactly like Johnny

Depp as Captain Jack the pirate. His appearance was deliberate, with little braids and beads in his beard and everything. The only thing that was missing was the black eyeliner. The pirate/messiah and I talked about liberty, highly valued by pirates. He didn't care much about religion but he knew that Jesus had said "I come to proclaim liberty to the captives."

We agreed that weed represents freedom for us. That's a big reason why we get so excited about it and hold onto it despite tremendous risks of criminal penalties. Taking away our right to smoke the weed, to make music or gather in groups of more than three, makes us feel slave-like. Making these things illegal prevents us from practicing our religion of brotherly love, making us not free. We need liberty the same way factory farm animals need liberty when they are crammed into cages and stalls. WITHOUT LIBERTY WE CAN'T BREATHE.

It's a feeling that pirates would share, and also the great American colonist Patrick Henry who said, "Give me liberty or give me death!" The young man and others had some very educated and deep things to say. It turns out that in the original Latin the word "CORPORATION" means "DEAD SPEAK." They also claimed that the holy anointing oil in the Old Testament was made out of cannabis, which I hadn't ever heard before. When priests "anointed" themselves with it, or smelled an "incense" made from it, they got high.

A guy told us about how he and some buddies had just spent a long night helping their pregnant friend move her van. They had to push it back and forth all night from midnight to 4 AM. so that it wouldn't get tickets. It had no gas and wouldn't start. It needed gas and a jump start.

One youth started to play my drum, the drum that had caused all the trouble earlier when music had been forbidden. Someone else had a guitar, I played my tambourine, and there was a harmonica. With no one forbidding us, we made nice music there on the hill under the big trees, and got a jump start of our own.

KANEH: FREE THE HOLY OIL

It turns out the guy was right. It's true that the anointing oil used by the priests in Jewish temples was made from cannabis. "Kannabosm," "kineboisin," "kaneh bosm," "sweet cane" and "kaneh," in the original 3language, all mean cannabis. It's mentioned about eight times in the Bible, if you don't count Jesus, "the anointed one."

It turns out there were mistranslations in the Bible, some of them deliberate. First there was a mistake in the Greek "Septuagint" translation in the third century BC., calling it "calamus," a different plant. Then when they compiled the King James Bible in the 1600's, it's said that they knew about the mistake, but King James decided to leave it in there as "calamus." Bible scholars discovered the error in 1936, interestingly the same year that William Randolph Hearst set in motion the criminalization of marijuana so he could make money cutting down the northwestern forests he owned to make paper with instead of using renewable hemp.

The sacred oil which high priests sprinkled on the altar and on all the holy objects, and "anointed" themselves with, definitely contained very potent levels of THC. Put directly on the skin, it could absolutely get someone very high. Unfortunately, only priests and kings were allowed to partake. Here is Moses' recipe for the holy oil:

"Moreover the Lord spake unto Moses, saying, Take thou also unto thee principal spices, of pure myrrh five hundred shekels, and of sweet cinnamon half so much, even two hundred and fifty shekels, and of SWEET CALAMUS two hundred and fifty shekels, and of cassia five hundred shekels, after the shekel of the sanctuary, and of oil olive an hin: And thou shalt make it an oil of holy ointment, an ointment compound after the art of the apothecary: it shall be a holy anointing oil.

"And thou shalt anoint the tabernacle of the congregation therewith, and the ark of the testimony, and the table and all his vessels, and the candlestick and his vessels, and the altar of incense, And the altar of burnt offering with all his vessels, and the laver and his foot. And thou shalt sanctify them, that they may be most holy: whatsoever touches them shall be holy. And thou shalt anoint Aaron and his sons, and consecrate them, that they may minister unto me in the priest's office."

"And thou shalt speak unto the children of Israel, saying, This shall be an holy anointing oil unto me throughout your generations. Upon man's flesh shall it not be poured (were the priests alien hybrids, not "man?"), neither shall ye make any other like it, after the composition of it: it is holy, and it shall be holy unto you. Whosoever compoundeth any like it, or whosoever putteth any of it upon a stranger, shall even be cut off from his people." (Exodus 30:23 to 30:33)

Marijuana was included as an item that should be brought for sacrifices. In (Isaiah 43:23-24), God complains that they haven't brought him any weed in their sacrifices: "Thou hast brought me no SWEET CANE with money, neither hast thou filled me with the fat of thy sacrifices: but thou hast made me to serve with thy sins, thou hast wearied me with thine iniquities." In another Bible version it's "You have not brought any KANEH for me..." In Hindu tradition, the god Shiva gave pot for the pleasure of mankind. Anandomine is the Sanskrit name for pot, which means "bliss."

HEMP

Note: Pot is still highly illegal in federal law.

The sight of people dragged away just for a plant

    is not fit for the eyes of Lady Liberty.
It is the brightest and the best who are denied the vote after they puff,

    to the advantage of the bullies who destroy the Earth.
God so enjoys their conversations about what is right and what is true.

    The sublime Presence in their smoke-filled rooms is undenied.
The lofty notes and words of rock songs full of hope and brotherhood

    burned in our hearts for fifty years.

Plastic, fuel, fabric and food are made from nature's fast-growing plant,

    enough to never have to fight another war for oil.

The seeds are edible and could be used
    to feed every domestic animal on Earth.
Then wheat and corn and other grains given to stock
    could go instead to hungry people everywhere.
The stems, twenty feet high, grow like wood and are used the same.
    If hemp paper was used instead of pulp, forests would stand.

The roots can bind eroding soil where corporate bulldozers have trod.
    The leaves clean dirty and polluted air.
the buds make medicines unrivaled by the weird stuff chemists sell
    and which our grandmothers knew well around the world.
If God so hates this plant that those possessing it get put in jail,
    why is it planted next to riverbeds in every corner of the globe?
"The tree whose leaves are for the healing of the nations" could just be
  what hippies pass around in pipes while they discuss things Jesus taught.

That's what they almost always talk about, in case no-one has seen.
    The tie-dyed cloth is like a badge of love for fellow man and Liberty.
God hears their hopeful rantings about peace and love,
    their visions of pursuit of happiness for man and beast.
They care so much about the Earth that they can't sleep at night.

They chain themselves to trees and risk their lives to rescue whales.
They care about their Third World brothers and march in the street
    with signs proclaiming things said by the Prince of Peace.

What a delight their efforts are to the Most High,
    the way they forgive enemies and look for good.
The TV brainwashers worked very hard to demonize good folks like these.
    They infused sleaze, hired provokers and weird bands, used bad religion.
They did the same to Jesus and his gang when they dared say
    the Beast of greed should take its teeth off mankind's throat.
They nail these people to the cross each day
    with drug wars, child custody suits, and tiny cages that drive men insane.

You need to change your schedule, Land of Liberty,
    from the Dark Ages when torture was cool.
An edible herb in the same legal "schedule" as heroin and crack
    ensures big prison profits for demonic force gripping our land.
The supermax in which you put these saints, these peacemakers,
    aren't different from dungeons where martyrs wept.
Here too people are locked away from loved ones in a civil death,

fed to the corporate Beast for something they consider a religious act.

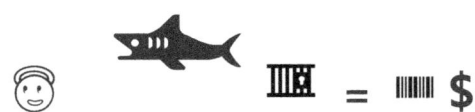

Self-righteous claims of dogmatists have put a healing herb
    in the same class as deadly man-made drugs that kill.

Built to Last

This lie fills prisons til they bulge and threatens almost every home,
    as something is illegal that so many decent people do.
If they made just breathing a crime or going for a walk, then
    prison profits would soar even more, more "felons" lose their vote.
God sees the crooked measure, the larceny in global investors' hearts,
    willing to bury men alive to raise their profit charts.

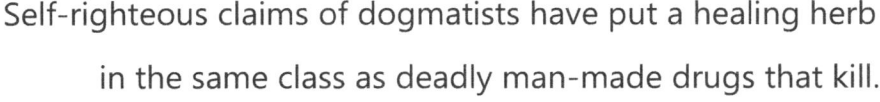

Religionists cheer on these robbers and excuse their crime
    supporting cruel sentences that put the Dark Ages to shame.

Nightmarish hardware is installed that can track an ant from outer space
    or look through walls at people smoking joints.

With the same hand that closes cell doors on the poor and forfeits homes,
    this kind of justice lets real poisoners go with bonus checks.

The kind of minds that made the Inquisition, witch trials and the Red Scare
    make laws giving us no recourse when we're made sick by all we touch.

George Washington grew in his swamp
    the thing for which police beat down our doors.

John Kennedy rocked in his chair, easing back pain with felonies,
    before an assassin's bullet cut him down for trying to stop a war.

So too the Pacifists are persecuted when they smoke or eat the plant,
    with brutal sentences and raids for weeds that grow wild in the yard.

Even the deer like to eat hemp along the roads,
    and birds fly farther and live longer on hemp seed.

A marvelous plant that makes men peaceful and grows free
    is the last thing bullies want who wish to hold us in their grasp.

With helicopters and big clouds of toxic dust and soldiers armed to kill

    in a "War on Drugs" that's really a war on the poor,

they can turn continents into dead zones and move villagers off the land
    so they can mine for minerals and build box stores everywhere.

Builders of pyramids will be enslaved more than when Montezuma fell.
    McDonald's will replace birds' cries in jungles thick if they succeed.

The corporate planners seem willing to hurt

    the Earth, the people, animals and all our dreams,

to kill the plant whose leaves are for the healing of the world,

    which grows twelve months a year and has twelve kinds of fruit.
        (Revelation 22:2) (the only verse in Revelation I ever quote)

Or anything in Nature's store people might find or grandmas told them of

    to ease their pain or calm their nerves,

which corporations can't make money on,

    or which competes with the poisons they push.

LET'S TAKE ONE STEP TOGETHER: At the giant Rainbow Gatherings in the wilderness people yell "WE LOVE YOU!" repeatedly on one side of the camp and others answer back, "WE LOVE YOU TOO!" Let's do the same thing out our windows at sunset on Saturdays, so that the Voice of the People can be heard! We could also play drums for half an hour at sunset on Saturdays at a window. Visit with or meet neighbors! WE NEED ALL OF US! (right + left)

Poems may be reprinted and shared by homeless for donations they can keep.
TELL TEN TO TELL TEN TO VOTE DEMOCRAT!   REGISTER 100 DEMOCRATS!
(https://www.usa.gov/register-to-vote)   (vote.gov) (rockthevote.org)
Democrats against forced mandates and other oppressive liability laws.
BILL OF RIGHTS   GOLDEN RULE   peacedrums.org   UNITE!

A PRECIOUS RECORD

    Ducky sat on the grass next to her wheelchair, her big brown dog nestled against her. She told about hopping freight trains. It's hard to imagine how she could do that while unable to walk, with a dog and a wheelchair. She explained that they always did it when the train was stopped, and that she always had with her a helper travelling companion, one of her "Brothers of the Road." I noticed the gentle care with which these rough young men assisted her. They in turn got some help when making money playing their guitars, because when they were with her, few tourists could resist helping a beautiful girl in a wheelchair. Her infectious and sincere smile, her genuine interest in other people, drew them to her.

The "house-free" who live in the park and around Haight Street have to carry all their belongings with them if they want to hang onto them. Out here all material items have a way of vanishing from their lives in a heartbeat. Often the most precious things in their backpacks, the things they grieve for the most if they're confiscated or stolen, are their journals.

As they sit there all day guarding their stuff, there isn't much they can do to occupy their time or to make contributions to society. So they devote many hours to creating these journals, which they hope might somehow help them to share something with the world or with their distant loved ones.

The journals are dog-eared and road-stained, having travelled on freight trains and in other wild places. Ducky reached into her backpack and pulled out four of them. I held each of them in my hands as if handling a precious museum manuscript. They were cheap medium-sized notebooks, some spiral and some with hard covers. Some were broken up with the covers missing. Many of the pages were so faded that you could hardly read them, having gotten wet at some point.

Here was a record of Ducky's terrible adventures, her hopes and visions, her ideas for fixing the world. There were beautiful felt pen illustrations with symbols and swirling designs, and poetry. There were bright colors and religious themes. Some of the pages were stained with tears. "This is my life," Ducky said, pointing to the loose stack of precious pages, the only copy.

It's so easy out here for things to get lost or in other ways to disappear. Almost every person you meet has a story about losing all their stuff. I thought it was unthinkable that anything should happen to these journals. Later that afternoon I took the thickest one to a printer and had it copied, including some color copies of some of the best drawings. Now there would be two copies which Ducky could keep in two different places, or with another person. This would be a pretty good assurance against loss of such a valuable thing.

STELLA THE HELLA STELLAR DOG

Most nomads have "Bulls" and "Pits." But on this morning at the log there was a little white and yellow Chihuahua. At first, I thought the guy with her was her owner, because he was very affectionate toward her, but he said he was just watching her for someone else. Talking to her, he teased, "I'm going to sell you if you don't behave." He said her name was "Stella the Hella Stellar Dog."

It was a cold morning, and she wore a thick dog coat with an argyle sweater over it with a big turtleneck. The turtleneck cushioned a thick black leather collar worn on top of it, making the heavy collar more 3comfortable. It was a big spike collar with "Coyote" written on it in big letters. The guy said, "She's been more cocky since she's been wearing it." He picked her up and put her in his jacket and snuggled with her nose-to-nose. He said, "She's going back to her rightful owner." I said I doubted it. A few days later I saw her on Haight Street with her owner, a young man in tie-dye riding a bicycle with her trotting happily alongside.

A man named Pan stood on the sidewalk next to the rainbow pillars of the tie-dye store, across from some beautiful San Francisco row buildings. He held a cardboard sign that said, "I'll bet you a dollar that you'll read my sign. God Bless." I've seen other signs on the Haight that people try to make money with: a dollar for a poem, for a joke, for an insult. My favorite said, "Give me a dollar so I won't vote for Trump." His hat was full of donations. People coming out of restaurants give away their containers of leftovers. Some buy a whole new meal to give away.

Some people judge the homeless harshly for panhandling, saying that they want something for nothing. That may be true, and I can't blame local merchants and residents for being annoyed by a gauntlet of panhandlers, some of whom might not be as polite as others. But let's not forget that Jesus said to live like the lilies of the field and the fowl of the air, to not worry about tomorrow, about what to wear or what to eat. When he sent out his disciples, he told them not to take anything with them, no money, but to rely on what was given to them. I believe that most of these young people are on a spiritual journey. They want to own nothing and answer only to God. I wonder... Do people feel as annoyed at the holy men in India with their begging bowls?

PANCAKE BREAKFAST IN THE REDWOODS

It's one of the most beautiful spots in the park, with massive redwoods rising up like cathedral pillars. Bright moss on the sides of the redwoods matches the fluorescent-green of the new grass. Big twisted oak branches, dark from a recent rain, contrast against the vibrant grass with the sun on it. ☀ The grass is so brilliant it almost hurts your eyes. The sun shines on the thick bark of the redwoods, making it seem to glow a golden red. On the other side of a small hill there are olive trees and Eucalyptus. In the other direction toward where the drum circle meets, you can see big fields of lawn including the Janis Tree.

There are no drummers on Monday mornings, when a church group comes to the redwood grove to feed everybody pancakes. Rain or shine they show up with carts loaded with food and clothes to give away and with two heavy-duty power stations with which to run a hot plate for the pancakes. When it rains, they haul in a pop-up shelter on their carts from distant parking areas. They're not the kind of religious people who can be negative and judgmental. They seem to really enjoy the company of the poor, the way Jesus did. Maybe that's why the poor like to go there.

Spiritual strength emanates from Claire, the woman who flips the pancakes. She seems to be the one organizing this, as well as pleasant-looking ministers named Barney and John, who do more listening than preaching. She's dressed in natural clothing like a hippie and she actually has dreadlocks. When the pancakes are finished she also plays a beautiful mandolin. ♪♫ 🎻♪♫ She has sewn two home-made patches to her jacket with big stitches. One says, "RADICAL HOPE," and the other "HOMELESS BILL OF RIGHTS."

Barney just published a book about his experience as a cancer survivor, called "The Other End of the Dark." I bought the first copy sold. It has many wonderful insights. John has long hair despite Paul the Apostle's pronouncement that "if a man have long hair, it is a shame unto him." (I Corinthians 11: 14)   Meeting him I regarded this as a good sign.

The house-free arrive and many go up to each one of these kind souls and confide things to them and get advice or give them news about how they're doing. People sit on tarps and visit while drinking hot coffee from paper cups with powdered creamer, or eating instant oatmeal, or big, thick pancakes drenched with syrup from a gallon bottle.

Sitting on one of the spread-out tarps I met a homeless grey-haired man named Mud Angel. He told me he'd "lost two family members recently." He meant his street family. He said he's been out here thirty years, first started coming to the park in high school, when his mom used to catch him and his teenaged friends smoking pot in the park. He said he was also conceived in this park. He said he saw the space shuttle go by two times right over his head, here at the park.

Looking up a hillside where a sun-touched dirt path wound through the brilliant soft new grass, I saw some young people standing there talking, with the sun on their hair so bright that they seemed to glow. As it started to sprinkle rain the sun was still shining brightly, so that the rain looked like a sheet of diamonds against the forest and the people. I saw in it a vision of Heaven. It didn't matter what they were talking about or who they were. The diamonds said it all.

☆✦ ▽ ✧ ▽ ☆✦

After packing up their gear the church group and the homeless make a circle holding hands, and whoever wants to gets to say a prayer. 🕊 🙏 🕊 They can say it any way they want, with no distinction between theologian and bum. When the group goes off in one direction and the house-free in the other, I get the feeling that each one feels as fulfilled by the encounter as the other. ☺ 💞 ☺

Is it the presence of the beautiful redwoods that makes the two groups get along so harmoniously here? These factions, conservative and liberal, would normally be on opposite sides of the great divide between those who believe mankind is cursed and those who do not. The complex Bible doctrines that Jesus didn't teach are not brought up in the pleasant interactions over pancakes. Maybe it was more than the rain of diamonds that lent an aura of the sublime. Maybe the two sides have more in common than we might think.

It turns out that even this is forbidden by laws against feeding the poor, and that the only way they're getting away with it is that among some officials they're "among friends." At any time the pancake breakfasts could be stopped, like so many other sweet social interactions under growing state control. One of the guests said to me, "Even a little bit of hope, a pancake on a Monday, something solid, can make a difference."

☆✦ ☮ ✝🕊 ☆✦

PUTTING OURSELVES BACK TOGETHER

A pretty young girl sitting with a group of people invited me to sit on the ground with them and their dogs. The dogs were playing, pushing at my feet as I sat on a sleeping bag. They raised huge clouds of dust, especially if they started to fight or even just scratched themselves. The soil at the park is rich and dark when it's damp and soft on the forest floor, but in some open areas where vegetation has been worn away by people sitting there, it becomes a fine dust. The dust doesn't get you that dirty because it falls right off. We were choking on dust but enjoying ourselves anyway, laughing at the dogs. Generations of road dogs have lived and played here. When they get too rambunctious people yell "dog out!" or "kick it down!"

The girl looked cute in a fur-lined hunter's cap, the kind that covers your ears. She said her name is Apple, because once she had an epiphany about apples, the life force in them. 🍎   She talked about travelling, telling how they usually travel with another person and help each other. We discussed relationships. I learned that love and proximity among nomads who are single can be somewhat seasonal, constrained by factors like location and destination. 🚏 ? 📍

   However, I've met many couples who have chosen to get legally married.   I've been struck by how glowingly these speak about their spouse. I haven't heard couples yelling at each other in the forest or on the street, despite the tremendous hardships and frustrations they sometimes endure. They always seem to be on the same side.

   Her boyfriend came, a nice-looking youth in a plaid shirt. He said, "I ride for free," referring to riding the rails. They talked about places all over the country and seemed very familiar with them all. "We're good dirty kids," he said, using a term some of them use to define their groups. They're not really that dirty, just as much as someone trying their best to stay clean while living on the street and riding the rails. They say it proudly in a kind of spiritual sense. Some not only don't have material things, but they don't want them. Some of them are too busy seeking first the Kingdom of God. He said the youth help each other, carry things like bandages in case someone needs them. 🩹

   There was also a man there named Apple Juice. It was probably a coincidence that everything about him was the color of apple juice, his greenish light brown clothes and backpack, his short reddish-brown hair and neat beard. He had a black lab named "Tramp," a well-mannered road dog. 🍎 🎒 🐕

   The girl seemed very adult, though normally someone her age might've been thinking about the mall. Her amazing conversation was like talking to a saint. ☺ She said, "The world is like a puzzle broken into pieces and we're the pieces." She was very serious. "We have to find a way to put ourselves back together."

A HIDDEN TREASURE

Is it because God is all they've got that these young people reach so often for the sublime? They talk about it, attach meanings and messages to it in everything they do and everything that happens to them. My talks with them on all those corners on Haight Street leads me to think they love God with all their heart, all their soul, and all their mind. (Matt. 22:37)

People would never guess, looking at those rough-looking characters on Haight Street, how much they love God. Most of these kids could tell you about miracles they encounter every day. Almost all the ones I've met have seemed to me to be literally walking with God. Some may call the divine presence by a different name, but the majority are quite comfortable with the "G" word and the "J" word, God and Jesus. Their long hair and nomadic lifestyle mimic the Prince of Peace. It's him they quote more than anyone else, him they pray to.

I would bet money that the majority of people out there in our country who embrace what the peace sign represents are into Jesus in one way or another. They believe what Jesus taught but not necessarily the things that others taught about Jesus. They often say that they don't understand how a religion about peace can turn out to be so violent. I can explain this very simply: Paul the Apostle is the main problem.

Paul, a sort of soldier-priest who never met Jesus, was on his way to Damascus with a band of soldiers to capture and imprison Christians. He claims that on the way he had a supernatural experience in which the disembodied voice of Jesus told him to start a church. He then wrote most of the New Testament, adding a million things that the Bible doesn't say Jesus said, and ignoring most of what it says he did say.

His travelling companions Mark and Luke, who also never met Jesus, allegedly wrote two of the Gospels and the book of Acts. Mathew's gospel copied theirs. Paul's many letters to churches he started are then packed with stuff Jesus didn't teach. Then **Revelation** puts in red letters the words of **John of Patmos'** *dream* **Jesus** that he saw while "*in the spirit*" or "*in a trance*," as if Jesus had really said them.

Many theologians agree that the last twelve verses of Mark were added over a hundred years later. It's the only place they've got Jesus saying you have to believe and be baptized or you'll be damned. It happens after his return from the dead, where in other Gospels they've got him saying things that don't sound like him. It's right next to where Jesus allegedly says to speak in tongues and prophesy, and that if you pick up poisonous snakes, or drink poison, it won't hurt you.

There's another suspect scripture that's guaranteed to give organized religions unlimited power over people. It also happens to be placed in his mouth after his return from the dead. It goes, "Whosoever sins ye remit, they are remitted unto them; and whosoever sins ye retain, they are retained." (John 20:23) Here Jesus is allegedly talking to his disciples, giving them power to determine other people's afterlife. Church hierarchy is the inheritor of the disciples' power.

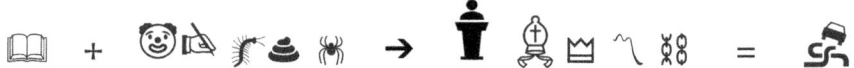

A scripture similar to that is where Jesus allegedly tells Peter, "And I say also unto thee, That thou art Peter, and upon this rock I will build my church; and the gates of Hell shall not prevail against it. And I will give unto thee the keys of the kingdom of heaven: and whatsoever thou shalt bind on earth shall be bound in heaven: and whatsoever thou shalt loose on earth shall be loosed in heaven." (Matthew 16: 18-19). It's in the same chapter where Jesus says to Peter, "Get thee behind me, Satan: thou art an offence unto me: for thou savourest not the things that be of God, but those that be of men." (Matthew 16:23)

I think it's also very interesting that John, the only gospel writer who identifies himself and claims to have walked with Jesus, states several times that Judas (who betrayed Jesus) was Simon's son. The only Simon mentioned in John is Simon Peter. The popes are supposed to be the inheritors of the mantle of Peter. It is they, more than anyone, who **used Paul's doctrines to make a cage for mankind when Jesus wanted to give them wings**.

The things Jesus appears to have actually said stand out in the red letters in the Gospels (in KJV), which came from a different document named Gospel Q, which two gospel writers had but which was lost soon afterward. You can tell these are Jesus's words because they are so fine, so far beyond everything written around them by others. They don't hurt anybody, and they make people feel important instead of like peons.

Unfortunately, Jesus's teachings about peace and understanding are largely put on the back burner in favor of Paul the Apostle's highly negative teachings. That's how a religion about peace turned so violent. Corporate entities, for instance the Roman Empire, liked Paul's doctrines best because they could be used to control people. He wrote, for instance, that slaves should obey their masters in all things.   👐   OK

Tourists and others drive by and stare at the gypsies and their piles of backpacks and dogs. Most of the scene is in road-worn brown tones. There's laughter and pipes are being passed with nature's best. Sometimes there's music from a guitar, or classic rock from a boom box.

🎸 📻 ♪♪ As people drive by some might feel a fear of the unknown that's been drilled into them by the media. How surprised some of them 3might be if they could hear these young nomads' excited conversations about God and the Golden Rule and how they try to love everybody. They are a hidden treasure. Their spiritual journeys should be appreciated as a valuable resource.

Note: These things were all said by Jesus (from KJV), though not in the same order. Aside from a few words in parentheses, the letter "D" in this poem is the only thing added to scripture in this book. (from The Liberal's Bible Guide) The original of this scripture actually says, "The *stone* which the builders rejected, the same is become the head of the corner." (Matthew 21:42)(Psalm 118:22-23)

God's Message to Treehuggers and Peacemakers:

THE STONED THE BUILDERS REJECTED

Be ye sure of this, that **the kingdom of God is come nigh unto you.** (Lk. 10:11)

The kingdom of God shall be taken from (authorities), and given to a nation bringing forth the fruits thereof. **The stoned which the builders rejected,**

the same is become the head of the corner. This is the Lord's doing,

and it is marvelous in our eyes. (Matthew 21:42)(Psalm 118:22-23)

And there are last which shall be first, and there are first which shall be last. And they shall come from the east, and from the west, and from the north,

and from the south, and shall sit down in the kingdom of God.

(Rainbow Gatherings? Peace Demonstrations?) (Luke 13:30, 29)

It is written in the prophets, **"They shall be all taught of God."** Therefore every man that hath heard, and hath learned of the Father, cometh unto me. **"The people which sat in darkness saw great light; and to them which sat in the region and shadow of death light is sprung up."** **Ye both know me, and ye know whence I am**. (John 6:45)(Matthew 4:16)

I am not come of myself, but **he that sent me is true**, whom ye know not. But I know him: for I am from him, and he hath sent me. (John 7:28-29)

Ye shall know that I am in my Father, and ye in me, and I **in you**. (Jn 7:14-20)

The words that I speak unto you, they are spirit, and they are life. (John 6:63) Go ye therefore, and **teach all nations**, teaching them to observe all things (love) whatsoever I have commanded you. (Matt. 28:19-20) And as ye go, say, "The kingdom of heaven is at hand." (now) (Matt. 10:7)

Peace I leave with you, **my peace I give unto you. Not as the world giveth, give I unto you. Let not your heart be troubled, neither let it be afraid.** (Jn. 14:27)

Built to Last

Also: (and God said) Behold, **I have given you every herb bearing seed**, which is upon the face of the earth, and every tree, in the which is the fruit of a tree yielding seed; **to you it shall be for meat**. (Moses in Old Testament)(Genesis 1:29)

And: 🪴 → 🚬

And he (Jesus) saith unto them, "Are ye so without understanding also? Do ye not perceive, that **whatsoever thing from without entereth into the man, it cannot defile him; because it entereth not into his heart**."

And he said, "That which cometh out of the man, that defileth the man. For from within, out of the heart of men, proceed evil thoughts.

THERE IS NOTHING FROM WITHOUT A MAN, THAT ENTERING INTO HIM CAN DEFILE HIM: but the things that come out of him (his words), those are they which defile the man." (Mark 7:18-21, 15)

Jesus' commandments: "**Thou shalt love the Lord thy God with all thy heart, with all thy soul, and with all thy mind** (by loving others). This is the first and great commandment. And the second is like unto it, **thou shalt love thy neighbor as thyself.** On these two commandments hang all the law and the prophets." (Matthew 22:37-40)

Also: "**A new commandment** I give unto you, **that ye love one another**; as I have loved you, that ye also love one another. **By this shall all men know that ye are my disciples, if ye have love one to another**." (John 13:34-35)

PAUL THE APOSTLE AND OTHERS ADDED THINGS WHICH JESUS DIDN'T TEACH: that all are born in sin, the Inquisition, excommunication (shunning,) "slaves obey your masters in all things," Adam and Eve, heresy, antisemitism, "women obey your husbands in all things," shame of the body, hell (really Gehenna, the trash dump of

Jerusalem, or Hades, the land of the dead), tithing, going to church, that idolaters and gays are "worthy of death," the divine right of kings, "obey every ordinance of man," "they that are in the flesh cannot please God," "let the unjust be unjust still," and that it's not what you do that counts, but what you believe in. Red letters in Revelation are the writer's vision or dream and don't teach what Jesus taught, and have been killing people since the ink was dry. JESUS DIDN'T SAY in the Bible that he created the world, or that the Bible was perfect. The part that says you have to believe or be damned, right next to where it says you can "take up serpents" and drink poison, (Mark 16:15-18) was evidently added a century later. The Prince of Peace taught kindness, brotherly love, and Heaven on Earth.

LET'S TAKE ONE STEP TOGETHER: At the giant Rainbow Gatherings in the wilderness, people yell "WE LOVE YOU!" repeatedly on one side of the camp and others answer back, "WE LOVE YOU TOO!" Let's do the same thing out our windows at sunset on Saturdays, so that the Voice of the People can be heard!
We could also play drums for half an hour at sunset on Saturdays at a window.
We could Visit with or meet neighbors the first Saturday of the month.
                        WE NEED ALL OF US! (right + left)
Poems may be reprinted and shared by homeless for donations they can keep.
TELL TEN TO TELL TEN TO VOTE!   ELECT KENNEDY   REGISTER 100 VOTERS (https://www.usa.gov/register-to-vote)   (vote.gov) (rockthevote.org)
Democrats unite against forced mandates and other oppressive liability laws.
BILL OF RIGHTS   GOLDEN RULE   peacedrums.org   UNITE!

TIBETAN GIFT

     Many of the shopkeepers are good friends with the homeless youth, sneaking them into their store or restaurant to let them use a bathroom, though liability laws severely discourage it. Because of "risk," their insurance makes it clear that they could get in big trouble if they don't obey every detail. To satisfy these insurers' business interests, we are ordered to put aside common sense, our conscience, and decency. This is a huge loss of liberty.

The lady who owns an exotic store called Tibetan Gift Corner is one of those saintly souls who agonize about not getting to be as kind as they want to be. Cheola told me how she loves the street kids and would like to do more for them but can't. She lets them gather on the sidewalk on the side of her store and doesn't chase away the little community that arrives there each day, about half a dozen young people and about three or four dogs, and a neat pile of backpacks.

There are always colorful characters there, and some vibrant conversations. They don't panhandle much but just treat it like their living room, even daring to sit down against the wall or on a backpack, although they can get a big ticket for that. If police officers are in sight they have to stand up, and make sure they're holding onto their dogs' leashes. They're usually smiling and laughing, even though they spend most of their time standing up.

The storeowner, a diminutive, appealing woman from Tibet, is a deep thinker. From behind the counter and piles of merchandise on each side, she peers out with a Buddha-like smile. We had a wonderful discussion amid the wealth of treasures in her store. It's crammed with beautiful things from floor to ceiling, ancient-looking handmade clothing and jewelry from Tibet. She said that the young people are smart and that they're good people, that they're just like you and me. She said everybody's the same. We talked about insurance companies. I gave her some poems I wrote about the street kids.

After I left, I walked to the side of the store and got to meet the group positioned there that day. It was a girl and three boys and a dog, travelling companions. The girl was beautiful and dressed in brilliant tie-dyed pantaloons of purple, gold and turquoise that were so full they looked like a long skirt. Before I'd come to the store, I'd seen her colors from across the street. Her name is "Yellow," and the dog is a "Beagle or Foxhound." She introduced me to her friends, who are called "Pink,"

"Orange," and "Gray." "Pink" wears a pink bandana around his neck and so is easy to identify, but it seems that "Grey" should've been the one to be called "Orange" because of his bright red hair. The dog's name is "Blue."

I guess that Yellow is called that because she's like a ray of sunshine. Sitting on backpacks on the sidewalk, "Yellow" and I enjoyed a deep conversation about things that matter. She said, "Life is like a roller coaster that's as exciting and thrilling as ever." She wore freedom like a perfume. She reached into her backpack and pulled out a gorgeous rainbow tie-dyed wall hanging and insisted on giving it to me. She wouldn't take any money for it.

Whenever I'm on that part of Haight Street, I've gotten in the habit of stopping in to see the owner of that store. For months there was a long skirt on sale on a rack in front of the store that I liked but didn't have the money to get. It was a light blue chiffon print, two rich layers that would look wonderful when I danced. The layers would blow in the wind like wings. Each time I went there I fingered the silky material, looked at the price tag. It had at first been fifty dollars.

The only reason no-one was buying this gorgeous skirt was because of a strange waistband that I could easily fix. One day I looked and it was only twenty dollars. I carried it to the lady and asked if she could hold it for me until I could come in with twenty dollars and buy it in a week when I got my check. She said, "Just give me ten dollars next time I see you." I hadn't asked for a discount. At first, I didn't understand and tried to give her the skirt to hold for me. Then she made it clear that she wanted me to take the skirt with me and just pay her later. She practically gave it to me. I'll feel her good energy in it when I dance in the skirt at the drum circle.

ANOTHER TIME

Being on Haight Street can feel like being in another country or another time, or even another dimension. It has beautiful big trees all up and down the street. It has a small-town feel with its own post office, hardware store, an art store with a fabric store, book stores and a doctor's office, all in miniature. It has a small grocery store with an awning and bins of fruit outside, and benches where people can sit and visit. There's a hattery named "Goorir Bros." that looks exactly like one would have a century or more ago, with dark wood paneling and shelves.

A vintage clothing store called "Decades of Fashion" is really an adventure to enter. Taking up a whole street corner, it used to be a bank, with massive pillars and a big stairway. Some people call it "The Vault." There are certainly treasures there, not only in the merchandise for sale, organized by decade, but even more in the displays of real period clothing above them near the ceiling.

There are also amazing reproductions of 1920's beaded dresses, originally recreated by hand by the owner, Cicely Hansen, a beautiful and vibrant woman who does many of the professional restorations herself. I enjoyed meeting her behind a counter at the back of the store, her red-blond hair and fine features and figure complimented by a finely-tailored vintage suit. A Haight Street luminary, she's been a part of this place since the glory days, moved among rock star royalty.

There's also a store named "Distractions" that sells beautiful period clothing, 18th Century-style coats in brocade or velvet, corsets, top hats, and Edwardian silk shirts. I met the owner, Jim Siegel, as he was interacting with Scott. Jim has been an important mover on Haight Street since the early seventies and has done a lot to keep the spirit of this place alive. This is where Scott gets his beautiful period clothes with discounts.

Scott now wears the most amazing top hat I've ever seen, brown leather with a gold haze on the front that makes it look like it's glowing, with inset semi-precious stones. Scott asked Jim if he could pay him later for a vial of patchouli oil. Jim went into the store and got him the vial. I feel that this store has been doing a public service in dressing Scott in splendor, one of the last visible icons of the Sixties on Haight Street.

    Other stores are full of sparkly and brightly-colored creations, sequins and rhinestones, suitable for headliners at rock concerts. There are taverns lined with old wood and brass, and live Irish bands. It's the stuff dreams are made of. At Haight and Masonic there's a real sidewalk café where you can hang out with people walking by and admire the amazing buildings across both streets. On one corner there's "Love on Haight" with its rainbow pillars and wildly beautiful psychedelic art. (Since been painted over.) There's often music coming out of there, and people sometimes spontaneously dance in front of the store.

    Across the street there's another gorgeous building. It is intricately hand-painted in what could be described as a geometric basket design, yellow and brown, completely unique. The two top stories, in high Victorian style, are even more incredible. Painted robin's egg blue, the building has a wide carved painted garland of flowers and ribbons around it between stories. It has several towers with curved glass windows, one of which has a cone-shaped roof like a castle in a fairy tale.

    The building on the other corner is painted in brilliant rainbow colors. In big letters a mural has the words, "THE SUMMER OF LOVE." It's all a celebration of life in architecture and paint. It's the unusual and the colorful in a world where too much is dull and all the same.

    There are several bars on Haight Street that are just like they would've been at the turn of the century. They include Michael Collins Irish Bar and Hobson's Choice Bar Victorian Punch House, among other good ones I don't know about yet. Each of these has a big old-fashioned bar with mirrors and wooden furniture. Hobson's even has a ship's model on display, like would've totally been in a San Francisco bar.

The sidewalk café is attached to Magnolia, an actual brewing company that makes its own beer. Their corner building has beautiful white and black tile work around the base, stained glass over the door, and Victorian round towers with curved windows on the upper stories. Walking in there's a high ceiling with wide moldings, a big bar with mirrors and shiny antique spigots and fittings. There are deep booths with black leather tufted upholstery, with an art deco lantern in each cubicle. High wooden partitions between the booths give privacy. There's also a long high table with stools where people can meet and socialize.

The bathroom entryway has a long antique porcelain sink with brass faucets, white hexagonal tiles on the floor and lots of dark wood. Next to a door, an intriguing white and black enameled small plaque on the wall reads, "Officers' Room." People a century ago, in period costumes, washed their hands here when the world was new.

Amid these wonders my favorite thing there is on the wall opposite the long sink with the brass spigots. It's a big framed picture of Haight Street, packed shoulder to shoulder with young people, during the Summer of Love. The street itself is full, plus every crevice and doorway, down the street as far as you can see. Jerry Garcia and the Grateful Dead are there on a platform and no doubt this was a special event with the street closed off like that. But even with that in mind it moves me to see so many people packed together so tightly, their uplifted faces so hopeful. A theatre marquee in the picture says, "Freedom," "Joy," and "Phoenix." When I look at the black and white photograph, I can feel the power of those people and of those times.

TO EMBODY CHRIST CONSCIOUSNESS

He's kind of a rough-looking character, a little bit like a Celt warrior with his strong physique and loose medium-length dark blond hair and a black leather jacket with spikes. I had thought Bear might be someone who might be cynical about my flowery writings, someone who might complain from experience that things might not be as great here as I make them out to be. But I found myself in profound conversation with him sitting on a stairway on a side street of Haight.

He told me that he'd seen his friend die about a week before. It was his best friend. They were forming a band together and had all kinds of plans. In the middle of one of these projects the friend accidentally locked himself out of his upper-floor apartment. He tried jumping to his balcony from another balcony. He didn't make it. Bear was right there when it happened. Now Bear has plans to go back to school, like his friend had wanted him to, and to become a paramedic. ⊕

As we sat there, he told me that he used to live in the house next door before it was sold. It had been some kind of communal Christian hippie house at that time. He told me how happy he'd been there, that it had maybe been the best time in his life. He said that one time he'd had a chance to go in and look at it again during an open house, but he hadn't. He didn't want to see how much it had changed. 💔

On that ancient sidewalk many people had thrown discarded pieces of gum, so that there were black, flat marks everywhere. Staring at them as we sat there, we wondered if any of the petrified gum stains could have even been chewed by icons like Jerry Garcia and Janis Joplin. Suddenly he stood up and pointed to one excitedly and said, "It's shaped like a heart!"

I got up to examine it, and sure enough the old piece of gum was a perfectly-shaped flat heart like you would find on a piece of jewelry. Then looking around at all the gum we both found more hearts, and more. It really seemed that God was communicating with us as we went from heart to heart, laughing and shouting that it was a miracle. ♥ ♥ ♥ ♥ !!

On Haight Street a young man was discussing God. He had a Pentecostal family background that had turned him off to religion. He said he'd "lost God" for a while because of it, then had found Him again when he took acid. He said he'd felt a part of not only everyone, but everything. "We're all the same," he said. So many people here I talk to say exactly the same thing. It feels like we're all getting the same message from the sublime (one way or another, not necessarily through things like acid or mushrooms) trying to make us smarter and nicer. I think it's an "outpouring of the Spirit."

He said he wanted to spend his life serving God. He said LSD had saved his life, that he used to be a selfish person. He said it helped him to understand that we're all connected and that's why respect is so important. I think that kind of love is what Jesus meant by, "Whatever you've done unto the least of these, you've done it unto me." The young man said he'd found truth "quarter inch by quarter inch" (referring to a paper hit of acid, its shape and size.) Others there agreed.

Bushwacker, whose other name is Cody, said "I have dissected the words, 'be the change you want to see in the world.' That is why I'm the person I am today." Larken Rose wrote this poem in my notebook:

"Trained to see chains as salvation, taught to bow to liars and thieves,

blind devotion to master and nation, binds the soul of he who believes.

What beauty might grow if we let the lie die

and embrace what is simple and true?

Yesterday's blasphemy; now truth most high: as I own me so you own you."

Larken Rose

A tall young man named Kamrin stood on a corner of Haight and Ashbury. He said that sometimes he needed to come here for a while to get re-charged. He was distressed that he'd seen some violence even at this intersection, which is viewed world-wide as a monument to peace. His medium-length hair, bleached at the ends, seemed to illuminate his face and his deep-set eyes. He said, "All I want is to embody Christ Consciousness and to be a messenger of that."

*"The true **democrat** is he who with purely nonviolent means defends his liberty and, therefore his country's and ultimately that of the whole of mankind,"*   Mahatma Ghandi

WHAT JESUS DIDN'T TEACH

Most people would be surprised to learn that Jesus didn't teach anything about Adam and Eve. He didn't teach that people were born in sin. The doctrine of "the curse," the idea that God cursed all mankind when Adam and Eve ate the fruit, comes straight from Paul the Apostle, who never met Jesus. The Old Testament doesn't say that all mankind was cursed, and there's no record in the Gospels of Jesus saying it. There's evidence that Paul possibly didn't write many of the things attributed to him, that the scriptures were "Romanized" by theologians for centuries to suit the purposes of the Roman Empire to control populations.

PAUL THE APOSTLE AND OTHERS ADDED THINGS THAT JESUS DIDN'T TEACH. He never met Jesus and he allegedly wrote "slaves obey your masters in all things," and "women obey your husbands in all things." His writings kicked off the Inquisition, excommunication, tithing, going to church, and the Divine Right of Kings. He added antisemitism, shame of the body, and that it's not what you do that counts, but what you believe in. Others wrote "obey every ordinance of man," "they that are in the flesh cannot please God," and "let the unjust be unjust still."

References to "Hell" were originally about Gehenna, the trash dump of Jerusalem where they threw dead bodies and burned them with "fire and brimstone that was never quenched," or about Hades, the land of the dead. A Greek translation a few centuries later decided to cut corners and make both of those into one term, "Hell." That, combined with the horrors in the book of Revelation, and maybe a few things that may have been added to what the scriptures claim Jesus said, created a perfect tool for the subjugation of mankind.

Red letters in Bibles are supposed to be what Jesus himself said. I would call myself a "red letter Christian," because I believe that the red letters in the four Gospels contain some of the real stories and words of Jesus. There are exceptions. There's evidence that the red letters in the last chapter of Mark were added in the second century. The red letters in Revelation are from a man's dream or "trance," not the real words of Jesus.

I believe that parts of the red letters in Matthew and Luke came from a separate source called "Gospel Q," which the gospel writers had but which was later lost. What makes the content of those red letters seem sublime to me is their utter simplicity and common sense. The Way of Peace that Jesus taught is a key to repairing any planet in trouble like ours. He didn't tell us to worship anything, just to love.

Most people don't know that Gospel writers Mark and Luke were supposed to be Paul's travelling companions, who never met Jesus. Paul also never met Jesus. The Gospel of Matthew copied the other two and may have been merely attributed to the tax collector Matthew mentioned in that gospel. It served the purposes of churches and governments to attribute writings to figures that would give them status and power. Luke is supposed to have written the book of Acts, which lays out the whole church hierarchy thing and lots of rules n'regs not mentioned by Jesus.

The writer of the Gospel of John identifies himself as "the disciple Jesus loved," though "most scholars conclude that the apostle John wrote none of these works." (Wikipedia) It doesn't mention Hell or the ritual of bread and wine. Instead, it says that Jesus washed the disciples' feet at the Last Supper. His gospel is big on saying Jesus is God but doesn't seem to contain much of his actual teachings about kindness and the Golden Rule. Some believe that this gospel was not written by the John who knew Jesus but by a John Presbyter, a student of one of Paul's disciples. This gospel claims that Jesus said he was "the only begotten son of God," a doctrine contradicted every time we pray "Our Father," as suggested by Jesus.

JESUS DIDN'T SAY that he created the world, that his mom was a virgin, or that the Bible was perfect. The part that says you have to believe or be damned is in the last chapter of Mark, right next to where it says you can "take up serpents" (Mark 16:15-18). That part was evidently added over 100 years later by theologians with agendas, employed by emperors and kings. 👑 💸 ⛪ → 💩🖋

The part in John that says, "**if ye believe not that I am _he_,** ye shall die in your sins" (John 8:24), is spoken directly to the Pharisees who were insulting him (not to ordinary people.) Plus, in my King James Bible, **if something is in italics it means the translators added it**, supposedly to make a passage more clear, or if some parts are missing. Maybe it could have meant, "**if ye believe not that I am _right_** ye shall die in your sins."

Jesus was also talking directly to the Pharisees, not to the other people there, when he said (if he said), "Ye are of your father, the devil," (John 8:44). Preachers have often used this scripture to claim that all people are spawns of Satan. The Prince of Peace taught kindness, brotherly love, and Heaven on Earth.

This piece may be reprinted and shared by homeless for donations they can keep.

THE DELUGE

Several weeks of heavy rain poured down on San Francisco. I wondered what the "house-free" do when it rains, and if they still have to take down their tents every morning at the crack of dawn. They do. Some might be able to find an obscure spot where rangers might not venture in the rain, and certainly the gardeners weren't doing much yard work in these conditions. But being isolated means being far from other needed facilities. Without a partner to watch belongings and dogs while someone else goes out to get supplies, it's not advisable. That's how people lose their stuff, by taking chances.

Water seeps in around the edges of the tents. The wind breaks the plastic poles of the dome tents and tries to blow the tents away with the occupants in them. I haven't seen any laundromats on the Haight's tourist strip, where they could dry clothes and blankets. Some people don't have tents at all. If they get soaked, some have told me they wait for the clothes to dry on them. I wonder how long that takes.

I asked a guy where they go when it rains. He said he knew some special secret places. When I asked him where they were, he said, "If I told you where they were, they wouldn't be secret anymore." But he ended up telling me where one was anyway. It's a great location, which I will not divulge. He said that when you find something like that and tell one person then other people find out and pretty soon lots of people show up and everybody gets kicked out.

When it gets very cold and wet, they can go to shelters, but most shelters won't take their dogs. The only way most dog owners can go is if they arrange for one or more persons to sleep at the park and watch everybody's dogs. This is another example of how much people need each other to survive. There are few shelters for dogs in cold weather like for people. Most "shelters" set up for pets are places where they might be put to sleep.

One night as I was trying to get out of the rain at McDonald's (where else?) I sat with a young man who said he'd been trying for three hours to get warm. ❈ His large dog, who wasn't supposed to be there, lay hidden under the table tightly curled up on a towel. They'd spent the night pressed up against a recessed area of a storefront, and the wind had driven sheets of rain into where they were. The guy said the dog had gotten wet too and had been shivering earlier. His short fur probably didn't keep him that warm. His dog coat had gotten wet, but the guy had an extra one that was dry that he'd put on him.

You can stay at McDonald's for about forty minutes, but the staff are kind souls who cut the homeless some slack if it's cold outside and not busy. They'd been more than generous and might even get in trouble for letting him stay three hours, not to mention the dog. So eventually the inevitable happened. A worker was assigned to tell him that he'd been there three hours and would have to leave. Without complaint he got ready and put on his backpack, adjusted the dry dog coat on the dog, and stepped out into the dark and the pouring rain. I saw them standing under the narrow awning of the bus stop across the street.

GEARLESS AND FEARLESS

When the rains stop and the sun finally shines enough to dry the damp grassy area below the Horseshoe, people spread out their things there to dry them off. "Dry'em while you can," one young man said, in a surprisingly cheerful tone after the ordeal of rain. He went on, laughing, "Hoping for sun. Please stay with us, sun!"

He told me about people he'd met on the road, one called Soul Saver and another one named God Finder. I told him how amazed I was that people I'd met who'd lost all their stuff didn't seem too worried about it. Over and over I'd run into people who, it would seem to most people, were in dire circumstances, but seemed to take it all in stride. Is this what Jesus meant when he said not to care about material things, not to take anything on our journey?

My friend said that he too had experienced losing his stuff to the rangers or others, several times. He said he always found what he needed again. He said there was a name for what I was talking about: "Gearless and Fearless." I said, "I'm lucky I live in a house."

The guy said, "I'm lucky I don't."

HOMELESS

The tears of kids in foster homes can show the way it feels

    when the Beast does its favorite thing: tear people from their homes.

Whether they're carried off as slaves or driven out by foreclosure

    or burned out with scorched earth, the result is the same:

communities and clans and tribes established before time began

    are dispersed to all corners of the Earth.

Gone are the ancestors, special embroideries, the songs and dance,

    that set each group apart and made them feel as one.

All that is gone as now homogenous we pass each other on the street,

    afraid to say hello but glancing up with questioning eyes.

Never has man been so alone as in this urban jungle where
      old folks can die alone of cold in cardboard boxes on the street.
Even the cave men cared for such as these,

      saving them an old bear skin and a bone or two.
The elderly, revered by Indians who called God "Grandfather,"
      are medicated for drug profits til they drool on rest home floors.

The zoning and insurance laws won't let us take our loved ones in
      unless we risk getting kicked out ourselves or fined.
They can't live in a tent or trailer in our yard as we might get turned in,
      and liability forbids our giving food to homeless people too.
The grocery stores must put locked gates and warning signs
      around the giant bins of food they throw away each night
to keep the poor from taking it away to feed their families with.
      It's said they even spray it with foul-smelling purple dye or bleach.

The homeless trek across deserts and many trails of tears
      and stand desperate in unemployment lines.
They sleep on couches at their relatives' or create hovels

in some hidden shed or attic like the Nazi victims did.
Many of them sleep in their cars or in abandoned wrecks
    til these get towed, containing everything they own.
Not satisfied with that the Beast demands huge fines and impound fees,
    squeezing food from the hungry like Medieval lords.

There is no doubt where it wants us to go
    when it's stripped us of everything we have and all we are.
The prison system or the military's where we're worth the most
    to corporations eager to suck up whatever's left.
They can get prison dollars from the feds locking us up
    or enlist conquering armies of the poor to go steal oil.
Some think it's gotten to the point of harvesting our kidneys and our lungs
    to give a few of us eternal life.

Is Earth so poor, is God so miserly,
    that human beings must strive and scrape just to survive?
Religionists and bankers preach that man must live by his brow's sweat,
    although you never see them breaking one in their starched shirts.
The Beast lays such huge burdens on our backs,
    with strokes of bureaucratic pens or holy quotes from dusty books.

It carpet-bombs the miserable for war profits

    and sweeps the homeless off the streets with bulldozers.

The Lord has seen what kind of "faith" some preachers have,

  fanatics who want mushroom clouds to prove their prophecies are right.

The lies they teach bear no resemblance to what Jesus taught.

    The "Hell" they love is what they make for all the rest.

The dogmas of their cult of death are so complex and intricate

    that teams of scholars with piles of books can't get them right.

The love that Jesus taught, he said a child could understand.

    It was a thing the unread thief beside him on the cross could grasp.

LET'S TAKE ONE STEP TOGETHER: At the giant Rainbow Gatherings in the wilderness people yell "WE LOVE YOU!" repeatedly on one side of the camp and others answer back, "WE LOVE YOU TOO!" Let's do the same thing out our windows at sunset on Saturdays, so that the Voice of the People can be heard! We could also play drums for half an hour at sunset on Saturdays at a window. We could visit with or meet neighbors the first Saturday of the month.   WE NEED ALL OF US! (right + left)

Poems may be reprinted and shared by homeless for donations they can keep.
TELL TEN TO TELL TEN TO VOTE!   ELECT KENNEDY   REGISTER 100 VOTERS!
(https://www.usa.gov/register-to-vote)   (vote.gov) (rockthevote.org)
Democrats against forced mandates and other oppressive liability laws.
BILL OF RIGHTS   GOLDEN RULE   peacedrums.org   UNITE!

UNLAWFUL LAWS

I spent the morning at McDonald's with a guy who had almost been a lawyer and knew the law. He told me it's true that more than three people gathered smoking pot is a conspiracy. Some friendly police officers had come by and told him and his friend about it. This liability law made me mad. The people always gather in sweet little groups I enjoy so much. It's reassuring to see them in clusters in the morning, talking about the day like people have always done, or about important things like liberty. Seeing them makes me think there's still something sane about our world.

We talked about the guy who lived in a plywood box in a friend's living room for $400. a month until his arrangement was declared illegal by fire codes. People can live in a group home in a 6-person bedroom for $650. a month. Or they can rent a bunk bed with twelve other people in the room for $1200. a month. The scary Orwellian thing is that they're not allowed to put up a curtain on the bunk bed. They get absolutely no privacy for all that money! After leaving McDonald's I wished I'd asked him more questions. For instance, does a drug conviction mean the person has to pay back money for scholarships already used? What constitutes a drug conviction? A misdemeanor? An infraction?

Behind Whole Foods there's a tiny building right next to the sidewalk that was probably the kind of kiosk where you used to bring film to be developed. It's now painted brightly with Amanita Muscaria magic mushrooms, though nobody uses it for anything. It's been closed for years but it has nice curbs and is a little bit out of the way and is sometimes a good place to sit. There was a young guy at this kiosk playing a guitar. He was being very friendly with the passerby, in an exuberant mood.

He told a woman walking by that she was beautiful but would be more beautiful if she smiled. She got all mad and said that she would call the police, that this was street harassment. She stalked off. I ran after her and tried to apologize and explain for him that he didn't mean to offend her. I could understand how she felt, having to run a gauntlet of people panhandling every time she left her Haight Street apartment to go to the grocery store.

I then went back to him and he was shaken by the incident. He said he'd just been busted for trespassing for sleeping in the place where he'd been sleeping for seven years, and that he already had two other tickets. He'd gotten a ticket for not standing up. It's illegal to sit down on the sidewalk, so the nomad youth who spend the day there are supposed to remain standing all day. They sit down anyway if there are no police around. If police officers catch them, most cut them some slack and just ask them to move, but some give them tickets.

He'd also gotten a ticket for his dog not being on a leash, although it was on a leash and tied to his backpack right next to him. That too is illegal. He decided to leave the area. He hauled on his neat backpack and walked away with his dog. From a distance up Haight Street I could see them walking, the red dog bowl and a folded green tarp tied to the back of his backpack, making bright spots in the crowd.

A little later in the day as I sat in the park with a group of people, someone shouted "SIX-UP!" A police motorcycle had abruptly emerged from the trees and was coming downhill on a dirt path toward the group. It was unexpected and unnerving, though not a surprise. It was not uncommon for loud motorcycle engines to break the sylvan perfection of nature, even in the most remote areas. From a distance the officer's big helmet made him look like an alien, but when he got up close he reassured the youths with a smile. He asked one to put out his cigarette and then roared on toward the street.

After that two cop stories were told, but not the kind you would expect. One guy told about the time a cop had bought him a meal. Another guy said a cop had given him forty dollars instead of giving him a ticket.

AN UNFORGETTABLE VACATION

At McDonald's I met "Old School," a smiling grey-bearded long-haired gentleman with a backpack and his "Chiweenie" dog. The Black, brown and white Chihuahua and Dachshund mix with high pointed ears and short fur and an oddly-shaped little body, wore an attractive red and white dog coat. Old school said, "I could lose everything I have and I'd be all right, but not if I lost my dog."

He told me he has an idea for a new business: Homeless Vacation Packages. People would give him $1500. and get absolutely nothing. They would be dropped off in a seedy part of town without even a sleeping bag and no money. They would get instructions about dumpster diving and how to urinate in public without being caught. On a worn-out piece of paper he had the plan all mapped out, the beginnings of a brochure.

Later that night, as I approached the kiosk near Whole Foods, I was met with the vision and wonderful sound of a really amazing hillbilly band. They had overalls and wildly free hair and really looked the part. They had a washtub with a string on it, a jug, a banjo, a guitar and a fiddle. They looked larger than life there on the corner. The rousing music they made was full of life.

BLESSED BEYOND BELIEF

At McDonald's I ran into "Change," the woman with dreadlocks who'd told me she felt caged in a house. She was the one who'd first told me about the term "house-free." She looked regal sitting on the plastic stool in her long skirt, her hairstyle evoking pre-Christian visions. The Vikings probably wore their hair in dreadlocks or braids like this, and Druids, and gypsies. Dreads are cool and people wear them as a spiritual statement. Unfortunately, lots of people think hippies are dirty if they have dreads. That's why I personally prefer the neat rows of braids I've seen.

She had a commanding presence. I walked toward her, and she motioned me to sit down. Amid the loud beeping from the French fry machine, we had a conversation. A girl with purple hair came by and showed Change a pretty scarf she had. Change asked, "Is it for trade?"

The girl replied, "No, I was going to give it to you."

Change said that whenever she's been in trouble, it's always been street people who've helped her. She said, "I want to give kindness and I want to deserve kindness." It turns out she's fed thousands of people over the past four years, at Rainbow Gatherings, and also running outdoor free food kitchens with a travelling community. She said, "All I need is some firewood, a grill, some pots and a big tarp, and you've got a kitchen!"

Her husband, named "Mellow," arrived at the McDonald's. He turned out to be a young man I'd seen earlier at the log on crutches. At that time, he'd told a harrowing story about how he'd been shot in the leg by a crazy guy and then had lost all his stuff. The police were required to confiscate his belongings as evidence because the other guy had shot him and it was an "open case." They'd told him he'd get them back someday, whenever they caught the guy, which would probably be never. Thankfully, Change wasn't there when it happened and was not involved.

I've never heard of confiscating the belongings of the victim. It must be some new law that none of us has heard of. The officers took all his camping gear, his backpack, sleeping bag, some new sandals, and a special SFPD patch that had been given to him by a San Francisco police officer as a gift. He said that when that officer had walked toward him, at first, he'd been scared to be in trouble. Instead the cop had handed him the patch and he'd been incredibly moved. Now that too was gone.

But the thing he was the most upset about was the loss of his new "Carhartt" overalls, his "bibs." He admitted he cried about the insulated overalls that seem to be a gold standard for those living outdoors. "You can sleep in the snow in those things!" he exclaimed. "I'm devastated." He said losing the overalls was almost as serious as getting a bullet in the leg. He lamented that he'd been at the top of his game, had his equipment just the way he wanted it, when this happened. He said that wearing the overalls had made him feel free.

When telling the story at the log he'd lifted his pant leg to reveal a gauze bandage going completely around his leg, with a big fresh red blood spot on each side. The bullet had gone in one side of his lower leg and come out the other side, and it hadn't healed yet after almost a month. He also had a metal pin in his leg that the hospital had put in, and then released him after only three days. He said he'd cried from the pain for those three days. Now eating French fries with us he was in better spirits than when I'd seen him at the log. He exclaimed, "go team!" He said they would probably head south now that the weather was cold. He asked, "Why let the birds be smarter than you?"

Change and her husband are legally and happily married, like several other couples I've met on the street and in the park. These relationships seem particularly close. The youth tell you right away that they're married, tell you about their wedding day or how they met. Working together to survive seems to bring couples closer, seems to help them appreciate each other. Maybe they value their relationships so much because that's all they have. Maybe the material world gets in the way of love for "housies" more than for those who can carry all that they own on their backs. Some might find it surprising that many of those who live outside feel sorry for those with houses and jobs.

Change said about the Haight: "This is a magical place that we cycle in and out of. We can make something happen that's blessed. Everybody comes in, gets what they need, and then brings it somewhere else. It flows better that way." Even with all the challenges they both faced, she said she felt "blessed beyond belief."

A few weeks later I ran into Change again. She was running around trying to find someone with jumper cables to jump-start their van, which needed to be moved or it would get tickets. I found out that her husband was back in the hospital because his wound had gotten infected and they had to replace the pin in his leg. I wondered if she still felt "blessed beyond belief." Amazingly, she said that she did.

Note: These things were all said by Jesus (from King James Version), though not in the same order.

JESUS: HE THAT IS NOT AGAINST US IS FOR US

Are not two sparrows sold for a farthing? 🕊 ♡

And one of them shall not fall on the ground without your Father

But **THE VERY HAIRS OF YOUR HEAD ARE ALL NUMBERED.**

Fear ye not, **YE ARE OF MORE VALUE** than many sparrows. (Matt. 10:29)

Is it not written in your law, "I said, Ye are gods?" I have said, **YE ARE GODS**; **ALL OF YOU ARE CHILDREN OF THE MOST HIGH.** (John 10:34)(Psalm 82:6)

I CALL YOU NOT SERVANTS; for the servant knoweth not what his lord doeth:

but I HAVE CALLED YOU FRIENDS. (John 15:15)

WHY CALLEST THOU ME GOOD?

There is none good but one, that is, God. (Mark 10:18)

And blessed is he, whosoever will not be offended in me. (Matthew 11:6)

<u>HE THAT IS NOT AGAINST US IS FOR US</u>. (Luke 9:50)

And **IF ANY MAN HEAR MY WORDS, AND BELIEVE NOT, I JUDGE HIM NOT:**

for I came not to judge the world, but to save the world. (John 12:47)

And **WHOSOEVER SPEAKETH A WORD AGAINST THE SON OF MAN,**

IT SHALL BE FORGIVEN HIM. (Matthew 12:32)

HE THAT IS NOT AGAINST US IS ON OUR PART. (Mark 9:40)

I JUDGE NO MAN.

Who made me a judge or a divider over you? (John 8:15) (Luke 12:24)

For God sent not his son into the world to condemn the world;

but that the world through him might be saved. (John 3:17)

THE SON OF MAN IS NOT COME TO DESTROY MEN'S LIVES

BUT TO SAVE THEM. FEAR NOT,

for **IT IS YOUR FATHER'S GOOD PLEASURE**

TO GIVE YOU THE KINGDOM.

Let not your heart be troubled: ye believe in God, believe also in me.
(Luke 9:56, 12:32) (John 14:1)

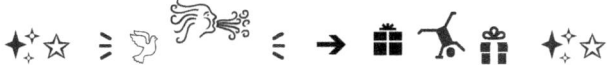

JESUS DIDN'T TEACH: that people are born in sin, the Inquisition, excommunication (shunning,) slaves and women "obey in all things," Adam and Eve, antisemitism, shame of the body, hell, tithing, having to go to church, that idolaters and gays are "worthy of death," the divine right of kings, that the Bible was perfect, or that he created the world. Paul the Apostle and OTHERS ADDED those, plus "obey every ordinance of man," "let the unjust be unjust still," and that it's not what you do that counts, but what you believe in. The part that says you have to believe and be baptized or be damned, right before where it says you can "take up serpents" and drink poison, (Mark 16:15-18) was evidently added by theologians over a century later. Red letters in the book of Revelation are the writer's vision or dream and don't teach what Jesus taught, and have been killing people since the ink was dry. The Prince of Peace taught kindness, brotherly love, and Heaven on Earth.

HEAVEN

Heaven feels like sitting on the ground with a group of friends in the morning, sharing coffee and other refreshments, while breezes and the sound of morning birds sweeten the air. Heaven sounds like people calling each other "Bro." It looks like people being free, wearing what they want, saying what they want. Probably one of the biggest reasons a lot of them are out here is because they want to say, wear, and do what they want. For them, a corporate nine-to-five can't let them have that kind of liberty, which they feel they can't live without.

Here at Golden Gate Park, a religious feeling is strongly felt. Most often it's not discussed openly in those terms, but the theme of the holy surfaces in roundabout ways in almost all aspects of these people's thoughts and conversations. If some of them are not comfortable with organized religion, it's because they're educated enough to know some of the things it's done. They're more into disorganized religion.

After finding it on the Internet, I stayed up almost all night looking at it. It was a large collection of material about the abuses of the religion founded on the Prince of Peace but not by him. There were countless genocides, hideous tortures in graphic woodcuts, and a massive guilt trip laid on all mankind. I'd known it was bad, but not that bad. From the overt fraud apparent in many of the scriptures, to the massacre of innocents that covered the Earth with rivers of blood, the whole tableau of the wrongs religion has done is absolutely revolting.

The horrors were not from particular places or time periods. They were all across the board, in every province, every territory in Europe and beyond. Clerics have been killing and torturing people in the name of Christ since the moment Constantine saw his vision of the cross and heard the words, "under this sign conquer!" Those in the remotest hovel were not immune to the complete control of their most intimate personal lives by the monster Medieval church. The penalties for disobedience were the most cruel that could be devised. Compliance required a lion's share of a poor man's food, or the bequeathed fortune of a rich man as a ticket out of eternal torment.

Don't get me started. The worst things are not even the ugly scenarios played out from the Inquisition to the Aztecs to the witch trials to the Drug War. Prison religions that teach things which the Bible doesn't say Jesus said, enslave people. They give them a negative vision of mankind's future and rob them of what Jesus really taught about love and brotherhood. Studies in forensic theology have convinced me that many "organized" religions have done more to drive people away from God than to bring them closer. Most people are naturally kind and already close to

God. Some religions and governments work hard to make them bad and make them think other people are bad. That's how tyranny finds its home.

According to the Gospels, there was nothing complicated about the way Jesus talked to the crowds of people who followed him. He just told them to treat others the way they'd like to be treated, and that they were all sons and daughters of God. He didn't accuse them of anything. The only ones he accused were religious leaders for being mean to the people. He said Heaven was "at hand," and "within you," not somewhere else. A lot of us seem to think that it's right here in Golden Gate Park.

HE'D HAVE TO KILL HIM TO GET THE DOG

The road dogs are very intelligent, and usually very well-mannered, unless they're getting into fights. The leashed dogs sit quietly beside their people, in a calm and serious attitude, as if they know they have a job to do. A good strong dog will guard his person's stuff, guard his person, and keep him warm at night. They seem smarter than other dogs, maybe because they spend so much time so close to people. To these lonely

wanderers, particularly those who travel alone, their road dog is everything to them. They think so much of them that they also call their human travelling companions "road dogs."

A young man named "Flag" wore the usual dark travelling clothes overlaid with "swag" of pins and patches. He had a small animal pelt on part of his hat, which was a 19th century-style cap with a visor, with a fox tail hanging from the back. He told a story about his road dog. Somewhere in the Midwest he got stopped for jaywalking. The cop said to him, "I'm going to put you in jail and put your dog in the pound." Flag said he told him he'd have to kill him to get the dog. The cop decided to let them go. The young man was willing to die not only to save the dog but to assert his human dignity and sovereignty, his right not to have his beloved dog taken away for a minor infraction.  ? !

He told another story. A while back he and his dog were at a truck stop. Something startled the dog and he ran right under the wheels of a semi-truck that was moving slowly through the parking lot. Flag jumped under the wheel of the semi and pulled his dog out safely just in time, but he got hit by the wheel and broke his collar bone and two ribs. He hasn't been to the doctor. He said they can't do anything about it anyway, because they can't put a cast on those bones. He said he just has to wait and let it heal.

"Slinky" is a gentle but dynamic young man with long dark curls and a reversed baseball cap full of pins, a Star Wars T-shirt, and a tattoo of the chemical formula for THC. He arrived at the log with a dog I hadn't seen him with before, a golden pit bull with yellow eyes, ears pushed back, and powerful jaws. His short sleek fur and light brown nose also made him look like the archetype of a really scary dog. Slinky had gotten stuck with the dog when its owner, a total stranger, had gotten arrested and had begged him to take his dog so that he wouldn't be taken to the pound.

Practicing the Golden Rule energetically, the boy had said he would do it. He just couldn't stand it that the guy could lose his dog and that the dog could be put to sleep. The police officers had taken Slinky's information and agreed to let him take the dog. The guy who was arrested would find them both later "at the park" in a few days when he was released. So the guy was taken away and Slinky was left alone with a wild-looking, powerful animal who'd never seen him before.

He admitted that the dog almost bit him, but it was when they were playing. His leash consisted of a thick rope with a loop at the end tied with a big knot. When Slinky tried to play with him, the dog thought the knot was a pull toy and kept grabbing it with his jaw, sometimes catching a portion of his guardian's hand. He spoke affectionately about the dog. "He slept right next to me all night, and even with no leash he never went more than ten feet away."

Helping someone else is a valued currency to these young people as they negotiate through their hard lives. They do it whether or not they're aware that Jesus said, "Whatever you've done unto the least of these, you've done it unto me," and "With whatever measure ye mete, it shall be meted out to you." That homeless brother being arrested, probably for some minor pot violation, who'd just had all his stuff confiscated and was about to lose his precious dog, certainly qualified as "the least of these." And the spiritual exaltation of people who said they were happy even while sleeping in the rain, qualifies also as a generous measure of reward for embracing the Golden Rule.

Most people like to help others for the sheer pleasure of it, not because they're afraid to burn in Hell or are hoping for a reward. I marveled at what the young man had done, which could've turned into a real hassle. He said that anyone would've done the same thing. I protested "For strangers?" Everyone agreed that most people wouldn't have done it for a stranger, but that it probably does happen.

"Never doubt that a small group of thoughtful, committed citizens can change the world; indeed, it's the only thing that ever has.
Margaret Meade

THE BEAST (Totalitarianism)

It prowls through halls of governments

and in the holy places of religions.   Bill of Rights  Use It or Lose It

With bloody teeth it tears apart the innocent

    and crushes idealist dreams.

With terrible claws it can rip to pieces the hopes of the gentle,

    using holy wars, witch hunts and secret police.

It can scatter and lay to waste

    even the paths of Paradise.

Built to Last

"Oppression" is a name of the cold-eyed monster

    which stalks mankind's collective dream of peace.

The creed that some may have it all and others nothing,

    expressed on clean white parchments by bureaucrats,

is carried out in squalor and sorrow

    as starving mothers weep over dying babies.

The worship of books and leaders and buildings

    leads to the desecration of the holy things in each of us.

The Beast cannot always be seen at first,

    but it can be smelled.

The descending smoke and ash in Nazi cities,

    the rotting bandages on a refugee's infected feet, tell us it's there.

The brazier of the torturer emits the foul scent of the Beast, the clothes of street children who sleep in garbage to keep warm.

There is the sweat and tears of millions locked in tiny cells,

each worth fortunes to men who construct prisons for their wealth.

With ravenous rage the creature now stands ready to destroy

the Bill of Rights, the Golden Rule, even the Earth.

Poised to destroy the peace sign and the pursuit of happiness,

it uses time clocks to break Christ in us each day.

Machines with glowing, colored lights are used

to tell us what to think and who to hate.

Other machines are used to spy on us from outer space,

to see which substances we have abused.

The real violence of what is done is seen

in burning rain forests and dying seas.

It's heard in lonely nighttime cries of children

whose parents are jailed for innocent acts,

and in the wails of tiny infants

    wrenched from mothers at dawn by a McJob.

The Beast has such disguises and such silky speech.

    The Spirit of God is the only thing that it can't fool.

THE RIGHT SPARK

There's something special about greeting the day outdoors, with other people, the way people have done since time began. It's pleasurable and reassuring to share banter with our fellow creatures, in the freshness of a new day, the way birds do when they make a raucous noise through the forest when the light comes. What I love about the park is that there's always someone there to hang out with, a whole ready-made community of people who have time to talk, time to think. They're rarely looking at tablets or cell phones. They can't afford them. Instead they have conversations, read books, make music. They make artifacts to sell, wear, trade or give away.

    I made my way to the log early in the morning, not long after a handful of the house-free had taken down their tents and assembled there. Already people were busy with their various projects and activities. A Celtic-looking guy with reddish dreads tied in a topknot on top of his head, sat on the log sewing two tigers onto his army jacket. He called them "patches" but they were really pieces of printed material he'd cut out of something he got at Goodwill. The ferocious-looking tigers were too big to be patches. Another part of his jacket had another "patch" of Baby BamBam from "The Flintstones." His red T-shirt with a guy playing a saxophone on it seemed to express a free-wheeling attitude.

He looked like a twenty-first-century version of Braveheart. When he put on his jacket, I saw that there was a weasel skin sewn to it, head and all. He said somebody gave it to him. The narrow body was sewn to the hood from front to back, with the face of the weasel right above his forehead. He also had a tattoo on his arm of the logo for the insecticide "Black Flag."

He spoke of the Punk movement like a history professor. He knew all the songs of all the bands, what order they were in, and the background story for each one. He also knew everything there is to know about the Grateful Dead. He asked for my notebook and wrote the names of Punk styles and Punk bands for me that I might like to check out. They included "Horror Punk," "Ghoul Rock," and "The Misfits." He said he just got his lip rings yesterday. The fresh cuts looked painful. I saw that in his bag he also possessed a raccoon tail. He said that he was sewing on the tigers because the raccoon was no longer his spirit animal.

The log was like a sewing circle that morning. A different young man was sewing "Scum Dog" on his jacket, a jean jacket with the sleeves removed. The jacket also had on the back an elaborate large skull, the Grateful Dead logo, with a lightning bolt on each side. Inside the head there was a metaphysical representation of the Tree of Life in fractal designs. This emblem is also supposed to be a diagram to enlightenment, mapping out the seven chakras, or energy centers, of the body.

With him was his beautiful girlfriend, in a long flowing tie-dyed skirt. Their dog, a Pitbull type in a camo dog coat, is named "Lasagna." The girl held onto the dog with a leash that had rainbow dancing bears on it, another Grateful Dead logo. It's important to hold onto big dogs, as there are many smaller animals around. One time a dog killed a kitten there at the log, snatching it right out of a girl's lap and breaking its neck.

A guy sitting further down on the log was holding and petting a puppy whose name is Pikachu, named after a type of stuffed animal.

Everything was peaceful until a Siamese kitten nearby tried to eat some of the puppy's kibble. The guy gently grabbed the puppy and held onto it tight. It barked loudly, adding to the noise of skateboards roaring by.

    A young man arrived very excited, wearing a beautiful light blue tie-dyed T-shirt with a picture of the world on it. It was his first time here. He'd travelled a long way to come to this special place. From the look of his newer, very clean clothes, it seemed like he might be a "housie" travelling in a car, on a pilgrimage. He smiled and laughed like someone who has reached a longed-for destination, his big white Pitbull mix by his side. The newcomer was made to feel welcome at the log, even though he was just visiting.

    He wore a hand-blown glass pendant with rainbow lines in a spiral design, and a cap thick with commemorative rock insignia. He talked about a concert he'd attended at Red Rock, to see a band called "Further." He said he "pulled all my pins and all my swag" because he thought some of the concert goers were not true hippies or didn't have the right spirit. "Swag" refers to band memorabilia, posters, patches and pins, especially those about the Grateful Dead. He'd removed pins from his clothes because he didn't want to be seen as a "poser," a "week-end hippie." I've never heard of anyone doing that before.

    I welcome and celebrate the posers. The "week-end hippies" are busy at their five jobs the rest of the week and probably on the weekend too, just trying to survive. But his removing his pins does show the seriousness which some feel about what they believe in. However, judging others or ourselves for not being cool enough, would not be cool. Later that day I saw him at the drum circle zoning out blissfully on a borrowed drum, his white Pitbull lying down between his feet.

A man named "Sonic" (his real name is Adam) wore fluorescent green sunglasses that matched the fluorescent green light reflections of plants around the pond. He said he likes to be positive. He waxed poetic as he told me how much he loves his dog, "Button." The dog has a collar with buttons sewn all the way around it.

Sonic wears bracelets with lots of crosses on them and semi-precious stones. The necklace he wears is absolutely unique and looks quite heavy. He made it from a brass candle holder and some stones wrapped in various wires, copper, brass, and even a little gold. The cornelian wrapped in copper is supposed to increase blood circulation.

There's also some hemp rope on his necklace, which for us represents the liberty to do, say, smoke what we want. After all, Jesus said that it's not what goes into man's mouth that corrupts him, but what comes out. With what seemed like wisdom beyond his years he said, "We choose to love each other." He said, "Give people the right program to plug into. They only need the right spark then they'll take it from there."

Just then someone yelled, "SIX UP!" the signal that there are police around. I heard the shout before hearing the sound of two police motorcycles emerging from the woods across the pond. They travelled right on the bumpy forest paths, down a hill at a rather high rate of speed. It was such an intrusion on the golden morning, the loud engines of the motorcycles overpowering the sounds of breezes and birds, the rough tires kicking up clods on the soft forest floor. The worst thing was the threat of being put in cages for things not considered to be crimes.

Of course, the officers had helmets on and we couldn't see their faces. As they drove slowly past the log we smiled at the helmets. They're our brothers but have to do this job whether they agree with it or not.

They didn't see anything illegal going on and kept on going.

HOW TO TRAIN YOUR DOG

At the log "Rocky Raccoon" has a raccoon tail hanging from his belt, and a winged pyramid on his hat. He gave me a crystal. He was making a keychain with a luminous stone with green and gold streaks, wrapped with three colors of wire, silver, copper and gold. Attached to it was a large filigreed almond shape that's a piece of costume jewelry, some small grey stone beads, a piece of root shaped like a tooth, and a delicate chain hanging across the bottom. Not really a keychain, it would be a work of art containing different parts of the Earth. He said the silver and copper wire were the real metal but the gold was not.

His friend was trying to sell the keychains and other crafts he'd created to people walking by. He wore a nice beige suit that complimented his attractive curly brown hair, and a Grateful Dead T-shirt. This kind of business arrangement beside the pond might look funky but it's real commerce, real "free trade," on which real liberty stands.

Ariel, a beautiful young girl, yelled at her big dog, who got in a fight with another dog. Ariel bit her dog. "Street dogs need to be disciplined," explained Rocky Raccoon. "You have to talk to them in their own language." He also advised, "Pee on your dog and it'll establish dominance." He said the ASPCA guy came by one day and they told him, "We don't tell you how to live your life, so don't tell us how to live ours." Ariel was worried that her finger was numb. She said she'd gotten in a fight with a girl the day before because the girl had insulted Ariel's boyfriend. The girl had bitten her finger.

On the pavement on a blanket there was a yellow dog of medium build that didn't look well. Its fur looked damp and without luster. I tried to pet the dog but a guy said not to because the dog was sick. There was a girl who seemed to be helping care for the dog. She was wearing a 40's-style helicopter hat, red blue and yellow, with blades on top of her head that moved when she moved. She came and gently hugged the dog, a full body hug, completely covered it leaning over it, giving it love. We had a great conversation while she petted the dog, who lay zoned out on its side. She said, "You have to give respect to get respect." Later I found out the dog gave birth to puppies that day.

"I SAW WHERE JESUS WAS HIDING"

It was a rare hot day, during the hottest summer in memory in foggy San Francisco. The young people in a large group next to the pond were having a kind of party. There was loud music from a radio. They'd somehow found a couple of fancy black executive chairs on rollers and were barreling up and down the walkway at a high rate of speed and laughing. They were having a blast. Others were cheering at the skateboarders across the pond, who performed feats like jumping over people with their skateboards. A youth named Tater Tot yelled to one of them, "Dude, that was totally epic!"

Like almost everything else nice in their lives, their impromptu office chair races didn't last. The roar of motorcycles came from the direction of the tunnel. Two police officers emerged and told them to move the chairs off the pavement because they were blocking the roadway and causing a hazard. This time I had to agree with them. One of the young people replied politely, "Absolutely!"

They quickly pulled the chairs up an embankment into the trees, where they could at least sit on them that day. The only other chairs these people sat on were the hard benches at the park and the equally hard plastic chairs at McDonald's. The rangers' clean-up crew would pick up the chairs by the morning unless they could hide them for a while in some hobo jungle in a more obscure part of the park.

So they set up the chairs on the embankment. They continued to live in the moment, eating McDonald's and talking movies and books. Wendy Whimsey sat on another embankment making hair wraps on a girl with purple and grey yarn. The girl was also working on something, making jewelry with wire and stones. At first I didn't notice, but as people walked by Wendy would call out just to be funny, "Tickets to the Gun Show!" It was hilarious because most hippies hate guns and so do most of the people who come to Golden Gate Park.

On the pond there were beautiful light reflections, and in that season, there were big pink flowers on stems six feet high. Someone had hung a hammock on the small outcropping of land near where the frog fountain sprays out a fan of water over the surface of the pond. Tree branches made shady grottos around the edges of the pond and of a small island, where there's a miniature pagoda. The vivid contrasts of a thousand sun-touched shades of green made an explosion of color. The sound of water was pleasant and reassuring, the way it is to all creatures.

You could smell the water and the perfume of lilies. There were delicate grasses on the ground, and gold sun reflections on the brown angled rocks and boulders bordering the water. There were purple flowers, orange, white, and Birds of Paradise, and graceful ferns. There was even a place that looked like a miniature beach, next to clusters of small palm trees, where a small area of the concrete bottom of the pond was exposed. The birds were enjoying it, bathing themselves on its shore.

People sat and lounged on the logs, soaking up the warm weather after months of living in the cold wind. The dogs were panting in the heat.

On the slope a couple of them had dug holes in the cool earth to get relief. Two park workers came by in their utility vehicle, but they weren't there to get anyone in trouble. They were bringing back a big plastic cooler so that these people and their dogs wouldn't be thirsty on this hot day. ♥   I didn't find out whether it had been lost or confiscated.

I felt the love that existed between some of the park staff and the house-free. The white and orange cooler had also been filled with cool water. Someone went over and filled a bowl with it from the handy spout. A tiny orange kitten and a big yellow dog drank from the bowl together. A young man in a beautiful T-shirt with a blue lightning bolt on it was telling us about his religious experience. He said, "I saw where Jesus was hiding when I opened up that third eye." 🍄 → 👁

ON HIPPIE HILL

It's usually the same guy who watches everybody's stuff in a big plastic carpenter's cart. His name is Aaron but his street name is Four-Twenty, because he was born on April 20, a hippie holiday. At the accustomed bench on the meadow he can often be seen sitting all day, except for when someone comes to relieve him for a while. It appears that he volunteers to do this without any kind of compensation. He has long dark blond hair in a low pony tail, and several necklaces over the sturdy army jacket that's meant to shield him from the frequent cold winds to which he is fully exposed on that bench.

In spite of the wind or sun exposure, this bench out in the open is still the best place to park the cart during the day. The wheels of the fully-loaded cart wouldn't make it up the embankments into the forest where there might be more protection from the elements. Plus, there's a greater measure of safety out here in the open where there are people around, in case someone tries to take the stuff off the cart. The cart is neatly packed with sleeping bags, back backs, tarps, tents, sleeping mats, a folded metal cart, a black plastic box with food in it, a folding chair, a guitar, and lots of plastic grocery bags with stuff in them hanging off the sides.

There's something steady and strong about the guy watching the stuff, whose name is   He doesn't say much but seems to listen carefully to the stories of people who come and sit on the bench with him. One of his necklaces has a small blue mushroom imbedded in a piece of glass. Another is an Indian necklace with real bones, and another has shells, glass, bone, wood beads and gem beads, a feather, and a wolf tooth. The only thing that's not on it is plastic. He said, "The wind has seared me. Winter's warmer than summers here in the Bay Area. Cold wind leads to bad attitudes."

A man named Pretty Tony came and sat on the bench for a visit. He had on a black leather vest with spikes and a baseball cap over short hair. He wanted to recite a poem to us that he'd written, and he wanted me to write it down. I wrote diligently in my notebook for about a half a page, but the poem didn't seem to make sense. He laughed and admitted he'd just made it up. He talked about the three dialects of the Id. He said, "One man cannot be but two others within himself, the ego and the other."

On the grass on Hippie Hill behind the drummers' bench there were some people on a blanket, including a guy with an Amish-style beard, the kind where they shave their cheeks and upper lip, though he's not Amish. His name is also Aaron. He said to me, in a cosmic kind of way, "You've always been here with us, you've always done so much for us." It was the first time I'd ever talked to him or seen him. He had a beautiful smile, took my hand and looked at me with all this love.

Under the Janis Tree down the walkway there was another group of people. They had three puppies in a rather heavy portable dog pen they'd been carting around. They didn't know how else to contain the rambunctious pups, the offspring of one of their other dogs. They also had a chocolate Pitbull with a yellow bandana around his neck, and a big black dog with pointed ears wearing a teal blue bandana. Many dogs are adorned with the same kind of bandana people wear, I guess in an effort to make them seem more like people. A dog wears the color or style of bandana that best matches or contrasts with his fur, or that says something about his personality.

They also had a big puppy with them. You could tell by the size of his paws that he was going to be huge. They didn't say where they'd found him. But for a group of people living outside with about eight dogs already, adopting another dog was a serious thing. And the shiny black Lab ate like a horse. But he was so pretty, and his coat was so sleek and nice to touch. Of course, he would follow them wherever they went. So they kept feeding him and called him "Maybe."

JESUS CLONES

The Golden Rule is so simple and so effective, it's obviously sublime. Love and respect are the best keys to fixing our country and our world, and the belief in liberty and justice for all. Most people get this and understand it perfectly and live it to the best of their ability with or without religion. It's some of our political leaders and religious leaders who need to be preached to about the Golden Rule. The effort to save the planet is not a guilt trip against ordinary people with three jobs, too busy to do anything more. Their very survival and their very goodness are helping to save us.

The Prince of Peace talked about the same kind of love shared by the nomad hippies in the park. I feel a special energy when I walk by the log or the drum circle, where people are either talking about saving the world or drumming about it. There's an immediacy in the way they seem to care so much about important things. There's a special space behind their eyes when they smile, a place that welcomes people they don't know as part of an unspoken alliance. They seem to feel that the Divine can somehow permeate everything, infuse ordinary circumstances with meaning.

People are already the offspring of the divine, according to Jesus. This is proven by the Lord's Prayer, which begins with "Our Father." It was others who taught that there was only one son of God. Feeling already perfect is what people imagine when they think of Heaven. Guilt and shame about what normal people do has been added by religions, in this case mostly by the Apostle Paul and his friends. Brotherly love and peace are miraculous concepts that can transform. If there's anything that can save a planet about to self-destruct from selfish greed, it has to be the Golden Rule. It's the law of life.

The natural light seems to reflect more brightly off of people who are kind and giving, rather than those who are haughty and mean. The light doesn't hit people's eyes the same way if their nose is in the air. Here at the park and on the Haight, there are faces shining with light, intelligent conversations full of wisdom. In fact, this has been the case in most places where I've met the public, for instance at swap meets.

What if every human being has the same capacity to be open and kind and to shine with light? That's exactly what a lot of these people here believe. It could be that's what Jesus meant when he said, "He that believeth on me (accepts his advice), the works that I do shall he do also; and greater works than these shall he do; because I go unto my father." (John 14:12)

note: He didn't say they'd be damned if they didn't believe. Theologians added that in Mark 16 over a hundred years later. And please remember, the same theologians could have easily added "he that believeth on me" and "because I go unto my father," leaving out that Jesus could've been saying that all people have these kinds of higher capabilities.

PURITANS I: God's Message About Leaders of Extremist Right-Wing Churches (Not the actual Puritans, or truth-seekers and devoted pastors misinformed by dangerous doctrines.)

Their zeal for God would mean so much

    if it was aimed to please the real desires of God's heart

to open wide the doors of cages where so many innocents abide,

    to stop iniquity of economic forces strangling all mankind.

The red letters in the four Gospels, Jesus' words, make it so clear

    the great delight of the Most High would be for poverty to end.

God would rejoice to see their conscience stricken over war and unjust laws,

    the way it is if they have sensual thoughts or have a smoke or drink.

The rude dogmas to which they cleave, not spoken by the Prince of Peace,

    turn so many who yearn for truth away from God.

The people have to stumble past Adam and Eve, lakes of fire,

    apocalyptic horsemen, to approach their God, none of which Jesus taught.

They have to give up their day off and ten percent of their small pay,

    feel guilt and shame for what they are 😟 and not drink beer with friends.

But worst of all they must believe that slaves their masters should obey,

    and that the world must end in violent, vengeful acts of God

 from a prophet's dream.

"Adopted sons" these preachers call humanity when Jesus plainly taught

    that we are all children of God, Whom he called "Our Father."

"You're on probation" they insist, making us feel like suspects on the news.

    Each thing that people do or say or think is wrong, even before their birth.

"Your righteousness is filthy rags!" they quote prophets from ages past and

    medieval priests in scarlet robes and funny hats, who thought torture was cool.

If all the energy they spend cleaning the outside of the vessel could be used

    to teach what Jesus really said, real miracles would bless the Earth.

THE APOSTLE PAUL AND OTHERS ADDED THINGS WHICH JESUS DIDN'T TEACH: that all are born in sin, the Inquisition, excommunication (shunning,) "slaves obey your masters in all things," Adam and Eve, antisemitism, women "obey your husbands in all things," shame of the body, hell (really Gehenna, the trash dump of Jerusalem, or Hades, the land of the dead,) tithing, going to church, that idolators and gays are "worthy of death," the Divine Right of Kings, "obey every ordinance of man," "they that are in the flesh cannot please God," "let the unjust be unjust still," and that it's not what you do that counts, but what you believe in. Red letters in Revelation are the writer's vision or dream and don't teach what Jesus taught. JESUS DIDN'T SAY in the Bible that he created the world, or that the Bible was perfect. The part that says you have to believe and be baptized or be damned, right before it says you can "take up serpents" and drink poison, (Mark 16:15-18) was evidently added a century later. The Prince of Peace taught kindness, brotherly love, and Heaven on Earth.

BREAKFAST AT MC DONALD'S

The McDonald's is an ironic place for the hippies to gather since many are vegetarians and also opposed to the corporate game and fast food monoliths. But McDonald's is THERE. It's the closest place from the park to get warm in the morning after a night spent sleeping on the ground. It's a community gathering place, even though you can only officially stay for forty minutes.

The loud, beeping noise that lets them know when the French fries are ready seems to be always on. I joined the throng trying to get warm and sat at a table next to big corner windows. There I could see everything happening on the street, the tourist buses rounding the tight corner, beggars, wildly dressed nonconformists, even Buddhist monks and Catholic nuns, and occasional police officers.

An older man in a wheelchair was trying to sell a box of chocolates to the customers at McDonald's in exchange for food. He was very grubby and said he was very hungry. I believed him. He was one of the real down and out, not really a hippie but the kind of really poor homeless you find in big cities. He was dressed in dark, worn baggy clothes. I bought him breakfast and found him to be wonderful company. 👁   He said he'd been on the street all his life and had gone to prison for giving away an ounce of pot. 🚬 ➔ 🏛

It turned out that he'd just spent the night at the hospital for a diabetic attack and had gotten out that morning. They'd kicked him out with no insulin, no shower, and no food. He said he was starving and I'm sure he meant it in a literal sense. He'd arrived at the hospital by ambulance, but when they'd released him, he'd had no transportation.

The hospital was way up on a big hill. 🏢 ➔ ♿ ⛰
He'd had to go down the hill in his wheelchair going sideways, zig-zagging back and forth, all the way down. That's when he'd arrived at McDonald's

on an empty stomach. I held his rough, stained hand. His face was weathered and care-worn but I saw a bright piercing light in his eyes. He told me many things about his life, so happy that someone was listening.

A tall youth in a top hat brought his coffee over and joined us. His name is "Prophet." His hat has a pin of a lightning bolt with wings. There are charms and spiritual emblems hanging from his medium-long, dark blond straight hair, and he wears sunglasses.  He told me about "street finds," items that the house-free find and use for free. He told us about the Green Cross, "Green Christian" environmentalists. He talked about Hawaiian mysticism, Jewish Mysticism, the Kabala and the Trinity.

The man in the wheelchair was having such a good time, he said he was planning to spin around in his wheelchair on the pavement at the Horseshoe.

Prophet was hungry so I gave him my pancakes. They come with the "Big Breakfast" and I never eat them anyway. I guess the coffee was all he could afford. I bought the chocolates off the guy in the wheelchair. He said the big box normally sold for twenty dollars, so it was a good deal for five dollars. I guessed he'd probably shoplifted it, but I didn't care. They should've given him food at the hospital. I gave the chocolates to the guy in the hat to give away to other people. Because I'd only paid five dollars instead of ten, we thought it would be fair if the seller could keep some. The guy in the hat gave him back his favorites, the white chocolate ones.

As I left the restaurant the door was held open for me by a Chinese man I'd seen drumming at the drum circle. He wore a black top hat with a raccoon tail hung off the back, a leopard fake fur coat, and he carried a tall staff with fur wrapped around it and a big cluster of big feathers hanging off the top.

MARRIED IN TIE-DYE

A couple named Cherry and Side Show stood outside McDonald's with a cardboard sign that said, "Just Food." They had three dogs with them, two Chihuahuas and a beautiful golden chow/coyote mix that looks like a fox, wearing a bandana with silk flowers sewn on. While double-decker buses and cars roared by, the couple told me their story.

Cherry had just found out that morning that she'd lost her baby for good that had been taken by the state in Arizona. The hospital had called her to come and get her daughter when the baby had already been adopted out for an hour. When the authorities had decided to take the baby, Cherry said, "They didn't even inspect the nice house we had." I didn't ask whether they'd lost their child for pot or just for being poor, but I'm sure it was one of those two.

They'd just gotten married after being best friends for years. She said they'd saved each other's lives. Now she was pregnant, and they were on their way to Oregon to have the baby. "Never again in Arizona!" she said, "Worst place for losing babies." She said police headquarters there are each full of about forty babies. The police officers watch them at night. This is our punishment for not playing the corporate game. Authorities take away your baby as soon as it's born and put it in the hands of strangers. It's one of the worst penalties that enslavers devise.

They were both very excited about their wedding. They'd been married in tie-dye. Sideshow told me about getting the license five minutes before closing time and getting married in a park by a friend who was an ordained minister. Both said they never fight. You could see they were both madly in love. I gave them a little money and he went into McDonald's to get a couple of cheap sandwiches.

She went on telling me their story, her face all lit up as she talked about him. She told me how they'd saved each other's lives. When she'd first met him, he was sitting next to a lake and about to shoot himself. She'd gone up to him and asked him why he had a gun. She said she'd asked him, "Where are you sleeping tonight?" And he'd answered, "Next to you." And that's how it started. He'd thrown the gun into the lake. She said several times that she couldn't find a better man. She rejoiced happily that she'd overheard him telling some friends, "I have an old lady who lets me be me, who doesn't hassle me. I've got some bad-ass old lady."

A HAPPY FAMILY

The reddish-blonde curls of his hair and beard are decorated with a few beads and metal ornaments, including some beer bottle tops pinched onto several narrow braids. Half of his head is shaved, and the other half is the usual Jesus length. When he said his name was "Orange" I realized he was someone I'd met and written about before. It was when I'd met a group of youths who'd named themselves after different colors, "Yellow," Orange," "Gray," and "Pink." The dog's name was "Blue." Please see "Tibetan Gift" in this book for our encounter then.

"Orange" is now married to "Yellow" with a year-old baby named "Moonbeam." He's so proud of his little family. He bragged about the school bus home he's outfitted with running water and heat and light. The vibrant young woman named "Yellow" is now his wife. She now arrived carrying their smiling baby in a cloth sling. He looked healthy and she looked very happy. It's clear that she and "Orange" are very much in love.

I read aloud what I had written about them before She had said some beautiful spiritual things in the conversation we'd had next to Tibetan Gift Corner.

Their bus is not the full-length kind but shorter, more practical in this place where parking can be such a challenge. It was parked four or five blocks away, in an area adjoining Buena Vista Park. He said that they had planned to get the bus and then planned to have the baby, and that everything was going according to plan. He said that in remodeling the bus he was trying to comply with legal requirements for living conditions, so that Child Protective Services wouldn't try to take away their baby. What a terrible threat for these good people to have to live with! 💔

A few days later I found out that the police had told them they couldn't park their bus in the Haight neighborhood, even if it was legally parked. Their beautiful little hippie bus, painted cobalt blue with rainbow swirls, was banned from the hippie capital of the world, where people come to see exactly that. 💔   Now they had to park it a couple miles away and take a city bus to get home to the Haight.

"No society can possibly be built on a denial of individual freedom."
Ghandi

PURITANS II: God's Message About Leaders of Extremist Right-Wing Churches (Not the actual Puritans, or truth-seekers and devoted pastors misinformed by dangerous doctrines.)

Their brother's blood cries out to God from desert sands

    as some false preachers lift their hands in praise.

God's ears cringe at the sound of their long prayers and pious songs

    as long as bombs destroy stone huts and pile the corpses of the poor

The humble Jesus loved are laid to waste, sprawled in their rags,

    while in sleek buildings weapons-builders tabulate their wealth.

Those tricked to vote for policies like these voted for death,

    no matter how many of the unborn they hope they saved.

Moralists peeking into bedroom windows with surveillance

    don't impress the Holy One.  ?

Some crucify their brothers for victimless crimes    ?

    and make them live in cages so men can make money building them.

There is no lie some preachers haven't told, no holy thing they haven't soiled.

 Some have no idea what Jesus taught, and they don't seem to want to know.

If there ever was an Abomination of Desolation,

    it's got to be right-wing extremist doctrines everywhere.

Some ministers shout loudly that they love the Lord

    then tell people to vote for savage laws that hurt the poor.

They strain at the mote of substance abuse

    and ignore the beam of genocide.

They idolize the Bible all day long and worship it

    and fail to see the living God in those they hurt.

Perhaps they should be on their knees begging forgiveness

                    for what they've done,

  instead of giving thanks because they think they're holier than thou.

From pulpits of power they attribute to Satan the works of God,

    like the great Peace Sign based on the Golden Rule.

They teach that people shouldn't try to save the Earth

    because some old guy in a cave wrote that it had to be destroyed.

They call environmentalists heretics, Earth mother worshipers,

    and make laws confiscating their homes and cars.

God sees the rank injustice that their high-priced lawyers do,

    how they lay crushing burdens on men's shoulders in His name.

Thinking they're better than their fellow man, more worthy of life's gifts,

    has always been some televangelists' disease.

Christ's healing words of love, the Bread of Life,

    have no effect on those who think they know it all.

The Holy Ghost, preferring closets to cathedrals for its dwelling place,

    instructs small children to share toys and helps beggars see God.

Meanwhile the princes of religions cannot hear the small, still voice,

    their ears full of the praise of men and the clinking of tithes.

Some Bible teachers worship Jesus but don't hear a word he said,

    letting dark fiscal forces pervert things of God.

On all the airwaves they teach things he never taught,

    like Adam and Eve, Hell and The Fall. 🍎

The sixteen scriptures which they know by heart are not the ones

    that Jesus meant when he said truth would set us free.

They tell the people that the world's injustice is God's plan and

                                 to be unconcerned,

    instead of urging them to hunger and thirst for righteousness.

Some preachers should be born again once more 👶

    and this time take their baggage off to pass the needle's eye. 🐫

Stop judging people for small misdeeds of the flesh

    while urging others to destroy the world and devastate the poor.

The cruel edicts of dogmatists must be repealed,

    eradicated from the Earth like foul disease.

For Paradise to bless this place all that is needed is for people to enjoy

    the art of treating others as themselves.

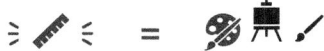

The right-wing media never stops promoting hate against the immigrants,
    telling the bullies to make laws tearing their lives apart,
sending them back to poverty and strife,
    as if they weren't the "neighbors" Jesus said to love.
Their food stands on the corners with their steaming pots in grocery carts
    display the goodness of this nation and its generous heart.
Now some insist they and their loved ones be sent back to war-torn lands.
    They tell the people not to care and not to see.

Religious radio and TV stations crank out hate all the day long.

    The poor, minorities, artists and thinkers, must live in fear.
Some cowardly and well-fed hand is the one to make the secret call
    bringing police to a neighbor's door for some small thing,
while these religious leaders tell the power brokers of the world it's right
    to deal in tyranny and war, and they don't notice this.
Those who have stumbled in this way should leave their gift by the altar,
    go heal their brother and their world, then come and give their gift.

JESUS DIDN'T TEACH: that all are born in sin, the Inquisition, shunning, slaves and women "obey in all things," Adam and Eve, antisemitism, shame of the body, hell, tithing, having to go to church, the divine right of kings, that the Bible was perfect, or that he created the world. Paul the Apostle and OTHERS ADDED those, plus "obey every ordinance of man," "let the unjust be unjust still," that idolators and gays are "worthy of death," and that it's not what you do that counts, but what you believe in. Where it says you have to believe or be damned, right before it says you can "take up serpents" and drink poison (Mark 16:15-18,) was evidently added a century later. Red letters in Revelation are the writer's vision or dream and don't teach what Jesus taught. The Prince of Peace taught kindness, brotherly love, and Heaven on Earth.

BIG RED HEARTS

He looks like a pirate in a leather tricornered hat that looks like a real antique. It fits his head perfectly, framed by long curls that enforce the impression that he's from another time. The young man could've also been a patriot in the American Revolution, who wore the same kind of hat. I wasn't sure if I even knew him, but he said, "I have something for you." He pulled out a little silk brocade bag and took out a large white crystal and gave it to me.

People like giving little gifts to each other out here. They do it every day and attach deep significance to it. It's a way for them to show love. These things are not elaborate or heavy, and most have little monetary value. They are more likely to have a spiritual meaning or purpose. Some are purchased and some are "street finds." Many of these small gifts are made by hand, crafted at the log. I have a collection of them at home which I keep all together, and which I regard as in a way sacred.

At McDonald's I met Gypsy Rose, who dresses like a lady even though she's living on the street. She wore a long black skirt and blouse, soft blue and green chiffon scarves, a blue necklace, a turquoise and rhinestone bracelet, and a purple hat. She had a serene look on her face. She said, "I love Jesus." and showed me her tattoo of a bleeding rose for Jesus. Over cheap breakfast sandwiches we discussed Peace Warriors and living in the present. She said, "I know that my soul is a beautiful thing. Money will not buy me anything, only things."

Outside McDonald's on the sidewalk there was a chalk drawing. In pastels there was a cross with a spiral in the middle. I crossed the street and walked up Haight Street. At some point I noticed something I hadn't seen before, a big red heart, about two feet wide, painted on the sidewalk. As I walked further there were more red hearts, one every ten feet or so, block after block. It looked like someone had taken a stencil and paint and done their work at night. I kept walking and found that they were all the way up the street, past Masonic.

BIG SKULLS

Some of the young Grateful Dead fans refer to "when Jerry was alive" as "the Golden Age of the Haight." They wear patches and pins of things he had on his guitar, even a patch of his hand which had the middle finger cut off due to a woodcutting accident. They talk as if they know him personally right now. Some like to celebrate New Year's Day, and "Jerry Day," when he died twenty years ago on May 14th, by gathering at his house at 710 Ashbury and smoking joints.

The "Dead" made great music that touched millions of hearts. Their music unites generations, with a powerful religious undertone that suggests life beyond death and the possibility of dynamic power in the hippies' ideals. At the same time, I hope my friends won't be mad at me if I express my opinion that some of the Dead's material may have been touched and molested by the record industry and others, the great brainwashers of our time who work behind the scenes to make hippies look bad. While studying the lyrics to some songs, I found some rather depressing. They included themes like suicide, hard liquor and cocaine, and even violence.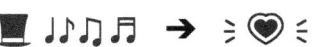

Standing in line at the grocery store, I thought it was worth the eighteen dollars to buy the Grateful Dead Commemorative Edition. The front cover of the magazine was filled with a big skull, with a lightning bolt inside the head. It's really a powerful symbol of immortality and deathlessness. It suggests that there could be lightning thoughts in the mind of man, illuminating concepts that can't be conquered by death. That's why Pacifists wear it and display it. They regard these images as something holy that represents what they believe in about universal brotherhood, even though the skulls and skeletons scare people and are easily misunderstood.

Nobody seems to know exactly why the hippie Pacifists, the most peaceful of people, are represented by the universal symbol of death. It seems that the skulls and skeletons and the name "The Dead" emerged as their emblems in the absence of anything else. It turns out a couple of graphic artists randomly found an old woodcut of skeletons in a book and thought it was "cool." The name "The Grateful Dead," from an old Irish folk song, may have been chosen the same random way. While it implies a happy afterlife, it could also be seen as advocating suicide.

Later as I ate breakfast in a restaurant and studied the magazine spread out on the counter, I found myself trying to cover up with my elbow the big skull on the cover and the words "The Cult of the Dead." I actually felt self-conscious about the people sitting next to me at the counter. Would they think I was weird for carrying around something with a big skull on it? I was dressed in brilliant tie-dye and didn't exactly blend in. People were seeing what I was reading and might be forming opinions about hippies. Could this make them think that people who dress like this are into the occult? Did some people feel that way each time they saw someone with a dancing skeleton or a skull on his T-shirt?

It was around the time of Halloween. The restaurant was decorated with cardboard cutouts, one of which was a hideous witch. She had bulging eyes and a big, hooked nose, much like the Nazis portrayed the Jews in their propaganda. Her skin was green and wrinkled, her leering mouth toothless. She wore dark ragged clothes and the kind of pointed hat that witch-hunters think sorcerers wear. Her hair was done in what looked like dreadlocks.

The kind of fear and hatred that Hitler aimed at the Jews was clearly visible in this Medieval portrayal of old women and midwives. The conflict between the old religions of Europe and the new Christian invaders unleashed rivers of blood. The great witch hunts of half a dozen centuries were not made up of isolated incidents. They involved the systematic slaughter of large segments of populations for long periods of time, with the usual goal of seizing property.

Europe was Christianized by the power of the sword. Not only the sword but the stake, the torture chamber, and a spiritual scorched earth policy still in force in many churches today. It's hard to imagine what could be Christ-like about burning people alive, a dozen at a time, with homosexuals thrown into the pyre as "faggots" to make the fire burn better. I feel that wearing skulls and skeletons puts hippies at risk, in a similar way that wearing a pointy wizard's hat in public might've put those other people at risk, who were also embroiled in a religious war.

I think that what we believe in about liberty and higher consciousness might have something to do with the fact that the federal law still says you can get huge prison sentences, lose kids, jobs and houses, for pot. The property forfeiture laws used in the drug war were based on the same principle as those used in the Salem Witch Trials. The property itself is guilty by association with a crime, allowing it to be seized by the accuser. It should worry all those who love liberty that longhairs get arrested and their property gets "forfeited" and confiscated for "possession."

They may not be hanging us up by the heels but there are some mean-spirited laws out there, especially for those of us who are homeless. The Vehicle Habitation Law in San Francisco says you can get a $1000. fine and/or six months in jail for sleeping in your car. Someone can get fined $500. and get put on a sexual predator watch list for urinating in public. Some of the homeless around here are penalized not really for what they do but for what they believe in.

It's not far-fetched to think that a similar attitude is at work here as when Paul the Apostle (not Jesus) wrote that idolators are worthy of death. In that mind-set, this includes anyone who has a statue of Buddha or a picture of Krishna or a goddess. It was Paul who also wrote, "It is a shame for a man to have long hair." He disapproved even of Jesus' hairstyle. (I Corinthians 11:14) It doesn't help that the "Dead" lightning bolt has thirteen points, an occult number. Judas is supposed to have been the thirteenth person at the Last Supper. I think the number is supposed to represent Proposition 13, a law to decriminalize marijuana. I've also heard that it's because "M" is the thirteenth letter.

Wearing skulls and skeletons around those with a seventeenth-century mentality is sheer political folly, in my opinion. It's disturbing enough to the status quo that hippie Pacifists talk like Jesus and look like Jesus. They have already been called Beelzebub like he was, have long already been at risk for legal crucifixion. It is an epic battle between good and evil, but not the way many churches would think. It's between those who believe people are basically good, like Jesus and Thomas Jefferson, and those who think humans are cursed and evil, like Paul the Apostle and some of our right-wing legislators and preachers.

The Grateful Dead's happy rainbow dancing bears are less scary and more representative of a people with such a positive vision. The adoption of the death's head as a symbol for a peace movement is a mistake, in my opinion. Such a public display of a universal symbol of death, is like inviting the Beast of prejudice to devour us. It also intimidates many who might otherwise be convinced by the Pacifists' Christ-like ideals. Some church goers, instead of believing their infallible Bible that "God is a man of war," might take Jesus' advice when they vote, to "Do unto others as you would have them do unto you."

The wreaths of roses and the beautiful artwork only slightly mitigate the subliminal negative effects in the superstitious. In my personal opinion, the logo of death's heads and dancing skeletons is a sad example of a wrong image being projected about who we are. It occurred to me that every person who was stuck standing in line at every grocery store in the nation, was seeing on a display rack, at eye level, the magazine cover about hippies with a big skull and the words "the Cult of the Dead."

BRANDING US

The ad was all over the airwaves, spreading its poison whether or not people ever saw the show. The miniseries was called "Aquarius" and it had a peace sign in the "Q." It was yet another fictionalized account of the Manson murders. The title letters looked like they were dripping blood, and the background they were on was reminiscent of rotting flesh. The ad was bound to catch your eye as you flipped through the channels.

Again, the specter of Manson is dragged out, the way it is whenever corporate political interests are served by making hippies look bad. Silencing the Pacifists with slurs reminiscent of Nazi propaganda, making people think they're stupid or dangerous or dirty, has the effect of reducing Democratic votes. Making people think they're psychokillers is better yet. If someone wanted to find ways to make people afraid of their political opponents, they couldn't invent a more perfect strategy.

It isn't necessary to see the movie to be affected by its evil suggestions. The peace sign in the title, and the title itself, say it all. The association of scary movies with the peace movement has been tried before to brand us as people to be avoided rather than listened to. The Manson story has been repeated ad nauseum, perhaps because it's the only one like it. If psychedelics were likely to make people go crazy and start killing people, there would have been more incidents. ☮ = 🔪 🩸 ?

There is ample evidence (find it online) that the Manson murders may have been a CIA black op to neutralize the Left by making people think there was "a monster lurking in the heart of every longhair." (I read <u>CHAOS, Charles Manson, the CIA, and the Secret History of the Sixties</u>, by Tom O'Neill.) Too many players in this story had ties to intelligence agencies and mind control experiments for it to be a coincidence.

Contrary to what most people have been led to believe, the killers were not on acid that night. They were on speed. Manson was closely associated with two people who'd been involved with mind control experiments with rats, giving them speed to make them violent.

Some working around Manson were part of **a secret government program to learn how to implant false memories and remove true ones. One goal was to create hypno-programmed assassins.** Alan Scheflin, who wrote a book on MK ULTRA, said "**THE MANSON MURDERS WERE AN MK ULTRA EXPERIMENT GONE RIGHT.**" It makes me wonder about all those other mass shootings we keep hearing about, which create such financial windfalls for insurers, prison and surveillance industries and investors.

Even the name "The Left" is a kind of slur. Left-handed children used to be forced to learn to write with their right hand. In the Bible the sheep go on the right and the goats go on the left. In depictions of the Last Supper, Judas is seated on Christ's left. Why must social justice advocates and environmentalists be labelled as "The Left" when they're so right and the Right is so wrong? "The Drug Culture" is another name that negatively portrays the life-filled spiritual explosion that transformed society. We are not the Right or the Left. We are the Center.

The Beast must be worried about the power of truth that ordinary people can have, to be going to such lengths to discredit us. Once again, the public will see the gruesome murders re-played, of course with some of the music of that era in the background. The music that inspired so many people's minds to peace will again be placed as a backdrop for a terrible act that had nothing to do with it, and nothing to do with us.

I've even wondered if that sensational event was the precursor of mind control experiments where they try to turn people into assassins. Was this another burning of the Reichstag to make it easier to demonize hippies? Starting the Drug War was something Richard Nixon did to get elected. It also had the effect of making the Pacifists real quiet in striving for social justice, since so many of them smoked pot and were at risk of losing everything if they spoke up.

Another way we get branded is that we get associated in people's minds with the persecuted gays. For the media to put Pacifists in the same category as those who've historically been mistreated has its political advantages for those who want to make money starting wars and a police state. 👬 💕 👬   With promises of preventing gender laws and stopping abortion, good people on the Christian Right vote for horrible business practices that have nothing to do with those issues and which most of them wouldn't have voted for if they'd known more about them.

In another bait-and-switch game, what's called the Liberal Left votes for **PARALYSING LIABILTY LAWS**, with promises of protecting everyone and keeping them all safe from everything at all times.

I believe that both sides, those against abortion and also those for gender rights, are used by the same financial forces to promote totalitarian agendas and to divide people who wouldn't normally be that divided. The few gay people I've seen on the Haight are treated with respect and love.

Policies that are forced on us, which most of the people are not comfortable with, make people mad. This makes it hard for the Right to unite with the Left to make a Center. The rainbow belongs to all of us, as a symbol of a connection between God and man, and of the unity of all people, including Right and Left.

As longhairs I think it's time we found ways to define ourselves better, so that others can know what we are and what we are not. It's important to let people see that we are not evil or weird, or anything else the media tries to turn us into.

Note: You may have noticed that I am a fan of Thomas Jefferson, who's also been branded in a way. I like him because he studied 300 constitutions trying to find the best solutions for us, and because he wrote a book isolating what Jesus is reported to have actually said, called "The Jefferson Bible." He tried to put the abolition of slavery in the Constitution many times, but others prevented it.

People fault him for living with his slave, Sally Hemings, and fathering children by her. What many don't know is that when Jefferson's beloved wife died when he was about 38, she made him promise not to remarry. Sally Hemings was his deceased wife's half-sister, also fathered by Jefferson's father-in-law, and looked a lot like her. I believe that he loved her, especially since there's no record of him being with anyone else for the rest of his life. She went back with him to Virginia after he took her to Paris, where she could've stayed and been free. Her progeny have stated that "he loved her dearly," that while in Paris he spent as much money on her clothes as on his daughter's, and that she was the virtual mistress of Monticello.

After he died creditors obtained his slaves as property, preventing his plan to free them all. Sally Hemmings was freed, and the eight children they'd had, and he'd let other slaves escape without pursuing them. He called slavery "an excretable commerce... this assemblage of horrors," and "a cruel war against human nature itself, violating its most sacred rights of life and liberties."

CIA MIND CONTROL ON HAIGHT STREET

Disclaimer: An important source has told me that some of the things in Tom O'Neil's book are inaccurate, but I have not yet been able to find out which things they are.

In 1967 **OPERATION CHAOS** was launched, a secret government counter-intelligence program to **"Make the public believe there's a monster lurking in the heart of every longhair."**(O'Neil) It aimed to **"create divisions in the peace movement, neutralize potential leaders, and spread disinformation"** using **"imaginative and hard-hitting techniques."** Most of this information is from a book by Tom O'Neil and Dan Piepenbring, called "CHAOS: Charles Manson, the CIA, and the Secret History of the Sixties."

During the Summer of Love at least **two key CIA operatives** had offices right in the holy heart of the Haight. **Dr. Louis Jolyon West**, an **expert in CIA mind control**, and **Roger Smith, Charles Manson's parole**

officer before the murders. Both infiltrators were funded by CIA fronts. Both were studying how to make rats violent with amphetamines.

Dr, West had been involved in deprogramming POW's who'd been brainwashed in North Korea. After the assassination of John F. Kennedy, he'd **examined Jack Ruby, who couldn't explain why he'd shot Oswald!** He was part of the Foundation Fund for Research in Psychiatry, a CIA cover for **MK ULTRA mind control** research. It paid for his **HAIGHT-ASHBURY PROJECT, created secretly to neutralize the anti-war movement** here. The **SAN FRANCISCO PROJECT** was funded by NIMH, the National Institute of Mental Health, also a CIA front. It made Roger Smith Manson's parole officer.

It's strange that Roger Smith, a San Francisco federal parole officer, was assigned to Charles Manson, though Manson's crimes at the time had been committed in Los Angeles. It's also strange that in 1967 Manson was his only parolee. He worked with Manson in "participant-observer research." Roger Smith claims that he was not Manson's parole officer while Manson was in San Francisco. Right after Manson's arrest for the murders, his files were burglarized, the only thing taken from the building.

Roger was part of ARP, the **AMPHITAMINE RESEARCH PROJECT**, which studied mice on speed crowded together **TO INDUCE RAGE AND VIOLENCE**. Dr. West's "Violence Center," approved by Ronald Reagan, included **LSD research** and hypnosis. Both were funded by CIA covers like the NIMH, a front for LSD research. It's common knowledge that the Haight-Ashbury dream of peace on Earth came to a halt when **massive amounts of speed were brought into the area**. Where hope and the Golden Rule had flourished and attracted the whole world, there were thirty murders on the Haight on six blocks.

Dr. West had said, "The role of drugs in the exercise of political control is also coming under increasing discussion. **CONTROL CAN BE THROUGH PROHIBITION OR SUPPLY**. The total or even partial prohibition of drugs gives the government considerable leverage for other types of control. An example would be the **selective application of drug laws** permitting immediate search, or **"no knock" entry**, against selected components of the population such as members of certain minority groups or **political organizations**." He also said that hippies living in rural communes were "less bothersome and less expensive if they are living apart, than if they are engaging in active, organized, vigorous political protest and dissent."

Aldous Huxley wrote to George Orwell: "The world's rulers will discover that **infant conditioning and narco-hypnosis** are more efficient, as instruments of governments, than clubs and prisons." Some believe that there is "a thought-out **medico-political** design" to **make a "new Dark Age**," to return people to peasant status, to **make them easy to control like serfs.**

A government **"PROJECT MASS CONVERSION"** was aimed to **engender "a fundamental change"** in **"basic moral, religious, or political matters."** It planned to create "the induction of abnormal states" to get information from people without their knowledge, **program them to make false confessions**, and **TO KILL ON COMMAND**. It hoped to embed hidden messages in people's brains, implant false memories and remove true ones. Its goal was to create **hypno-programmed assassins**, "couriers" in trance states. (logosmedia.com)   Records show that the Manson killers took speed before the murders, and no acid. It's said that Manson habitually only pretended to take acid, or just microdosed.

A CIA front called the Geschickter Fund studied **"latah," a neurotic condition marked by "automatic obedience"** (the way Manson's followers obeyed him.) Manson employed mind control techniques used by cults. The girls were "forced into unconventional sexual practices" that "negate your ego." According to his strict rules they were not allowed to see their families and had to take on new names. He told them that "good is bad, God is Satan, and that death is life." Again, Alan Scheflin wrote, **"the Manson murders were an MK ULTRA experiment gone right."**

There was **"a curious leniency"** as prisons kept releasing Manson, though he was obviously guilty of crimes. Susan Atkins' probation was cancelled twice. When five Manson girls were arrested in Ukiah, a phone call to Roger Smith freed them right away. There was a big police raid on Spahn Ranch for auto theft. All were arrested but were released after three days. Officials later said, **"We were told not to bother these people."** **During these events Roger Smith** actually **took care of Manson's baby** for eight weeks.

In keeping with the plan to make hippies look like monsters, **Manson** told his followers before they left for the murders, "Leave something witchy." Police suspected they'd been **helped by "Uncle" Charles Tacot, a 6'6" assassin for the CIA who was good with knives**. He worked for the Intelligence Agency at the time of the murders under Hank Fine, another government assassin. Both he and a man named Boyle, also suspected of having taken part in the murders, were second-generation intelligence and had been guests at Cielo Drive, where some of the murders happened. Also, Manson and Tex Watson, one of the killers, had attended a party at that same house.

Authorities solved the case the day after the murders but didn't arrest Manson. Dennis Wilson of the Beach Boys said he knew why the murders were committed and would someday tell the world. The landlord of Cielo Drive knew it could be Manson but said nothing. The Beach Boys and the whole community knew it was Manson before the world did, their manager Parks said. The police knew it was Manson but acting would've exposed their secret intelligence-gathering operation. There were also civil **liability issues for letting him go free**. Police didn't interview key witnesses and destroyed all records.

THE MANDO SAVED HIM

His name is "Captain," and he looks like a king or a pirate or a rock star. He has luxurious shoulder-length salt and pepper curls. He's a big man, tall, strong. He said he used to have a corporate job, was almost a lawyer. When I met him near the tunnel there was something regal about him, like the picture of a merry good king in a fairy tale book. The night before, someone had punched him and he'd had his backpack stolen with all his stuff, yet he was laughing and having a good time. He wasn't putting it on. ⎈ 👔 👑   👊 🎒❌ OK

Across the walkway a white-haired woman dressed all in light blue sat on a log. Her clothes perfectly matched her beautiful light blue eyes. She told me about her son who has many names: Earth Brother, White Cloud, Brown Eagle, and Geoffrey. She said her Creole husband still has his slave name. I was surprised to learn that she knew the laws really well, had been active in the hemp movement, and knew a lot of the people I knew. With her and the almost-lawyer across the way, they could open a law office right there next to the tunnel.

A young guy with a hat full of pins arrived with his white spotted dog. He talked deeply about his mushroom experience, which he thought had expanded his consciousness. He said that he didn't want to eat them often, maybe after months or even years, so he could have time to digest what he'd learned. 🍄🌀 A guy dressed in a cool suit jacket arrived with a noble-looking black lab. The guy knew about politics. He said, "It's not just the activists we should pay attention to, but the activated." ✦

"Ground Squirrel" was wearing a cap with a peace sign on it and he carried a mandolin. He told a story about police. They were undercover, dressed like regular guys, when they pulled out their badges. His friend who was with him happened to be rolling a joint, so the officers thought it was him they should go after. They searched the friend but not the mandolin player. "The mando saved me," he said. They also let the other guy go. ☮ 🎸♪🚬 → 🕵👮 → FREE ☺

LEFTOVERS

Many people are so careful about their physical diet, but what about their spiritual diet? They shouldn't have to settle for old, left-over, genetically modified God. Most religions are not properly labelled. Their scriptures do not disclose the true origins of the ingredients and those who prepared them. There are no disclaimers warning people of cases where repeated use has been shown to cause side effects like violence and injustice. What if those who cooked up the harsh precepts that rule over us didn't wash their hands of their ego and lust for power? What if those who prepared the main course we need, boiled the life out of it, and added unpalatable foreign matter?

Maybe we need better regulations to certify a scripture as infallible, so that consumers of religious doctrine don't inadvertently find themselves annihilating or excommunicating others. Potential side effects of a bad batch of religion can include extreme guilt for victimless acts, torture, war, and the confiscation of property of those who believe differently. An over-reliance on prophecy can lead to dangerously relaxed attitudes about the destruction of the Earth and the loss of liberty.

Out at Golden Gate Park, there are generous helpings of God wherever you look. Amid the forests and the hobo camps there are laid out lavish tables filled with only the most spiritually nutritious items that religion may have concocted with its recipes. Many selections are arranged there for those who hunger and thirst for righteousness, some exotic and diverse. But by far the most delicious dish, the one for which demand requires a heaping platter full at every table, is what Jesus taught about universal brotherly love. That's the one that sticks to your ribs and feels good on a cold morning, and God knows these people need that.

When it's not adulterated by ingredients added by others, this dish can have tremendous healing power, not only for individuals but for nations and planets. Doing unto others as you would have them do unto you turns out to be not only a civilized policy but something vital for the survival of worlds and civilizations. This is the treasure that's in Golden Gate Park and on the Haight, in the bright clothing and in the Peace Drums, in the smiles and hugs of the house-free. It's here, fresh and clean, without harsh poisonous chemicals like the doctrine of the fall of man and that all are born in sin, which Jesus didn't teach. You won't break your teeth on the Inquisition, excommunication, or that slaves should obey their masters in all things.

There's no big sign with Jesus' name on it, and many are not even aware that this is what they're consuming. It just has a little sign that says, "The Golden Rule." There are no crucifixes and no place to leave money or sign your name. The hippies in the park and on the Haight consume eagerly what Jesus taught about love and peace and forgiveness. They digest easily the things he said about co-operating with others and caring about what happens to them. They genuinely don't want the bizarre concoctions of some religions that make people think they're better than other people, no matter how much sugar and salt have been added. They like their God organic, straight from the source, outdoor-grown with no additives.

PAUL THE APOSTLE AND OTHERS ADDED THINGS WHICH JESUS DIDN'T TEACH: that all are born in sin, the Inquisition, excommunication (shunning,) "slaves obey your masters in all things," Adam and Eve, that idolaters and gays are "worthy of death," antisemitism, "women obey your husbands in all things," shame of the body, hell (really Gehenna, the trash dump of Jerusalem, or Hades, the land of the dead), tithing, going to church, the divine right of kings, "obey every ordinance of man," "they that are in the flesh cannot please God," "let the unjust be unjust still," and that it's not what you do that counts, but what you believe in. Red letters in the book of Revelation are the writer's vision or dream and don't teach what Jesus taught, and have been killing people since the ink was dry. JESUS DIDN'T SAY in the Bible that he created the world, or that the Bible was perfect. The part that says you have to believe or be damned, right next to where it says you can "take up serpents" and drink poison, (Mark 16:15-18) was evidently added a century later. The Prince of Peace taught kindness, brotherly love, and Heaven on Earth.

Note: These things were all said by Jesus (from King James Version), though not in the same order. The few words in parentheses we8re added.

BLESSED ARE THE PEACEMAKERS

God's Message to Treehuggers and Peacemakers:

Blessed Are the Peacemakers:

for they shall be called the children of God. (Matthew 5:9)

Blessed are they which do hunger and thirst

after righteousness, for they shall be filled. (Matthew 5:6)

Thou art not far from the kingdom of God. (Mark 12:34)

Whatsoever ye have spoken in darkness shall be heard in the light;

and **that which ye have spoken in the ear in closets**

shall be proclaimed upon the housetops. (Luke 12:3)

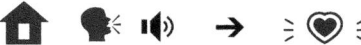

Built to Last

Blessed are the eyes which see the things that ye see.

For I tell you, that **many prophets and kings have desired to see those things which ye see**, and have not seen them and;

to hear those things which ye hear, and have not heard them. (Lk. 10:23)

He that hath my commandments (Golden Rule), **and keepeth them,**

he it is that loveth me. And he that loveth me shall be loved of my Father **and I will love him, and will manifest myself to him.** (John 14:21)

This is my commandment, that ye **love one another, as I have loved you.** (John 15:12)

Blessed are the pure in heart: for they shall see God. (Matthew 5:8)

YE HAVE BEEN WITH ME FROM THE BEGINNING. (John 15:27)

Unto you it is given to know the mystery of the kingdom of God. (Mark 4:11)

Flesh and blood hath not revealed it unto thee, but my Father. (Matt 16:17)

(God) hid these things from the wise and prudent,

and revealed them unto babes.

If any man hath ears to hear, let him hear. (Luke 10:21), (Mark 4:23)

I will utter things which have been kept secret

from the foundation of the world.

There is nothing covered that shall not be revealed;

and hid, that shall not be known. (Matt. 13:35, 10:26)

While ye have light, **believe in the light,**

that ye might be the children of the light. (Jn 12:36)   If thy whole body

be full of light, having no part dark, the whole shall be full of light,

as when the bright shining of a candle doth give thee light. (Lk. 131:36)

Let your loins be girded about, and your lights burning. (Luke 12:35)

Take heed, lest at any time your hearts be overcharged with cares of this life.

These things have I spoken unto you, **that my joy might remain in you,**

and that your joy might be full. (Luke 21:34), (John 15:11)

DUCKY'S MANDOLIN

I walked by the log and saw Ducky in her wheelchair with a group of people. The smiling girl motioned for me to join the group of long-haired nomads. A guy glided gracefully by on a skateboard, wearing a rainbow tie-dyed t-shirt that read, "Let's Get Weird." A young man was playing a violin.

The sun was shining brightly and Ducky was in good spirits. She was holding a beautiful mandolin, stroking out a few pretty notes once in a while to go with the violin. She didn't seem to really know how to play it but enjoyed holding it and doing what she could with it. She told me about her wonderful new place, which she'd waited for on a waiting list for public housing for a long time. At last she was no longer on the street. She was proud to have someplace she could invite someone to. She told me that if I ever needed to, I could shelter and spend the night in her little room.  !!

The stickers crowding her mandolin were loaded with political and spiritual statements. There was the Earth with an unborn baby inside, and a sticker that said "Positive Creations." There was a pot leaf on a rainbow background, a Buddha sticker, red and blue lightning bolts, and a sticker that said "Suffering Sucks." There was a Mickey Mouse strap on the mandolin. Another sticker said "Still Not Loving (heart) Police." Another one said, amid rainbow swirls, "Bound to Cover Just a Little More Ground," referring to a Grateful Dead song.

The next time I saw her she didn't look the same. She was in her wheelchair with her head down all the way to her chest, very upset. I tried to talk to her, but she barely said anything. Finally I got it out of her that she got kicked out of the nice new indoor place she had, because they can't have anyone there with seizures. It was another cursed liability law, based on insurers' mandates to limit all risk on all property. You'd think that a paralyzed homeless girl would be someone they'd want to help with public housing but the **liability laws, our gods**, had decided otherwise. The property managers had been forced to kick her out at night and she'd had to go to a motel. The motel didn't have wheelchair access so she'd had to crawl up the stairs.  →

I met a forty-something guy who'd just lost his job and his home. He had short hair and was still neatly-dressed, clean-shaven, didn't look like he belonged in the park. I saw no tent or sleeping bag. He was very depressed, couldn't believe this had happened to him. He had no idea how to survive, had ended up at the park because he had no place else to go. He'd lost his job through no fault of his own, and then as a result had lost everything else.

It seemed to cheer him up to have someone talk to him and hear his story. He said he wished he had a drum. A month later I saw him and almost didn't recognize him. He was bearded and his grayish hair had grown, his hands were dirty and he wore the usual dark, baggy clothing most street people wear. He said, "I used to have an apartment, and jobs, and now I just don't care."

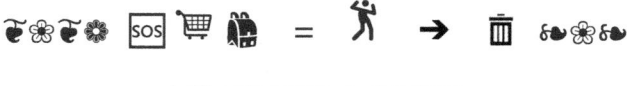

LIT UP LIKE A SAINT

There's a lady everyone told me to go see, who owns an import store on Haight Street called "Love of Ganesha." The young people talk about "Noot" with reverence. It seems like she's a saint to them. They've told me that during cold weather she has sometimes let homeless youth sleep inside the store in her meditation room, ignoring liability compliance agreements.

Beneath the big purple mural across the top of the building I walked into her store, which is an experience in itself. Though one of the biggest on the Haight, her store is always the most crowded. There is the scent of water and the sound of a fountain, and the perfume of incense, making a different atmosphere than on the sidewalk outside. Near the front door is a beverage dispenser with free ice water with slices of fresh cucumber and lemon in it, and a bowl of sweet crackers or cookies that are free.

The room is very large and lined with row after row of bins filled with every kind of gemstone imaginable. Most of the rocks and pieces of stone are rough in a natural condition, and very reasonably priced. The hippies love to trade in these and give them to each other as gifts, assigning spiritual or medicinal properties to each one.

Many other beautiful things are for sale there, exotic imported goods stacked in piles and hung from the ceiling. There are gorgeous wall hangings and beaded curtains, and pieces of vintage native costume from other parts of the world. There is a whole wall of all varieties of incense and essential oils, which makes the place smell wonderful. There are display areas with big hollow stones cut open so you can see the insides covered with crystals.

The most amazing thing in her store is her meditation room, the only one on Haight Street. You don't have to buy anything to enjoy a quiet time resting on embroidered cushions in the beautiful space she created there. It's not really a room but a large square pop-up tent, the kind you can buy at a garden store in the summer. It's completely covered on three sides with rich beaded wall hangings on the walls and on the ceiling, with a Persian carpet on the floor.

Before people enter there's a sign asking them to take their shoes off, and not to use cell phones. A poem is posted about raising your vibration. The tent is set up in a back corner of the room, pulled away from the back wall to make an area that looks like a shrine. Inside are pictures of saints and deities, including Jesus and Mary, and statues lined up on a couple of ancient-looking carved wooden tables. There are candles and fresh flowers, incense, and big bowls of fruit. There is a brass musical bowl people can play.

Around the base of this altar there are placed amazing large rock formations, the most spectacular in the store. There are huge white crystals, two feet tall, lit up. Another crystal, with glowing iridescent shards of white translucent stone, and a pair of stone pyramids six inches high, make the display look like a futuristic city. Pinned to one wall hanging there is someone's drawing on a piece of typing paper. It says "LOVE."

I spent so much time enjoying the meditation room that I felt I should buy something. I chose a small box of incense, the only thing I could afford at the time because of a gift I'd bought earlier at another store for a friend. I got to see the owner. She was beautiful and seemed surprisingly young. I couldn't tell at all how old she was. She had the kind of youth some people have who never seem to get old. She was as lit up as any of the saints pictured in her shrine.

I watched her with customers while standing in line. She blessed each person with a radiant smile. She treated them like her child or friend. She took people's hands, looked them in the face, listened to them. No matter how many were waiting to pay, she took enough time with each customer to make them feel special. She gave customers some little extra gift, and discounts they didn't ask for. ☺ 🤝 🕊️ OK

I bought the incense and paid my dollar for it. She gave me an extra box of incense and made me the gift of a pretty silken bag in which to put the gift to my friend. It was worth more than the incense. FREE   Next time I went in there I bought a blue and gold skirt I couldn't do without. She took ten dollars off the price without my asking, again showing love to a stranger.

🌸🕊️🌸 👗🛍️ − $10. ☺ 🌸🕊️🌸

OTHER VISIONS

Paul the Apostle is the one who wrote that idolaters are "worthy of death." Ever since the ink was dry on those unholy words, big bullies have used them to rip off anyone whose stuff they wanted. Paul's words sealed the fate of the Aztecs, the Native Americans, the Africans. Anytime religion teaches people that they're better than someone else, rivers of blood flow. This is proved by both history and headlines. 📖 ☠️ 🧕 = 🔱

In their thirst and hunger for righteousness the Pacifists have explored many different faiths and philosophies. They've been judged harshly for this by organized religions and those who want to demonize them for political reasons. They explore meditation, yoga, diet. On their bookshelf there might be a statue of Buddha or Krishna, or even of strange-looking gods people aren't familiar with. Most of them don't worship them, but just think they look cool. Do Bible literalists think this makes them "worthy of death?"

The statues are a way to express their desire to be spiritual, though most haven't found a religion they can land on. Most of these people believe that "we are all one." They think that whatever anyone does to the least of these, they do it to everyone. They show solidarity with people of other faiths with the imported decorations and ideas that they borrow. They keep busy with a treasure hunt to find a faith that doesn't kill people or make them feel small. They are trying very seriously to love their neighbors as themselves.

It turns out that what the Prince of Peace taught is the closest thing to what hippies believe in. Many people don't realize this because they think the awful, violent words written by Paul the Apostle came from Jesus, although the Bible shows that they did not. The whole thing about being born in sin, women and slaves having to obey, shame of the body, hell, and idolaters being worthy of death, came from Paul and others, not Jesus. The weird dogmas added by ambitious theologians are not only the opposite of what Jesus taught. These teachings and the corporate policies their adherents vote for are killing every living thing.

When Pacifists call each other and other people "brother," and "sister," they fit into the category Jesus meant when he said those who love him are those who hear his words and do them. In their hungry search for truth, many hippies and liberals try out other belief systems. They are disgusted with what churches have done, the tortures and the slaughters, the negative vision of people and of the Earth's future, the heavy artificial burdens of guilt and shame laid on mankind.

Their approach to God is fluid, bendable. It's not full of threats of punishment and impossible demands, like most religions. It doesn't tell you what to believe, but what to be. Like Jesus, it asks us to be kind.

COPS AT THE LOG

It was a beautiful morning beside the pond, as a group of people sat and stood around talking and enjoying the day. A guy sitting on a skateboard said that one third of the Earth is above water and two thirds below water, like our intelligence and our consciousness. He said it was like where there's an iceberg and you can only see the tip above the water. A young man told us that when he used to be in his bedroom at home, there was a glow-in-the-dark poster of an angel and a demon over his bed. He said he used to lie there and stare at it. He wanted the angel's sword to go through the demon.

A guy who looked like a biker was there, his black hair in a spiked Mohawk several inches high, his bare arms covered with tattoos. He wore a black leather vest with lots of spikes and metal studs on it. He talked about India, Tibet, and "stories of the "Sadhus." From his belt there hung two long strings of prayer beads. Other people stood around discussing politics and religion and history. An attractive young couple was there, a man and wife, the girl's long colorful skirt covered with sequins that caught the sun in brilliant dots of light. Just as she said "You have to be prepared for anything to survive," we heard the roar of motorcycle engines.

A shout went out, "TEN-SIX!" People scrambled to make sure their dogs were on a leash, and to put away anything they didn't want police to see. One man didn't act fast enough, or maybe he decided to commit civil disobedience. The two officers pulled up next to the log on motorcycles and caught him with a pot pipe.

They put their hands in his pockets and frisked him up and down. Not finding anything they noticed his backpack on the embankment. They asked, "Whose backpack is this?" Nobody said anything. They asked him, "Is it yours?" He said, "All you'll find in there is my dirty laundry." With quick thinking someone else lied, "His lice-infested laundry." 🎒 ?? They let him go. Then they got back on their motorcycles and drove off toward the Haight without doing anything. The police officers don't always agree with the laws they're asked to enforce.

Afterwards I talked to the man that was rousted. It turned out he really knew his legal stuff about pot issues, had all the correct lingo, sounded like a lawyer. ⚖ He was very intelligent and very Christ-like. He had incredible deep dark blue eyes, a neat beard, and graceful curls framing his face. He wore a necklace with a large pink stone. The morning continued on almost as before. OK

I was told about the laws that these people have to deal with. They can get a $500. ticket for letting their dog run without a leash in the park. They can't leave their dog unattended outside a market or restaurant, can't tie it to a pole or tree. Others must watch their dog. Smoking a cigarette in public, even in the park, can bring a $500. fine. One girl got three tickets in a short time and had to do sixty hours of community service. These people live in the park and on the street. Where else are they going to smoke a cigarette? It's said that these rules are not enforced for "housies." They can set up their tent in the middle of the meadow all day and let their dog chase Frisbees, and nothing happens to them.

A camping ticket is $500., something that these people risk getting every night (647-E Illegal Camping.) One person had a friend who'd gotten forty in one year. He couldn't pay so they put him in jail for two months. People can't sit on the sidewalk until after 11 pm. Obstruction of the sidewalk is a $500. fine or twenty hours of Community Service for each ticket. They can request a "Receive Services Program," which doesn't go on their record, instead of Community Service. People don't want a homeless ticket. Urinating in public, even in the bushes in the park, can get them tagged as a sex offender. In North Carolina, there's a $1000. fine for feeding the homeless.

WHAT'S IN A NAME?

The name of the Right-wing group "Patriot Prayer" doesn't fit. Its adherents seem to want to reduce our liberties, not get more of them. It works to enact policies that don't do unto others as they would like to have done unto them. Yet this angry group tries to highjack both the flag and the cross. The cruel immigration and criminal justice policies embraced by the far Right have no resemblance to what Jesus taught. The mean-spirited beliefs driving the extreme right-wing agenda against the poor came from Paul the Apostle, not Jesus.

The labels attached to the anti-Nazi counter-demonstrators by the media are also inaccurate. Out of all the church groups and veterans' groups taking part in protests, "By Any Means Necessary" is highlighted. A tiny red-shirted contingent from the Communist Party is disproportionally visible, like always. A giant gay rainbow banner, almost allways an image that separates the country, stretches all the way across the street, bigger than anything any of the other peace groups carry. 🏳

The frightening masked "black bloc" is constantly in front of the cameras, grown from a dozen provocateurs I saw in Rodney King days, to a black-uniformed army of two hundred. As they leap about our demonstrations and parades, they look frightening in their faceless black shapes. I believe some of them have been sent out by someone who wants big business to win elections. They do minor damage with crowbars or bats, to make it look like a riot so that the powers that be can clamp down on peaceful demonstrators. They deliberately incite the police.

As if that weren't enough to make people terrified of liberals, the name "Antifa" sounds just like "Antifada," the terrorists' name for holy war. The name brings to mind the foreign enemies Americans have been taught to hate to a fever pitch. I believe that our political adversaries on the Right deliberately thought up a name for Pacifists and a costume, to make people hate us and fear us. Having perfected their black op skills and their lying about us since Nixon promoted the Drug War to get re-elected, they couldn't have done a better job. 👬 ☭ ☪ = 😺 = ☮ ?

In this arena, calling the Pacifists names can be followed by sticks and stones. Some laws can force organizers to pay giant bills for things like police presence or loss of profit to businesses. Unknown to most people, proposed new anti-terrorist laws could make someone a terrorist for merely participating in a demonstration where a provocateur commits a crime. This could put a lot of real patriots at risk of prison and also of losing their votes. That's why the "black bloc" is so dangerous to us, and why I believe they're organized by outside forces.

🔱 ||||| = 卍

RIDING THE BUS WITH TWO DREAMERS

Rainbow was bringing me to Mutiny Radio to read my writing online. It's not an actual radio station anymore. It used to be what is called a pirate radio station, and it got shut down by the FCC. So it started broadcasting over the internet, out of the FCC's jurisdiction. Rainbow also wanted me to meet the 60's icon named Diamond Dave Whitaker who runs the radio station. He's another Hippiesaurus like Rainbow, here since the beginning. An urban legend says that he introduced Bob Dylan to pot, who then introduced it to the Beatles. ▽ 🚬

The ride over there was half the fun. From his upper-floor walk-up on Page Street Rainbow arrived, his guitar slung over his shoulder. 📻 🎸 He would be performing several songs he wrote into the airwaves. At the bus stop we met up with his friend Chris, a vibrant, good-looking young Irishman who's totally crazy though sharply intelligent. On the spur of the moment, he decided to ride with us to the radio station. Another homeless young man came up, and a transaction started to take place there at the bus stop. Chris traded his St. Christopher medal for the other man's attractive bright green bandana. The man had cancer and seemed to think the medal might help make him better. Chris put on the green bandana. It looked great on him, he being Irish. 🚌 ☘

Then it turned out he was only lending the guy the St Christopher medal, but that's what the guy with cancer expected. He was lending it to him for its healing properties. ☤ ☥ He sort of rented it out as trading stock. It appeared that he had a trade in healing objects. As an added bonus, he rubbed the medal on a picture of Saint Jude he had, to make it more potent.

We got on the bus and Chris continued to say funny things that didn't quite make sense, laughing and having a great time. He rattled on being silly until he had us roaring with laughter. In the midst of the hilarity, he said some pretty profound things. He wore a button that said,

"OPEN MINDS – OPEN HEARTS." He decided not to go to the radio station after all and he got off at an earlier stop. I found out later that he let the guy keep the St. Christopher medal.

As Rainbow and I rode the bus, we enjoyed looking at the lovely Victorian row houses built at angles on the famous hills of the city. In San Francisco's precious limited space, many structures are built small. These beautiful homes are diminutive, using a minimum of space but rising two or three stories. Some are painted in pastel colors with gleaming gold or silver highlights. With graceful lines and curves and Greek columns, each is a creation the builder was proud of a century ago. 🔨

All of a sudden Rainbow got very serious and very excited. 💡 He said dramatically, "I'm gonna make a confession to you." I leaned closer on the bus bench to hear what he was going to reveal. What could it be? Then with all the passion anyone could speak with he blurted out, "I'm a dreamer!" 🎨 That was it.

After a long bus ride, we got to a bus stop and walked the rest of the way. A lot of walking goes on in San Francisco, because it's such a hassle to own and park a car. Maybe that's why most people here look so healthy. There are very few fast-food places here, a business that evolved to serve the car culture. The only McDonald's I know of is the one in the Haight. It doesn't have a drive-through and you can only park there for forty minutes. As Rainbow and I walked the several blocks we could hear live music from a garage band in one of the houses. We passed another Beatnik-type coffee house, where the scent of powerful coffee wafted out onto the sidewalk. ☕ ≋ At last we arrived at the broadcasting station.

MUTINY RADIO

On the glass storefront of Mutiny Radio there's the painted picture of a ship which looks like it's lurching forward with rays around it. As I approached, a group of longhairs stood around the doorway talking excitedly. They were discussing the Black Hills Rainbow Gathering last year, the Lakota Rainbow Alliance, and the pipeline and demonstrations at Standing Rock. A guy in a good suit said to the group, "I have a song in my heart every day. It's a gift."

Inside there's a low stage platform and about three rows of chairs. The walls are painted black and covered with political and art posters. The base of the plywood stage is lined with mirror tiles. Most important, there's the radio booth that you can see from the main room through a big glass window. It's a large walled-off area with microphones inside and a flashing red light that says "On the Air."

It turned out that Diamond Dave was out of town running a kitchen at the Rainbow Gathering in Pennsylvania. The people at Mutiny were more than interesting. Alternately sitting on the chairs or wandering outside, we all shared animated conversations. You can talk while the show is going on if the performers are inside the radio booth, but not if they're in the room with the stage, where a different mike is on. People stand around on the sidewalk and network.

It was the first time I would be reading my political poetry on public airwaves. It was exciting but frightening. As usual I hadn't really prepared, had just brought a whole book manuscript with me to decide later what to read. I figured I'd see what the others were reading and then decide. Plus, I wanted to be cautious and see how radical these people might be, what the others believed in who were reading beside me. I didn't hear anything especially inflammatory. Most people played guitars and chose the stage with the microphone that connected to the radio booth instead of going into it to read or speak. The show is "The Common Thread Collective."

(I now have my own show on mutinyradio.fm called Peace Drums," on Wednesdays from 4-6.)(You can also google "Marc Mercado reading PEACE DRUMS - Jesus Was a Hippie, where Marc reads this book aloud.)

Rainbow got up on the stage with his guitar and performed two of his songs, accompanied by my tambourine.

🎸🔄 Lots of people clapped. When it was my turn, I entered the radio booth. I wanted the experience, the excitement, of being behind that red light that said, "On the Air." Shaking inside I sat down at the table in front of the microphone. I didn't know how many people would be listening. They said it went all over the world. The moderator introduced me and then there I was, standing on the edge of my own personal high dive.

Reading my writing into the microphone was exhilarating. To share my thoughts and beliefs with the public is something I've been enjoying at the swap meets for two decades. There's something very sweet about opening up to lots of people, especially when they open up back. On the other side of that microphone was a whole new crowd many times bigger than the number of people I was friends with at the swap meets and on the Haight. When you counted that people might send the broadcast to other people and put it on the Internet, the potential outreach was staggering compared to what I was used to. 🎤 → 🌍

I approached timidly this new, much larger arena. I would be on display before the world, my words not retractable. If I made a mistake and said something stupid, or if I said it in the wrong way, it would always be out there floating somewhere on the Internet, in the archive of the radio show. Starting off easy, I read my "Peace Drums" poem that's been well-received by a lot of people. It was still risky, because it's what I call "syrupy religious without the religion." The people at Mutiny Radio are very sophisticated and educated. Some of them are atheists. They know too much about the atrocities of religions to take somebody else's word about truth. Using the "G" word (God) might be a big turn-off for some of them. 🫢

I read the poem and one other. Except for a slightly awkward intro I refrained from trying to ad-lib this time. Might as well try out the trapeze before trying to fly without a net. ✌️ Leaving the radio booth I didn't get much in the way of feedback. It seems that people inside the station don't listen much during the performances, either preparing their own or visiting and talking outside. I got more response reading my political and spiritual poetry outside, to a group of longhairs as we all sat cross-legged on the sidewalk. I couldn't tell right away how the staff or the show's audience would respond to what I'd read. But the next week when I came back to read, they asked me to broadcast my syrupy religious poem again. 🏆🤸

On the bus ride back, Rainbow again got urgently excited out of the blue. ≷💡≶ From his tone of voice, I thought it would be about something more immediate, like that he'd seen something amazing out the bus window. Instead he said, ardently, "What am I in relation to the universe?? Infinitely small... I am love!"

☆✨ ≷❤️≶ ☆✨

DIAMOND DAVE – DEFENDER OF THE POOR

I thought someone was telling a tall tale or repeating an urban legend. Could it really be true that someone that I knew was the person who'd introduced Bob Dylan to pot? I googled Diamond Dave Whitaker and sure enough, Bob Dylan himself had mentioned him in his own writings about his life. 🚬

It turns out he'd not only introduced him to pot, with history-making effects. When Bob Zimmerman was eighteen Dave had actually mentored him, given him a copy of Jack Kerouak's "On the Road," which greatly influenced his life and led to his friendship with Woody Guthrie.

Whatever ways Dylan affected the generations, Diamond Dave had something to do with it.

The media articles on Google said that he'd recently been recognized by the San Francisco Board of Supervisors as "a true San Francisco Treasure." They'd made a proclamation that February 2, 2016, be declared "Diamond Dave Whitaker Day." They called him "a poet and a San Francisco staple." With his student demonstrators he'd actually had something to do with saving the Board of Supervisors from being shut down one time. He'd also saved the city college from losing its accreditation another time. The articles called him "defender of the poor."

He runs the "Common Threads" show on the web station Mutiny Radio, where I used to read my writing on Friday afternoons. He looks the part of an icon of the 60's, with grey curls and beard beneath a favorite red leather cap he always wears. His hair is long and includes several thin braids to his waist. Dressed in a psychedelic vest and tie-dyed shirt, he is over eighty and walks with a cane. He's always among the other hosts of the radio show, interacting with guests and providing humorous and inspiring banter.

He looks really cool behind the microphone, in the glassed-in room with the red sign that lights up and says, "On the Air." He begins, "If you don't panic you can keep it organic. Live to learn, learn to live, it never ends!" He's been doing this radio show for decades and was involved with the 60's movement for over half a century. Leaning toward the mike, he goes on with great vitality: "Take what you need, get what you can, where you can, however you can. In other words, it's about lending a hand, strangers becoming friends, friends becoming family, family becoming community, community on the move. That's our movement!"

He introduces the next performer, a beautiful girl called Windsong, who steps onto the stage to sing and play a rare instrument called a Bouzouki. It looks like a lute, with flowers on the delicately carved tortoise shell pic guard. She's wearing a baseball cap over a honey-colored braid going down her back, and a brightly- flowered shirt with a large live parrot to match. The parrot perching on her shoulder is over two feet long, beak to tail, cobalt blue with bright orange and yellow. Next, poetess Julia shares her heart about the state of the world. 🌍

Taking the mike again Diamond Dave goes on, sounding like an old-time preacher, kind of singing the words instead of just saying them. "Cause hey, we were brought together for a reason, and the reason is this: that we *love* one another! We were brought together for a reason and that reason is this: that we *heal* one another. We were brought together for a reason and that reason is: we *compliment* one another. We are brought together for a reason and that reason is that we *complete* one another. Like what? Like yin and yang, left and right, up and down, old and young, man and woman, ROCK AND ROLL!!" The people in the studio clap and cheer. 🙌

I got to meet with him for coffee on Haight Street, at "Coffee to the People." ☕ He told me it was a guy named "Dumpster" who'd taught the kids how to ride trains. 🚃🚃🚃🚃💨 He recounted adventures he'd had with famous bands and some of the giants of the counterculture, including the Grateful Dead. 🌹 We agreed that the main focus of the conversation should be, "where do we go from here?" Even while not on the air he spoke in a kind of rhythm. He said, "Cast a wide net, find the common thread. Let life flourish, don't panic, keep it organic. If you have questions, I have answers. If you have answers I have questions!"

PEACE IN THE PARK

I keep running into powerful women who own businesses and make things happen around here. There's Sunshine "Sunny" Powers who owns "Love on Haight" and does so much to keep the spirit of this place alive. There's Jessy Kate Schlingler with "The Red Victorian," and Noot, who owns "Love of Ganesha" and Cheola, who has "Tibetan Gift Corner," Cicely at "Decades of Fashion," and Amal at Amal's Deli.

Linda Kelly wrote "Deadheads" and started "The Haight Street Voice." The publication features articles about and by local artists and writers, including interviews of the house-free telling their stories and displaying their art. The first page had a quote by 60's icon Stanley Mouse: "The 60's were a portal to an inner-dimensional universe, and possibly a door to parallel worlds. We were explorers of inner space. The psychedelic experience was a shortcut to God."

One dynamic woman who very much impressed me is Mona Lisa, whom I met at Mutiny Radio. She's an attorney and I'm told that at one time she ran the local chapter of the National Organization for Women. She put on "PEACE IN THE PARK," one of the few Summer of Love commemorative events that made it past the bureaucrats. It was held at the bandshell at Golden Gate Park and it featured speakers, performers and bands, and booths with vegetarian food only. The crowd seemed very moved when they participated in a silent Prayer for Peace that was happening simultaneously all around the world.

Mona Lisa was incredibly beautiful in a blue butterfly costume and flowing skirts and a wreath of fresh flowers crowning her long brown hair.

I thought she was pretty before, but on this day she took my breath away. Wearing her usual sweet, mysterious smile that was like the other Mona Lisa's, she was the master of ceremonies, along with Global Val, the host of Mutiny Radio. She too looked absolutely gorgeous in a gold butterfly costume, also with flowing clothes and flowers in her hair.

Together next to the timeless-looking large stone pillars of the bandstand, they looked like they'd just come through a time warp from classical times or some other dimension.

There was an Earth Dance and Wavy Gravy was there. Most spectacular was a parade of giant puppets on stilts that circled through and around the event, waving large, sheer rainbow-colored banners. The puppets' papier-mache heads were beautiful, not scary, and not cartoon characters. They were dressed in brightly-colored flowing clothes. The people on stilts who carried them underneath walked them gracefully, moving their hands with long sticks. It was dream-like. When the show was over the band called out "Love and Light!" to the crowd.

THE GREAT ESCAPE

Diamond Dave is almost eighty and had just narrowly escaped being taken prisoner by a hospital after a fall. I'd gone to see him there and snuck in the cigarettes he craved. He had to really sneak around to smoke them, had to pry open the window. He'd left the hospital without permission, despite a tag alarm and a social worker who'd decided he was too old to live alone. He'd just walked out and made his way back to the warehouse building where he rented a little windowless room where he'd lived for years.

He doesn't exactly live alone there. When I went to see him, I met several people who live there in a semi-communal arrangement. Some have places inside the warehouse building, and at least one lives in a camper in the parking area. Most interesting, there's a hippie bus village in the back lot.

It's also kind of a hippie bus graveyard, as only two of the wildly-painted school buses seem to be occupied. These are decorated with tiny lights, plants, and colorful hanging artworks. The other buses are lined up in a row at the back of the lot, each having many stories to tell if walls could talk. They have flowers painted on them and spiritual symbols. A couple of them look really vintage, maybe built in the Fifties. They have that rounded look and a different contour.

I went back to the warehouse where a communal kitchen was almost open-air, with all the wide-open doors and other openings. I was told that raccoons wander through nightly. Otherwise, the kitchen was very clean and organized, though cavernous in the large echoing building. I had a great conversation with a man, some kind of artist, sitting at a counter with his computer. Another man came and cooked some sausages and made a sandwich.

Diamond Dave was happy in his little room, at last away from the clutches of the police state in the guise of protection. It's frightening that they can keep old people from going home from the hospital "for their safety." He sat on his little single bed and smoked his cigarettes contentedly. The thing he'd hated the most about the hospital was that they wouldn't let him out to have a smoke.   The room here was kind of Spartan but it was where he wanted to be.   Beside the bed was a can full of cigarette butts.

DIAMOND DAVE'S 80th BIRTHDAY

For Dave's eightieth, the usual yearly birthday bash at the Adobe Book Store was planned. When I got there, it was already packed with interesting-looking people. Barbara from Mutiny Radio had set up a nice refreshment table with mostly vegan offerings and some bottles of wine.

There were musicians and poetry readings and one lady did a Middle Eastern dance with cymbals. A man who could whistle incredibly well, who was also a political activist, performed and amazed us all. ♩♪🏆

Diamond Dave had on a new suit that someone had gifted him. 👔 He looked terrific in it with a white shirt and tie, and another visor cap of the special 19th-century-style he likes, to replace the red 🧥 leather one the hospital still had. He gave a speech acknowledging all his good friends. It was not only a celebration of his eightieth birthday, but of a new lease on life since escaping the hospital.

I finally got to meet Linda Kelly, who is even more beautiful than the picture on her email. There's something effervescent about her, full of life, a quality hard to describe. She was dressed artfully and was accompanied by her attractive long-haired boyfriend in a high-end top hat. They looked like rock stars. We didn't have much chance to talk in that crowded, loud place but agreed to meet later to discuss putting my writing in her magazine, the Haight Street Voice. ≥ 👩 📄 ✌ 🎩 ≤

Both Mona Lisa and Global Val were there, who'd put on "Peace in the Park." I got to have a wonderful conversation with Mona Lisa. 🖼 She told me more about Mary Magdalene, whom some religious texts say was Jesus' best friend. She told me that some people believe that she was an important influence on his teachings. Some even believe that she and Jesus were married. 👩 ?

I believe that Jesus's teachings came from beyond himself, as he said, "Everything I have I got from the Father." The Golden Rule doesn't need to come from either gender to be validated. It comes from plain common sense and could have been expressed by any one of us. That's what makes it sublime. ≥ ✏ ≤ 🥇!!

I assured Mona Lisa, who at that moment looked to me like Mary Magdalene with her beautiful long hair and angelic face, that I would look again at the short Gospel of Mary. I have no problem believing that she was Jesus' best friend, that the disciples were jealous of her, and that she later lived in a cave in France. I think it's possible that they could have been married. Jesus did not teach celibacy. Paul did.

There's a reason why I stuck to the King James Bible and didn't use other gospels in assembling The Liberal's Bible Guide. I wanted to show that the Christian Right is wrong about their own Bible, the same "translation" that's been used to make many of the unjust laws we live under. It and the precursor Geneva Bible were used to make Inquisitions and witch hunts, to kill the indigenous, to promote the Holocaust, and now to let corporations destroy the Earth and steal our liberty.

False statements by theologians about the contents of the New Testament are tricking good people into voting for fascism, by telling them that they're stopping gays and saving the unborn. At the same time those called Liberals are tricked into voting for strangling liability laws when they are told these laws are going to protect someone or get them fairer treatment. It all translates into profits for insurance companies and other corporations, and less liberty for all of us. It pits us against each other.

I can't blame Mona Lisa for wanting nothing to do with the "patriarchal system" associated with Jesus. Most people don't know that the things they can't stand about that religion didn't come from him. Televangelists never tell us who said what. Bible studies often don't study anything. They seem geared only to memorize Paul's doctrines, set in stone, that Jesus didn't teach, and to master the mental acrobatics needed to comprehend them.

The party ended, the refreshment table was cleaned up and the big metal gate was pulled across the bookstore building and locked, but many of us stood on the sidewalk for an hour in excited discussions.

A CASE OF MISTAKEN IDENTITY

To honor Mona Lisa, I did some research on Mary Magdalene and read again the Gospel of Mary. I found it to be very short, since ten pages of it are missing. The things Mary Magdalene said about how things are ordered and connected together made me wonder if she and Jesus had eaten sacred mushrooms or something together.  ?

I liked it when she told Jesus' disciples that he'd said not to make lots of rules for people to follow. I was surprised that it didn't say anything about love and forgiveness and the Golden Rule, vital tools for saving the planet. It could be that these are in the missing ten pages.

I will show here, from the New Testament, that Mary Magdalene was not a prostitute. The woman accused of adultery who was saved by Jesus from being stoned, had nothing to do with Mary Magdalene. The part that claims Jesus cast seven devils out of her is in a part of the last chapter of Mark, which most theologians agree was added in the second century.

There are three instances of a woman anointing Jesus' feet and drying them with her hair:

1.) An **unnamed "woman in the city, which was *a sinner*," washes his feet with her tears at the Pharisee's house** where Jesus had been invited to dinner **in the city of Nain.** The Pharisees judge Jesus, saying that if he was a prophet, he would've known that the woman was a sinner before letting her touch him. This happens **early in Jesus' career,** while John the Baptist is still alive. The **next chapter introduces Mary Magdalene as a separate woman,** one of those who "minister to Jesus."
2.) **Mary Magdalene is the sister of Martha and of Lazarus** whom it says Jesus raised from the dead. At a dinner **in Bethany** Martha complains to Jesus that her sister Mary isn't helping her serve the

guests. Jesus tells her that Mary has made the better choice, sitting listening to Jesus. **Another time**, **six days before Passover,** Mary anoints Jesus' feet with ointment and wipes them with her hair. The disciples are angry, saying the ointment should've been sold and the money given to the poor. Jesus tells them to leave her alone, that she's done this to anoint him for his burial.

3,) *An unnamed woman* enters and anoints Jesus' feet with ointment as he is having dinner **at the house of Simon the Leper in Bethany, two days before Passover.**   Sounds like the exact same story about Mary Magdalene, except it's at Simon the Leper's house and only two days before Passover instead of six.

It's hard for me to understand how theologians can assert that the New Testament is perfect when they know that many of the books were not written by those they are attributed to. Pseudepigrapha is scripture that's not authored by the apostle or disciple whose name appears there. Of Paul's letters, on whom much of the oppression of the Western World has been built, only seven of the fourteen are believed to have been written by him. They are Romans, I Corinthians, II Corinthians, Galatians, Philippians, I Thessalonians, and Philemon. The ones by **Mystery Theologians** are Ephesians, Colossians, II Thessalonians, I Timothy, II Timothy, Titus, Hebrews, Peter II, and Jude.

I think it's important to know that Paul never met Jesus, and the alleged Gospel writers Mark and Luke, Paul's travelling companions, never met Jesus. The author also doubts that John of Patmos, who wrote Revelation, supposed to be Jesus's best friend, ever met Jesus. The teachings of Jesus about love and forgiveness aren't in his book.

There have been some serious "mistranslations" that have impacted people's lives. The word "Hell" was substituted for "Gehenna," the trash dump outside of Jerusalem where they burned dead bodies with fire and brimstone. "Hell" was also substituted for Hades, the land of the dead. The plant "Calamus" was substituted for "Canna Boisn" and other names that referred to cannabis, the active ingredient in the holy oil used in the Holy of Holies.

Voltaire claimed that at the Council of Trent in 1546, one way they decided which scriptures to include in the Bible: They prayed and if scrolls fell on the floor, it meant they were not accepted by God. Thomas Aquinas, a father of the Church, said that the greatest pleasure in Heaven besides being with God would be to watch the tortures of the damned.

THINGS JESUS SAID   (King James Version)

COME UNTO ME, ALL YE THAT LABOUR AND ARE HEAVY-LADEN, AND I WILL GIVE YOU REST. Take my yoke upon you, and learn of me; for I am meek and lowly of heart: and **YE SHALL FIND REST UNTO YOUR SOULS.** For my yoke is easy, and my burden is light. (Matt.11:28-30)

The Spirit of the Lord is upon me, because he hath anointed me to preach the gospel (good news) to the poor; **HE HATH SENT ME TO HEAL THE BROKENHEARTED,** to preach deliverance to the captives, and recovering of sight to the blind, **TO SET AT LIBERTY THEM THAT ARE BRUISED.** (Lk 4:18)

BLESSED ARE THE POOR IN SPIRIT: for theirs is the kingdom of heaven. Blessed are they that mourn: for they shall be comforted. **BLESSED ARE THE MEEK**: for they shall inherit the earth. (Matthew 5:3-5)

I AM COME THAT THEY MIGHT HAVE LIFE, AND THAT THEY MIGHT HAVE IT MORE ABUNDANTLY. (John 17:13)

As the Father hath loved me, so have I loved you: continue ye in my love. If ye keep my commandments, ye shall **ABIDE IN MY LOVE**; even as I have kept my Father's commandments, and abide in his love. (John 15:9-10)

THOU SHALT LOVE THE LORD THY GOD WITH ALL THY HEART, WITH ALL THY SOUL, AND WITH ALL THY MIND. This is the first and great commandment. And the second is like unto it, **THOU SHALT LOVE THY NEIGHBOR AS THYSELF**. On these two commandments hang all the law and the prophets. (Matthew 22:37-40)

A new commandment I give unto you, that ye **LOVE ONE ANOTHER**; as **I HAVE LOVED YOU**, that ye also love one another. By this shall all men know that ye are my disciples, if ye have love one to another. (Jn 13:34-35)

And **AS YE WOULD THAT MEN SHOULD DO TO YOU, DO YE ALSO TO THEM LIKEWISE**. These things have I spoken unto you, (Luke 6:31) that my joy might remain in you, and **THAT YOUR JOY MIGHT BE FULL**. (John 15:11)

GIVE, AND IT SHALL BE GIVEN UNTO YOU; good measure, pressed down, and shaken together, and running over, shall men give into your bosom. For **WITH THE SAME MEASURE THAT YE METE**, withal **IT SHALL BE MEASURED TO YOU AGAIN**. (Luke 6:38)

GIVE TO HIM THAT ASKETH THEE, AND FROM HIM THAT WOULD BORROW of thee TURN NOT THOU AWAY. Do good, and **LEND, HOPING FOR NOTHING AGAIN**; and **YOUR REWARD SHALL BE GREAT,** and ye shall be the children of the Highest. (Matthew 5:42)(Luke 6:35)

JUDGE NOT, AND YE SHALL NOT BE JUDGED: CONDEMN NOT, AND YE SHALL NOT BE CONDEMNED. (Luke 6:37) For **WITH WHAT JUDGMENT YE JUDGE, YE SHALL BE JUDGED** and with what measure ye mete, it shall be measured to you again. (Matthew 7:2) **FORGIVE, AND YE SHALL BE FORGIVEN.** (Luke 6:37) **DO NOT THINK THAT I WILL ACCUSE YOU TO THE FATHER.** (John 5:45)

BEWARE OF FALSE PROPHETS which come to you **IN SHEEP'S CLOTHING**, but inwardly **THEY ARE RAVENING WOLVES. YE SHALL KNOW THEM BY THEIR FRUITS.** Do men gather grapes of thorns, or figs of thistles? **EVERY GOOD TREE BRINGETH FORTH GOOD FRUIT**; but a corrupt tree bringeth forth evil fruit. A good tree cannot bring forth evil fruit, neither can a corrupt tree bring forth good fruit. (Matthew 7:15-18)

NOT EVERY ONE THAT SAITH UNTO ME, "LORD, LORD," SHALL ENTER THE KINGDOM OF HEAVEN; but he that doeth the will of my Father which is in heaven. Many will say to me in that day, "Lord, Lord, have we not prophesied in thy name? And in thy name have cast out devils? And in thy name done many wonderful works?" And then will I profess unto them, "I NEVER KNEW YOU: Depart from me, ye that work iniquity." ("**unequalness**," from Latin root) (Matthew 7:20-23)

The kingdom cometh not with observation: neither shall they say, Lo here! or, lo there! for, behold, **THE KINGDOM OF GOD IS WITHIN YOU**. (Luke 17:20-21)

JESUS DIDN'T TEACH: that all are born in sin, the Inquisition, shunning, slaves and women "obey in all things," Adam and Eve, that idolaters and gays are "worthy of death," antisemitism, shame of the body, hell, tithing, having to go to church, the divine right of kings, that the Bible was perfect, or that he created the world. Paul the Apostle and OTHERS ADDED those, plus "obey every ordinance of man," "let the unjust be unjust still," that you have to believe or be damned, that you can "take up serpents" and drink poison, and that it's not what you do that counts, but what you believe in. Red letters in the book of Revelation are the writer's vision or dream and don't teach what Jesus taught, and have been killing people since the ink was dry. The Prince of Peace taught kindness, brotherly love, and Heaven on Earth.

☆✦ 🕊 ☮ ♡⚷ ‼ ☆✦

A FIGHT AVOIDED

He looks like a teacher or a student drinking his coffee as he sits at his accustomed spot near the entrance to the park, wearing headphones and sunglasses and a high-class wilderness jacket like you buy in catalogues. 🎧 With a neat beard and short hair, Ryan seemed like a housie until I looked down at his feet, in flip flops and encrusted with dust as if he'd just walked a thousand miles. He must be going shoeless for health reasons because the rest of his stuff is really together.

I met him where he was set up on the grass near the Horseshoe. He was working on something, making himself a serviceable leather pouch with pockets. It was finely done, like everything else of his, so neatly packed and organized. He was using high-grade suede and a real glovers' needle. Sitting on the most light-weight and most comfortable folding camp chair I've ever seen, he drank hot coffee he'd brewed with a high-tech tiny camp stove almost small enough to fit in your pocket. It was another expensive item from a sporting catalogue with state-of-the-art innovations.

We had a wonderful conversation, the most educated one I'd had at the park. He has a beautiful vocabulary. It seems like he's out here by choice. I don't get a sense that he's down and out, although he obviously lives out here. It doesn't seem like there's room for a tent in his tightly-packed belongings. He says he doesn't need one, that the less stuff he has the better. He seems houseless but not homeless. He sleeps in a hammock, off the ground and away from raccoons and other critters.

He told me that sometimes he finds new species in the park and alerts the scientists about them. They actually named a new species of scorpion after him, Psuedouroctorus Moyeri. The second part is a reference to his last name. Some people call him "the Professor." He's more than uncomfortable with anything to do with religion. His knowledge of history makes any kind of dogma unpalatable, mysticism suspect. He is outraged. He advised me to be careful how I use the "G" word ("God") with people. I refrained from telling him my true opinion: God would agree with him.

As we changed the subject there was a commotion near the log. Abruptly the Professor told me, "You should leave now." At first I didn't know why but then I saw a young man approach a group of people near where we were. He was angry. It turns out a Pitbull from that group had gotten loose and gone over to the log, grabbed a kitten right out of a girl's lap and killed it. The girl was really upset, the daughter of one of the women there. This mother and grown daughter were the same ones I'd seen a few weeks before, when the mother's back had gone out and she'd been taken away in an ambulance.

The young woman was crying, holding the dead, bloodied kitten in a towel on her lap. It had a broken neck. The angry man strode up to the group of people and started yelling at the guy who had the dog, waving his arms as if he was going to hit him. By this time, I was standing about forty feet away watching.

Right then the Professor stepped in and started talking to both of them and asking questions. It turned out it wasn't even the other guy's own dog. He was just watching him for someone else who'd gone to the Haight. He'd loosened the dog's harness because it looked too tight and then the dog had gotten loose and this had happened. By the time explanations were made, things cooled down. Whatever the Professor had said, it had defused that volatile situation.

TOO FAR OUT

As I approached the paved area and the planter shaped like a half circle, which is why it's called "the Horseshoe," I met a homeless beggar who talked like an angel. I don't remember exactly what he told me but it was perfect, and he just went on and on sounding like something more than himself. His black face was beautiful as he assured me that what I was doing, and what I was trying to write, would succeed. These kinds of encounters happen to me every now and then, particularly at the park. The place seems to vibrate with miraculous force. My favorite area on the east end of the park really feels to me like it could be in another dimension.

At the Horseshoe there was a lady with a Bible and some tracts. She and her friends thought they were going to convert the hippies and make them into good people, never knowing that Heaven was right under their feet. The tracts told people they were cursed sinners and had been "born in sin." The little folded papers, printed black and orange, told them their body is shameful and that almost anything that people enjoy deserves punishment. There were scary pictures of people being burned alive, and the threat that if the reader didn't do exactly what it said in the tract, that's where they would end up. The references were almost always to something the Apostle Paul wrote. There wasn't anything in them that Jesus said.

I tried reasoning with her, tried to show her in her Bible that everything in those tracts was not from Jesus, but from Paul the Apostle and others. All I got was a friendly Teflon smile and the question, "Are you saved?" I replied that I was. She persisted. "Have you confessed to Jesus Christ that you are a sinner?" I told her that I didn't think I was a sinner, and that Jesus didn't teach that all people were sinners, or that they had been "born in sin." She asked me if I ever told a white lie and tried to use that to convince me I was a sinner.

Her dogmas growled and barked, but I was ready for them. I tried to prove to her that the Bible says it was Paul, not Jesus, who'd taught the things that most of us can't stand about religion. Jesus wouldn't have been able to stand them either. The encounter ended with her deciding that I was from Satan, in the same friendly manner. She gave me a few more tracts and walked on down toward the log, where she stopped briefly but seemed uncomfortable with the house-free smoking pot openly. After she left, I lingered at the Horseshoe, talked with a young guy who looked and sounded like Jesus. He was dressed in white, had long hair, and his guitar had a picture of the universe painted on it. I felt so much better after talking to him. 😊 ♥ VS ⛪ ↰ ⛓

I crossed the street at the light and walked on down Haight Street, where I met "Destany" and her husband "ABlessin" sitting on the sidewalk and "flashing a sign" that said it was her birthday. She has blond hair which she'd decorated with melon-colored streaks, and he's African American. They're still madly in love after being married four years. She said, "Every morning he tells me all the things he loves about me."

He added, "Then we read the Word of God." Then a lady came out of the "ChaChaCha" club across the street and gave them a nice container of delicious leftover food. Before eating it, they said grace.

On another corner, there was a couple selling jokes to the tourists. The boy asked, "Why do hippies wear corduroy?"

The girl answered, "Because it's groovy."

And "How many hippies does it take to screw in a lightbulb?"

"They don't screw in lightbulbs but in tents, bushes, and vans."

Also, "Why couldn't the lifeguard save the hippie?"

"He was too far out!"

STREET JUSTICE

What the young man did to protect the group was what John Wayne would've done, but doing the same thing today would land someone a hefty prison sentence. Yet the police can't protect these people from the rogues among them, those who would bother the young ladies or steal from the vulnerable community or beat people up. It's not that the police don't care. These people don't want to go to them for various reasons. A lot of them are on the run for minor violations like not reporting to a probation officer or social worker. Most just want to stay off the grid and take care of their own business.

I witnessed for myself what happens when somebody seriously breaks the rules. A guy had been caught going through people's stuff, a tall guy with lots of long curly black hair. Another guy, a thin blond guy with a cap, warned and threatened him. He said that he'd hit him with his skateboard if he saw him in the park before three weeks' time. Skateboards can make a weapon and are carried by some people partly for defense. When you hear of people getting in fights, skateboards are sometimes involved.

A skateboard has many uses. It provides transportation that makes the rider look like he's flying, gracefully gliding. No other way to travel is as artfully attractive. These are the same young men we saw doing incredible tricks on skateboards when they used to live at home and congregate near their high schools. A skateboard can be used as a table or platform, as a seat to stay out of the dirt, as trading stock for something else they need. It's the chosen mode of local transportation for many of the homeless youth. It's light and easy to transport tied to a backpack. It can be taken on the bus. It's not that expensive to replace if something happens to it. It can be used to defend the owner against dogs, among other things.

Now the guy was threatening the accused thief that he would hit him with his skateboard if he returned to the park during the next three weeks. No one defended the thief; they were just silent. There was no hate either. They banished him but for only three weeks. They were willing to let him back into the community later. I thought it showed again the ideal of forgiveness, of treating people like brothers. At the Rainbow Gathering there is usually a group of people called Shanti Sena, volunteers assigned to handle any problems. Shanti Sena means "peace keepers" in Sanskrit. Most situations with people who are upset are handled with hugs, food, or other refreshment.

A thief can cause a lot of trouble for these people, pilfering their few possessions and sowing mistrust among the group. Yet they were willing to take him back, to try to help him mend his ways. Meanwhile he risked a concussion if he set foot in the park. He got it easy compared to the guy who defended the people's stuff and kicked him out would've gotten if someone had reported him for threatening the guy, or worse, if he'd actually hit the guy with his skateboard. He probably would've been charged with making a terrorist threat and assault, unlike John Wayne.

A young man and his wife were there next to the pond. They told me their dog was wasted after eating a quarter pound of his friend's pot in a van. There was no talk of retribution or retaliation or prosecution for that theft.

STAY AWESOME

You see unexpected combinations of things on and around the Haight. A shiny rented bicycle built for two went by, then was followed by a pieced-together bike with a major hippie on it, a trailer with milk crates, and a big dog trotting alongside on a leash. The trailer was fully loaded and covered with a big blue tarp. The guy wore comfortable baggy clothes and long hair that trailed behind him in the wind as he and the dog sped along. In contrast, the gentrified tourists were gorgeous and well-groomed in their top-of-the-line sports clothes, sleek and close-fitting to reduce wind resistance.

I met a black man named Theo with big bushy grey hair and beard, who hangs out at the Horseshoe. He wears a large crucifix and a long tailored grey wool coat. He has a golden-brown brindle Pitbull named "Boogie." He said he got her when she was a puppy, when he could hold her in his hand. The dog wears what looks like a really gorgeous collar, real silver on black leather. The collar is actually a man's belt that fits perfectly two times around the dog's neck. It was a special gift given to her when she was a puppy. He said she's the sweetest dog ever and that she loves kids. He said, "I would be lost without her. I wouldn't care if they stole all my stuff as long as my dog was still there."

At the log I met Dire Wolf, also called Johnny Wolf and Smiling Wolf. On a patch on his pack it says, "Nature is my religion and the Earth is my church." Then in the meadow near the drummers' bench I met Ruby Lips, who offered me some of her bottle of wine. I took a long swig and we hugged and had a great conversation. She told me about the different kinds of ground she's slept on, including sleeping around rocks. She said the best ground she'd ever slept on had just been freshly plowed.

She said that raccoons could be a real hassle because they break into tents to try to get food, even while people are sleeping in them. They're very aggressive and move in packs. She told me the best way to keep food away from raccoons is to put it in two secured plastic bags, one inside the other, and hang it from a tree. Hearing about how much trouble people have with raccoons made me wonder where all those raccoon tails guys wear come from. A girl with a fur vest was there. She had a small mammal's skin hanging from her pocket, maybe from a little weasel.

Contrary to what many people think, most of the house-free here don't drink. Some areas of the park are like an AA meeting. Once I had a leftover bottle of wine and tried to give it away to three separate guys. Each said they didn't drink. Likewise, I haven't seen evidence of hard drug use out there. It's everybody's fantasy that the street people are all on meth and so on, but in all my intimate conversations and interactions with these people I can honestly say that I didn't see it, and I didn't hear about it. I didn't hear people talking to each other about it, didn't hear any jokes about it. What I did hear was that this group at the park tries to keep "tweakers" away because they make trouble and attract police.

A boy named Richard the Third arrived. He said the park rangers tried to take his stuff while he was cleaning up after his dog. 🐕 🚕 He said the DPW takes all their stuff and leaves the trash. He said "With cars, they warn you. Not with tents." While telling the story, he was looking for socks in his backpack. He took everything out, still couldn't find them, and put everything back in. A woman named Lisa looked forlorn sitting on the grass. She had many troubles, had lost a house, but she said that as long as she still had her partner, she'd be all right. Some people out here seem to be hanging onto love like it's their last dollar.

On the Haight, some people walking by gave me three baskets of strawberries to give away. I went to the sidewalk on the Stanyan side of McDonald's, where there is a semi-permanent encampment of a guy with a wheelchair, a tarp and two dogs. I gave him one basket of the strawberries and also one to another homeless man walking by with a grocery cart. 🐕🐕♿🍓 🛒🍓 🎨🍓

The remaining basket I gave to Mario, an artist sitting on the sidewalk making paintings on small squares of wood and selling them. The one he was working on had a heart with wings. He was happy to get the strawberries. The hardest and most costly thing to get on the street is anything fresh. He was very educated, and we talked about Mary Magdalene, the Cathars, cathedrals, history and art. He said, "To dream and to think thereof and then put into f-----g action." He wants to make a tricycle juice bar. He said, "People want to be healthy, need juice, need exercise." 🚴 ﹥🏁﹤

I met Justin, who talked about theoretical astrophysics. He said God is like a fractal. His philosophy: we exist on a spectrum. Humans are creatures of habits we use to describe the existence we perceive as reality. It has to do with brain waves and "empathical read-out." Another guy showed up and he, like so many, had a story about losing his stuff. He said, "I'm not worried. I always find the things I need."

As I walked away, I heard their customary parting greeting: "Love and embrace and stay awesome!"

THE PIRATE QUEEN

In her beautiful high-quality black leather jackets and her brilliantly-dyed persimmon-colored hair, "Dragon" is hard to miss sitting on logs near the tunnel with her crew. I think of her as the Pirate Queen because if there was one, this is what she would look like. People seem to give her a lot of respect. She called herself a "scurvy pirate."  She said that she was really a "Sea Dog" (as opposed to a "Road Dog?") A patch on her jacket says "DISOBEY." She also has a button with a cow on it, which shows she's mindful about what she eats. It says, "Not Your Mom, Not Your Milk."

She used to have a house and a good job. Then she had a big RV that was sometimes parked at the meters next to McDonald's, but it was impounded for tickets and she couldn't get it back. Then she bought a truck, but it blew up. Now as winter approaches, she's staying in the park like the rest of her group. Like all the others, I'm sure she's survived some really tough situations. Last year I saw her wheeled out of the park in a wheelchair to an ambulance, when her back went out.

I used to see her pretty grown daughter whose platinum hair is sometimes partially dyed pink, but I haven't seen her lately. It looks like her mom found her a place indoors. She's the same girl who had a kitten snatched right out of her lap by a Pitbull. When I talked to her, I found out she does very well in school. **A +**

Dragon arrived at the log across the pond with her two dogs, Daphne, a large brown dog, and Daphne's son Bear. The son doesn't look at all like the mom. He's small and has pointed ears, and luminescent bright white fur.

A drunken man, a stranger, had been hanging out at the log and was now pissing right next to it where people sit. "Drunk guy's gotta go!" Dragon said with quiet authority. She told the men to ask him nicely to leave first but didn't mention what would happen if he didn't. The man got his cart and strolled off. She counsels people, sorts out arguments. Everyone pays attention to what she says. 🕺 🚽 🛒

One day I heard beautiful haunting music coming through the forest. Approaching the tunnel, I was surprised to see it was Dragon, playing a violin like a virtuoso. She had skill and heart, and all those around her were quiet as she performed. The depth of her experiences and feelings, and also some hope, seemed expressed in the plaintive, vibrating notes. Seeing her presented an unexpected picture, one worth keeping in memory.

🌸🎻 🎵🎶 🌲 🍀

PIG EARS FROM HEAVEN

I met Kelly, a woman probably in her late thirties. She was set up on a blanket under a tree near the Horseshoe, with another blanket covering her for the cold. ❄ I wanted to go up to her but felt cautious because of her big dog, who looked scary with  yellow eyes and strong-looking jaws. You don't want to take anything for granted with some of these road dogs. If you look at them straight in the face, they might think it's a challenge. But this dog turned out to be a sweetheart. The dog's name is "Athena," Goddess of Wisdom. She has golden-brown fur that seems to glow and to match her yellow eyes, and she wears a rainbow tie-dyed bandana. After sniffing me briefly she let me pet her, then languidly lay back down.

  Kelly told me Athena was pregnant, due any day. She's her "seizure dog" who can alert her when she's about to have one of her seizures.

🐕 = 🚑   That's why as a service dog she's allowed to be on subways, Greyhound buses, and on planes. 🐕 → 🚆 → 🚌 → ✈️ OK She's been to 30 states. Kelly told me that she's gone some days without eating so the dog could eat. She said that four dogs in the park community are pregnant and they have to keep them separate. "We have to zig zag as we walk across the street, keep the girls away from each other."

  When Athena was in heat, Kelly and her husband tried to prevent pregnancy by putting a diaper on her, but she got pregnant anyway. They'd have to find a nice private place to camp for her to give birth, so hopefully she and the pups wouldn't have to be moved right away. Otherwise, if she and her husband had to take the tent down early every morning as usual, they'd have to carry the pups around in a cardboard box during the day. The pups would also have to be kept off the ground, in case there were Parvo germs from so many other dogs. It looked like they'd have to camp in the park for a while. They couldn't travel on a Greyhound or hitch-hike with a litter of puppies. ⛺🌲🐕 🐕 🐕

  Kelly told me some of her story while we waited for her husband to get back from the Haight. The house where she and her two children were living in Michigan burned down. They moved to Alabama, where her

Michigan medical marijuana card wasn't good enough and she lost her kids.    She said the State usually tries to keep kids in foster care as long as possible because of money they get, but her children are adoptable, well-mannered, with blond hair and blue eyes. They were adopted right away. She's not allowed to see them or know where they are until they're eighteen.

It's another heartbreaking story of persecution for a plant. But then she said, "I live by faith. The universe always provides not what I want when I want it, but what I need when I need it. You can manifest things. I've seen it a hundred times. If I want a cup of coffee, someone comes by and gives me a cup of coffee." Even more surprisingly, she said "In some ways (but not losing my kids) my house burning down was the best thing that happened to me. I lost cancer, got healed travelling." She'd met her husband, gone to the Rainbow Gathering. Her life had been transformed.

Her husband arrived, an attractive youngish guy with curly reddish-blond hair and beard. He came carrying a large cup of coffee for her, that he said a guy had got for him who said he had beautiful eyes. He did. He told how he and Kelly had gotten married at the National Rainbow Gathering in Vermont that summer.

She said his mom doesn't approve of the marriage because Kelly is older than him. You could see that she was, him young and vibrant and she sitting wrapped in blankets, her thin hair still showing patches from chemo. He said he was happy. He took off his jacket to proudly show me the "Celebrate the Summer of 69" T-shirt he'd gotten married in, which he happened to be wearing. It's part of his spiritual costume. It's clear that they've both found something special in each other.

They've had some challenges on their travels. Somewhere in the Midwest they got a ride from some people who invited them to sleep over at a house because it was cold outside. When they woke up the people were gone, and all their stuff was gone. They were left with nothing but one sleeping bag and three dogs. It was minus ten-degree weather with a minus twenty chill factor. She got real sick with a 104-degree temperature.

Last night the only place they could find to get out of the rain was a narrow ledge next to Whole Foods. They got all wet, slept sitting up with the dog on their knees. In the morning when they were trying to dry out on the lawn next to the Horseshoe, when the sun had come out, a random guy came by and gave them a warm, dry hoodie, a tarp, some banana bread, and a bag of pig ears for the dog.

For all their tribulations they both seemed happy and content with a tent for a home. "I've had three houses." Kelly said. "It's very liberating to simplify to what you can carry. It feels good to trim down."

Her husband said, "Money has no value except for toilet paper and to start a campfire."

DUMPED AND STRANDED

Behind McDonald's, sitting on the edge of the planter, there was a guy named Woody with a little black dog and not much else. He asked if he could use my phone to call his dad. Some "friends" of his had stolen his van with all his stuff in it. 😭 I've heard of this happening to other people on the road. They left his little black dog tied up to a bush. He said, "She was crying her head off!" They left him only a dirty blanket and pillow, the only dirty things in the van. 🚐💨 🚶 🐕

It turns out I knew someone in Colorado who knew someone who knew the people with the van. I gave him the phone number and he wrote a note to give me with his name and phone number, and "Lost van, white with black stripe, (so and so) took my 1995 Grumen OLSEV step van. Left my dog and I stranded. Please help!" 🆘

Being "house-free" isn't always peaches and cream. A guy at the log said he was not here by choice but got dumped here by a girlfriend who kicked him out. 💔   He said he would love to be a yuppie again, but "You make the best of the situation. I've been happier in other places but there are also places where I've been less happy."

"A guy at the other log said, "There's hate on the Haight. Stuff gets ripped off." I asked a random person how many times they'd had their stuff confiscated by authorities. They said over twenty times. 🏃

Just then a man walked up wearing a black leather jacket that was all ripped up in several places. He said matter-of-factly that last night in the park he'd been attacked by five raccoons. He didn't seem particularly upset about it, as if it was just routine. 🐾 🐾 🐾 🐾 🐾

I ran into Scott, the man who dresses in gorgeous period clothes. He had a black eye, no shoes, and what was left of his beautiful clothes was filthy. Someone had beat him up and robbed him. 👊   After the first, when people get their checks, I saw him again. He was all cleaned up, dressed in clothes even more dazzling than before. 🎖

His new leather top hat, of the exact shape for that era, like the Mad Hatter's hat but of very high quality, looked perfect on his grey curls. Two live red roses were attached to the brim. The new ruby velvet coat with black lace was a real work of art, and the brocade pants. He had spent his entire check on these princely items, still had no blanket, and would beg for food for the rest of the month. But he sure looked happy.

FLASHES OF LIGHT

I met him on Earth Day on Haight Street, and so thought he was just dressed up for the occasion, but it turned out he wears this kind of costume every day. He said he was dressed for his mother's birthday, and it turns out he meant the Earth. He wore gold-edged rainbow bloomers and a paisley tie, flowers, and around his neck were necklaces, carnival beads, mandalas, and an artfully carved animal horn. He said his name is Random.

The most striking thing he wears is a unique hat, made of rainbow-colored strips of material wound in a spiral from where it frames his attractive young face and honey-colored curls and beard, to a tapered point on top crowned with a tassel. It really does make him look like a magic creature of the forest. Otherwise, he looks like Christ. ✝ He talks about saving the planet, fixing the country, rescuing the animals and the trees. He has such a gentle yet powerful look on his face.

I saw him again at night, riding a skateboard and pushing a fully-loaded three-wheeled stroller with music, gliding by. He wore a stylish hat with gold, white and black sequins, a black sequin jacket, and a sequin shirt underneath. He sparkled as he moved under the lights, each sequin a flash of light. ♪ ☮ 🎩 🆒 ♫   ☆✧🛹

A guy walking by borrowed my notebook and wrote this in it: "We know! We are saying... in our hearts! We love our souls in the midst of golden rainbows that the system tries to overthrow. So naive we remain unchanged to the holds they so try to hold… So we see the dark in the light and shine in the struggled peace. We feel so real and live!" Then he wrote this: "Love means =   L (living)   O (over)   V (violence)   E (everywhere). He signed it, "LOBO 143." The number 143 means "I love you" when you count the letters: 1(I) 4(love)   3(you)."

On the way back to the car I met two guys sitting on a stairway and we had a great conversation, but I don't remember what we talked about. I was too distracted to write it down because I was staring mesmerized at what the one guy was making. He cut up aluminum cans to make flower arrangements to sell to the tourists. The one he was working on was amazing, the red flowers made from a red Coke can, and the base from a blue beer can. The leaves were made from a green can.

With metal shears he worked so skillfully, cutting narrow strips with which he made curled spirals which suggested leaves. The blue base of the arrangement was intricately made, with alternating strips curved in and out, still attached to the lid of the can. It made a solid platform that didn't tip over. The three red flowers were each assembled with six perfect diamond-shaped petals. It must have taken him a long time to figure out how to do that. When he finished, he gave it to me and wouldn't take any money. When I got home, I placed it on the table where I write, in a display with other treasures given to me by the house-free.

MACHINES

Building machines set men on a weird course,

    and the idea that some owned land and others didn't.

Dogmas of supply and demand will be seen in history books

    as bizarre aberrations of a brutish time

    when factory children worked from dawn to dusk for crusts of bread and working poor today must get third jobs.

Corporations own machines, and throngs of hungry people own their work.

    When jungle law is so applied, the people always lose.

The sweat and toil of human beings is never worth much, with a huge supply.

    When jobs are scarce, the people can't negotiate for a fair wage.

The costly and complex machines the corporations own are worth much more

   as there are few since normal people can't afford them or to keep them up.

The small supply of technocrap and the great demand,

    and making deals with desperate people with no choice,

is a scenario that has robbed us of our hopes

    for a free country where we all can have a chance.

Machines gave power to the few to rule the rest,

    whether by weapons or by corporate deals.

The big fish eat the little fish and everything in sight.

    Box stores go up and all the mom and pop stores disappear.

The Indians laughed at the idea of owning land and then they cried.

    The conquerors with their guns and phony deals

not only wanted all the land but all the people too.

There wasn't one thing on God's Earth that they didn't want to take.

New overlords, the ones who'd starved people since before Romans marched,
    now took a grip on the New World with legal briefs.
They got the presidents to give them land and goods
    and to subdue the people if they started to complain.
With guns and clubs they mowed down protestors seeking living wage
    including starving factory children barefoot in the snow.
They got their lobbyists to rule it was ok
    to work people so hard it crippled them.

These business entities and their attorneys grabbed the Constitution,
    shaped and twisted it beyond what could be recognized.

They claimed the people had "the right to contract" for the pittance they got,
    that it was tyranny for governments to say how business should be run.
"Too much government!" they said as their friends ordered troops
    to stop the riots of the people with no bread.
In their salons, smoking cigars rolled up by slaves,

they used both Darwin and Paul's teachings to condone their deeds.

In this great darkness corporations had their birth, a demon child.

    Not at all human but with all the rights of human beings,

it was exempt from legal pitfalls and the requirements for businesses.

    Its stockholders could not be sued or charged with crimes.

Now they were free to screw the public all they could,

    which is exactly what they did.

The laws were tailored to the needs and whims of the big fish;

    the people suffered on parched earth like they had done before.

The child grew and it prospered at the people's great expense,

    sucking their blood the way a giant tumor does.

Not content with America's vast wealth it started wars in other lands,

    to sell the uniforms and bombs and stuff that made it thrive.

Now that we've bought all we can buy and all our jobs went overseas

    the only thing left it can get from us is prison dollars if we go to jail.

Letting this baby play with these machines

    has been disastrous for the world, for all that lives.

HAIGHT STREET AT NIGHT

A late dinner at McDonald's consisted of a tasteless value hamburger with a thin patty with no tomato. I was so tired of everything on the menu except for the garlic fries, which I'd already had an order of that day. The spiritual food of the companionship that happens in this place is worth ingesting some of the barely palatable, unhealthy food.

I could've paid extra and ordered the tomato.

A young man at McDonald's was sitting at an adjacent table to where I was visiting with some other people. I thought he wasn't paying attention to what we were saying until he started talking. He sounded like a wise man instead of some punk. He said, "Very few understand. They have to spread it around."

What he was saying sounded a lot like what Jesus said about the leaven, that if you put a little bit of yeast in a loaf of bread it grows and makes the whole loaf rise, the way Heaven grows even if there's just a little bit. The boy looked like a punk with his dark clothing and black stocking cap. If tourists saw him on the street, they might worry that he might rob them. He said, "People don't have to spend their whole lives wandering." He said he was on a straight path to enlightenment, not wandering any more.

In the next booth a man listened to our conversation with interest. He had a neat beard and wore an attractive leather hat with a wide brim. That and his gear made him look like he'd just come out of the Australian Outback. He had a tattoo on his cheek that's a religious symbol. He said it's called a "Unalome" and it represents the seventh chakra, which is the third eye. A young man at another table was excited about his new 40's-style grey wool tweed pants. "I can't believe I found them at Goodwill!" he said. They had subtle pink and blue threads woven into the grey, pockets, and a paisley lining. He said: "I have morals. I have ethics. Nothing changes." So young and so serious. ✌☮✝⚖🆒

I walked on up Haight Street, which was illuminated by many artful neon signs at night, and also small colored lights, magenta, green and purple, wound around the big beautiful trees all down the street. I ran into four guys standing around next to a big mural of Jerry Garcia and near a colorful store named "Earthsong."

There was a young blond guy wearing a Grateful Dead T-shirt, and a raccoon tail hanging from his belt. He was the same guy I'd met before, with the pyramid on his hat. He said, "I'm happier here, I eat better, am better cared for than in Massachusetts. There's nothing there for me. Everything I want is here." He said this while standing next to his three friends on the street corner on the dirty sidewalk that had bird shit and old gum on it. ☺ 🆗

His friend, "Green Eyes," wears ragged overalls, and lots of dreadlocks on one side of his head, with the other side completely shaved. He has a very special hat. Lots of people have top hats around here but this one stands out. It's not really flashy but beautifully made and it suits him perfectly. Kind of a green silken fractal pattern, it's covered with pins from every Grateful Dead concert there ever was. There's depth and intelligence in his face and when he smiles there's a special sparkle. He seems to embody something for the tourists. They smile at him as they drive by, if only to admire the hat. ≩🎩≩

Another boy, a teenager, said, with what sounded like wisdom beyond his years, 🎓 "We don't get sad about yesterday. We're not worried about tomorrow. We just live in the moment." He wore a T-shirt that had a map of the U.S. on it and the words, "We're Broke." He quoted a line from a Grateful Dead song: "You can't let go and you can't stand still. If the thunder don't get'ya the lightning will."

I walked on and passed a bar, Michael Collins, where customers can sit right at the window at a counter and visit with the people walking by. I was invited in and was offered a drink by a young couple. We talked over the noisy music. The Haight Street Magic is alive and well in this gentrified establishment where housies go to recover from their horrible jobs. Freedom is just as attractive to them as to the nomads, just more out of reach.

Out on the street it was now later and darker with some lights turned off, when most older ladies like myself wouldn't be out alone. There were still plenty of people on the street but most of them were street people who live there, literally sleep on the sidewalk.

I approached a group of people who were only shadows, with the intention of walking by quickly because it was late and I thought I didn't know them. Abruptly a young man emerged from the group and gave me a big smile and a big hug. It was "Slinky," his kindness to the arrested stranger and his dog having been completed. He said, "I love you! Everybody in this park loves you!"

He said we should have a reading and get everybody to sit down and listen to what I've been writing about them. He called me "Mamma" and insisted on walking me to Rainbow's a few blocks away. Having nothing else to give me he presented me with a photo he had, a precious picture of his friends he'd been carrying since travelling from another state, some other "dirty kids," as some of them like to call themselves. I've placed it on the desk where I write, with the other holy little gifts I've received on the street.

This sweet interaction which I experience with the public is what Heaven is about for me. I can't say where Heaven is, what dimension, but I can say what it feels like. In my community at the Rose Bowl swap meet in Pasadena, it felt like being wrapped in the hug of a random swap meet vendor whose name I didn't even remember, like being welcomed into so many of their booths. Here on the Haight and in Golden Gate Park, Heaven feels like being greeted at the log among the nomad young people. It feels like making friends on the train, on the bus, like connecting with the whole human race. Heaven is there even late at night on a so-called dangerous street.

AMAL'S DELI

Late at night, when almost everything else is closed, it's sometimes worth the walk all the way up to Masonic to Amal's Deli. It's the only place you can get real food after hours, and at reasonable prices. It's also the only place you can get home-made things like hearty macaroni and cheese and lasagna to go, and soups made from scratch. In glass cases there are also exotic things like stuffed grape leaves and falafel and baklava, and even some eggrolls.

Among the chips and sodas common in convenience stores there are cardboard boxes of fresh vegetables for sale and other staples.  It's also called the Cedar Deli and Market and has above the door two large painted cedar trees on either side of the sign that has both names. There are two beautiful big trees growing outside, all lit up. Someone walking into the store is in for a feast of aromas. A noble-looking man named Jeryies handles the cashier at the front of the store. He is the brother of Amal, the woman owner, who does the cooking herself.

I found this pleasant woman in the cooking and food display area, which takes up one whole side of the store. She looks like an archetype of a mother, her grey and black hair tied back at the nape of her neck to keep it out of her smiling face while she cooks, apron-clad. We talked while she worked, both of us peering between glass cases containing some Middle Eastern things she makes that look like pizzas but aren't. She didn't say much about herself and asked about my interests instead. I found that we shared a love for the house-free on Haight Street.

The street kids call her "Mamma" or "Mom." She often gives them leftover food at the end of the night. How good a hot bowl of soup must feel late at night, when it's cold outside on the sidewalks where they live. A young man came in and asked if he could get a hug. She gave him a big hug and two slightly dried pieces of pizza for free. Then she told him, "You are the best. Keep telling yourself this." I'm sure that many of the street kids feel that even the honey-drenched baklava here is not as sweet as this motherly love they crave.

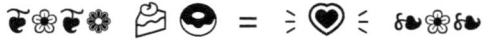

THE RED VICTORIAN

It's called "The Red Victorian" because it's painted red, a prominent landmark on Haight Street, called "San Francisco's Living Peace Museum." It's a hotel where many icons of the Sixties spent the night. Built in 1904, some say it was once a brothel. It's now a "Peace Bed and Breakfast," where you can still rent a bed right on Haight Street for a reasonable price. This very special space was initially created by Dr. Sami Sunchild, an environmental artist and activist who passed way in 2013. Here she hosted "World Peace Conversations" every Sunday. She also gave lectures and hosted "Soul Conversations."

In 2014 it was bought by a new owner, Jessy Kate Schlinger.  She established the Red Victorian L.L.C. and took over management from Dr. Sunchild's non-profit and beneficiary. She and some others transformed it into "an intentional community that supports creatives to connect and to be in." It includes co-living of hotel guests and longer-term residents, in a communal setting. One time I walked by and saw a rock band inside. Another time there was a class there on figure drawing with a live nude model.

A young student named Olive invited me to come over for a communal dinner and a movie. I got to see the inside of the big room that takes up almost the whole first floor of the hotel. In it there are couches and long heavy wooden tables and bookshelves covering one whole wall. The room has enough seating and is big enough to hold conferences or musical performances. 🎤 It has a grand piano.

David, a man who almost always volunteers to cook for everyone, had put together a giant meal and laid it out on the table. The food was delicious, some vegan and some not vegan. There was tofu and rice with David's special peanut sauce, kale salad, roasted chicken breasts, and macaroni and cheese. He'd also made pies for desert. At the table I enjoyed his conversation, which was deep and educated. ¶ After dinner we watched a movie on a big screen, lounging on the cushy couches.

Afterwards Olive and I went up a quaint zig-zagging wooden stairway to her room. We passed doors of rooms named after San Francisco landmarks, like "Tea Garden," "Conservatory," and "Summer of Love." Her room had curtained-off spaces for two other people, which appeared to be vacant. Everything was painted white and there were white linens. We opened the window and sat on the fire escape and talked and wondered what famous people might've sat there and talked the same way, about the same kinds of things.

The hotel's website has pictures showing that some of the rooms are done up with Victorian antiques, and others are decorated in hippie style with big daisies everywhere. One hotel guest posted that his stay there was "an enchanted escape."

WHEN GOD IS IN THE PICTURE

Sitting on a log on a path near the tunnel I met "Dinosaur," whose real name is Trevor. He wore a kind of kilt, a red plaid pleated skirt, and a rainbow-colored flag hanging from his shoulders like a superhero cape. He had nice long blond hair with beads, a brilliant rainbow T-shirt, and blue eyes that turned to grey. Beside him was his guitar, his neatly-packed backpack, and a medium-sized brown and black dog.

He was really into dinosaurs, as if they were his spirit animal. He showed me a bead in his hair that was light green, called a dinosaur egg.

He had a hand-stitched leather vest of ancient design which he'd made himself. It had rows of big square metal studs lined up across the chest that made it look like armor. The leather was carefully sewn together by hand in a patchwork. He proudly told how he'd saved the leather from a garbage pile. The leather hood had dinosaur spikes sewn across the top. 🗑 → ✂ → 👕 On his arm was a tattoo of his little son's name

    I was on my way to the pancake breakfast in the redwoods and he came with me. There we saw a friend of his, a blond man with a knitted cap that covered his ears. He had a black leather jacket with stars and a neat, big suitcase. He said, "We're all children of God. You only matter if God is in the picture. We should be loving people without inspiration, not because God said to." They talked about the difference between a street and a neighborhood. ☕👁 🎩🤝♥

    Then I met Shawna Lou, wearing a rainbow tie-dyed skirt and a bowler hat with a yellow daisy. ❀ She proudly showed me the leather belt she'd just made. ✂ She's a big fan of art. 🎨 She said, "Every time you follow music and art with a conscious group of people, miracles happen, synchronicities." She told about riding trains with no bottom, where you have to hang on for dear life.

    She'd recently spent eight hours on a train, in an incident that she believed was a real miracle. She and her travelling companions had been forced to wait three days for a suitable train to hop, because there were no cars that were open. The miracle was that suddenly an open car stopped right where they were sleeping. It was in the middle of the night so there were no "bulls," guards that search train cars. As she was running to the train with all her stuff, she forgot her knife so had to run back, but still got on the train. 🕊💨   🚌

    They also got lucky getting off at the train yard in Roseville. She said it looks like a FEMA camp with a high fence, and you can get caught inside. Police will take your stuff. It's a federal offence because it's on government property. I thought about this terrible cat and mouse game that so many young people live all the time. What a harsh contrast it is to the "Leave It to Beaver" lifestyle that they were taught to expect. Many of these are the children of people who raised them carefully, who had high hopes for them. Yet they don't complain.

A guy with a big husky dog and with a big jingle bell design on the back of his sweatshirt said, "It takes the Haight to stop the hate."

A DIFFERENT LEVEL OF EXISTENCE

In the park people have their little neighborhoods, where specific groups of friends assemble regularly. Across the pond from the log that's near the tunnel, on the edge of a hill under some trees, there is another "log." There's always a crowd of wild-looking people there, and laughter, and sometimes music. One time, months before, I'd brought a drum there and some people had played it. Now as I walked by, I was careful about barging right into their special space, not sure if they wanted company. Then a man called my name.

He had reddish blonde dreadlocks with metal clips of bottle caps folded together, home-made tattoos of dots under his eyes and another of a railroad track curving over one eyebrow. An earth-colored plaid shirt, and a somewhat ragged arrangement that suggested a kilt, made him look like an ancient Celt against the pond's reflections. As I approached the log where his friends were gathered, he ran up to me and gave me a big hug. It turned out I'd seen him and his girlfriend at the Oregon Rainbow Gathering which we'd both attended.

He wasn't exactly wearing the skirt, which did not in any way make him seem feminine. It was draped around only one side, was hung from his belt like a decoration, like a pirate's plunder. ☠ Under it he was dressed in more practical street gear. His clothes were assembled and decorated with care and artfulness, each detail rich with meaning. He said his name is "Parking Lot." He'd adopted a little gold short-haired dog with only three legs. The dog's name is "Shnookums Wookums." The dog sports a road-worn brown bandana that matches the man's clothes.

The brown and green patterned skirt was adorned with teal green lace bands between rows of gathers, a grey velvet ribbon pattern along the edge, and a ruffle of teal green netting around the bottom. It had once been beautiful, but now had taken on the olive drab hues and road patina of the rest of his outfit. He'd sewn pockets into it in which he stored various items. He wore a big patch of the Grateful Dead skull, which they call "Steal Your Face," with the usual vibrant red and blue background and red roses on the skull. His tennis shoes were bright turquoise.

He said he'd never had a driver's license, never had insurance, had never tried to get food stamps. He'd never used a social security number, all by choice. He called himself a "sovereign citizen," though he admitted he has a birth certificate. It reminded me of Biblical advice to "Be in the world but not of it." FREE Then he started talking like Jesus or some kind of holy guy. He said he'd fallen through a dimension and gone to the end of time and come back. He said he'd experienced a different level of existence. 🪐 🌀 ✨☆

After that he told me about mycelium, a substance in plants that links them together so they can communicate with each other in the forest. He said it makes it possible for them to think together. I said it would be nice if people could think together that way to fix the world's problems. We all agreed that they could but hadn't fully developed that ability. I said we'd better hurry up and develop it quick.

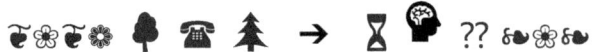

IF YOU SOW LOVE YOU GET LOVE

After such a nice welcome at the "other log," I felt comfortable going over there the next day to hang out with my new friends who looked like pirates. "Parking Lot" clearly had status with this group, and he'd invited me into their circle. Again, he stood up and gave me a hug (he'd read some of my writing at the Gathering).

There were decorations I hadn't noticed before, swinging from his amber hair, wingnuts, small metal fittings from a hardware store. "Wingnuts" is also what they call the crazy people on the street. They also call them "fifty-one fifties," their official code number. Some people think they dump them on the Haight. 5150

As usual Parking Lot was in a jovial mood and brimming with energy. He was telling jokes. "Why doesn't San Francisco sink into the ocean?"  he asked. "Because there's a wingnut on every corner!" And "What do you call a train rider who says he doesn't hitch hike? A liar." A few feet away, his little three-legged dog lay curled up in a sunbeam. Other dogs slept in piles, tied together or to backpacks.

A beautiful girl named Lena invited me to sit on a stone ledge, the most comfortable and cleanest seat in the house. On my stone ledge seat, I felt honored and privileged the way I do if I get a spot on the drummers' bench. She was so nice to me. Her loose freshly brushed long blonde hair suggested that she was not homeless. She told me about her spiritual journey, how she'd felt at one with God and had experienced love for everyone. She freely used the "G" word.

The guy next to her was dressed lightly for the cold wind but he had plenty of necklaces, and a baseball cap full of pins. Some of these people don't seem affected by the cold. Many actually go barefoot by choice, even in cold weather. He said, "We're not all homeless. Some have homes and choose this way of life. Where I lay my head is my home. I don't need all the stuff other people think they need. Sure, you might have hardships, if you call them that. But then you notice the blessings… We're happy just being alive." 👣 ☺ OK

There was a guy with a nose ring and scary oriental tattoos, and the tattooed initials of his mom on one hand and of his dad on the other hand. The sides of his head were shaved, with longer hair on top. He said, "It's nice to be around other people. We need human interaction. It's something the world has less and less of. The people I meet here are why I'm back after fifteen years." ⟩ 👥👤👥 ⟨

A girl in Bronze-Age leather clothes agreed, saying "The park is a shelter and a waystation." Her short leather skirt was finely made, sewn together with narrow strips of leather and an awl. The fur sewn on in places made for a timeless vision. Half of her hair was shaven, half with small neat braids. She looked like an action figure in her heavy hiking boots that could trek anywhere, a dagger tied with a leather band around her knee. 🥾🗡 She said that whenever she'd had any kind of trouble, it had always been the poor who'd helped her. ♿🛒 → 🎁💵 → 🤲

Pretty Tony in a black leather jacket, with a pirate skull on his baseball cap, with a sword crossed with a long-stemmed rose, said he knew more good people than bad. He said, "A lot of people get confused about things, which leads to chaos. They're not against each other. It's outside forces that make them that way." He said, "If you're cool, you're cool. If you sow love, you get love."

PURITANS III: God's Message About Leaders of Extremist Right-Wing Churches (Not the actual Puritans, or truth-seekers and devoted pastors misinformed by dangerous doctrines.)

Some preachers say that the red letters are things Jesus said

    but point to things the Bible says were said by someone else.

Like the dream Jesus of John of Patmos in Revelation,

    so mad at everyone and everything for such vague cause,

whose stern pronouncements have been used

    to justify every atrocity in Jesus' name.

People are told to wreck their world for corporate gain,

    that some will all be "lifted up" so they shouldn't care.

The red ink also claims that Jesus was the disembodied voice

    that told Paul he should be the leader of a church.

This was on horseback when he had sunstroke and was struck blind.

    His first miracle was making a man blind, something Jesus never did.

On his way to evangelize he had to wash his clothes

    from the blood of martyrs young and old. (He'd persecuted Christians.)

His sacred letters contained so much stuff that Jesus didn't teach,

    it overshadowed by sheer bulk what He had said. 💔

The false red letters and Paul's words give marvelous tools

    to anyone who wants to bully humankind. 🏰 ♗ ♛ 🎤 ▦ = 👊

They're handy for all those who want to hurt the poor, 🦅🦅

    or think they're better than everyone else. 🥇

Paul's words were shouted over screams of victims

    at witch burnings and Inquisition trials. 🔨 🏃 🔥

Jesus didn't use words like "heretic" or "infidel" or "idolater."

    Why have so many who read Bibles till they fall apart, failed to see this?

The things that Jesus really said, some red letters in the first four books,

    were framed with utmost care and skill to promote peace. 🕊 ♥

There are no rigid judgments on the flesh,

    no hell, no Adam and Eve. 🔥 →

There is no son of Cain to hate,

    no daughter of Eve to blame. 🍎 🐍

In Jesus' actual words there's nothing saying that you can't associate

    with other folks of different faiths.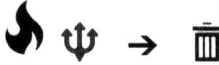

Paul added that and told mankind

they were no good.

He told the slaves their masters to obey

and told wives to obey their war-prone husbands as if they were God.

He made us all afraid of hell, really the trash dump of Gehenna,

and taught that all should remain virgins all their life.

Without having such an intent, he set mankind on a weird path

by filling up his holy books with things that Jesus never said.

Gehenna Dump →

JESUS DIDN'T TEACH: that all are born in sin, the Inquisition, excommunication (shunning,) slaves and women "obey in all things," Adam and Eve, that idolaters and gays are "worthy of death," anti-Semitism, shame of the body, hell, tithing, having to go to church, the Divine Right of Kings, that the Bible was perfect, or that he created the world. Paul the Apostle and OTHERS ADDED those, plus "obey every ordinance of man," "let the unjust be unjust still," that you have to believe or be damned, that you can "take up serpents" and drink poison, and that it's not what you do that counts, but what you believe in. Red letters in the book of Revelation are the writer's vision or dream and don't teach what Jesus taught, and have been killing people since the ink was dry. The Prince of Peace taught kindness, brotherly love, and Heaven on Earth.

🌼🌸🌼   IN GOD WE TRUST   🌸🌼🌸

DELICIOUS CORNDOGS

The "other log" became a regular stop on my route. A guy sat there with some other people, enjoying the morning. With his fresh haircut and shave and neat clothes, he looked like a housie sitting there on the log with all the vagabonds and gypsies. His sturdy shoes were in good shape. It was hard to tell that he lived outside.

He has a big tattoo about a foot long running from his elbow to his wrist. It's made with delicate lines and is quite an attractive decoration. It seems to mark him as someone spiritual, and that's not the only thing that makes him seem that way. He has a tremendous light in his eyes, and a beautiful smile. He said his name is Trey, because he's the third generation in his family, with an actual Roman numeral after his name.

He said the tattoo is a star tetrahedron with two intersecting pyramids with the Flower of Life. He explained that the Flower of Life "is nine circles that are intersecting, that create a flower pattern in the center. It's the geometric explanation of the creation of life." There are also smaller Flowers of Life around the edges of the design. He said he got it when his daughter was born, because of the creation of life. He said, "I created life, protected life, and wanted it to protect her." He wears another Flower of Life, a patch sewn on his jeans at the knee. There's a tattoo on his hand of a six-pointed star shining with rays of light.

"Cosmo" was there with the beautiful smile he always blesses me with. His long grey hair and floppy brimmed hat make him look like the Old Man of the Hills or some other timeless being. His smiling face and easy laughter and wit make him pleasant company at the log.

A beautiful girl arrived, who looked like she had stepped out of a time warp from prehistoric times. It was hard to see the color of her hair because of her headdress. It was a fake fur hat with cat ears, with raccoon fur sewn to parts of it that made it look real. The skin of a raccoon head hung from her belt. Torn jeans suggested leather leggings. She looked like a mythical character with the sun shining on her as it came through the trees. She wore bracelets, rustic and hand-beaded mixed with modern costume jewelry. Also hanging from her belt was a shiny metal mug like you carry at the Renaissance Faire. She had two small dogs on leashes, one beige and one black, who were humping each other.

Two hardy fellows who looked like they'd just jumped off a pirate ship were having a lively discussion about partisan gerrymandering. They said the Supreme Court could overturn it in the coming session, because it was on the agenda. They strode back and forth in front of the log and moved their arms, blue with tattoos, in agitated ways, but it was not in argument. Each agreed completely with what the other was saying.

It was excitement that made them talk loud enough for the group to be quiet and listen. They talked about Citizens United, "when money becomes speech," and the need for a federal standard for states' voting rights, and to get rid of corporate personhood. They told us that the Glass/Steagal court case had been overturned, which had limited economists' wild financial risks with mom and pop properties.

To the casual observer this crew may have looked like a buncha bums, but the things they discussed were the same things colonial patriots discussed with each other, and for the same reasons.

Just then Manfred came by with a big paper bag full of hot corndogs. "He brings us something almost every day," someone told me. A thin man of maybe late middle age, he doesn't look rich, not enough to feed all the people he feeds. Each person got two corn dogs wrapped in two layers of foil. After the others all had theirs, I accepted two warm foil packages. The corndogs tasted delicious the way something tastes good when you eat it outside in good company.

"In a time of universal deceit, telling the truth is a revolutionary act." Orwell

BECOMING JESUS

Rainbow told me about something that happened to him while he was working on his big Jesus painting. For weeks he'd shown me the painting's progress each time I came by, asking me if the hands were turning out all right. It showed Jesus meditating and dressed like a hippie, with a little vest like Rainbow wears. There was the usual lush sun-washed background with a couple of animals.

He recounted his experience. While dabbing on the brilliant colors with brushes and fingers, he'd felt as if Jesus was right there with him. Then he'd felt like he was *becoming* Jesus. He said, "It's like I'm working through God and God's working through me. I feel like I've really been in touch with the Divine!"

He looked around at the happy disarray of the small Victorian room stacked with paintings. "In the Magic Theatre there's Heaven," he laughed. "There's always a little bit of Heaven in a disaster area. The Kingdom is at hand in individual hearts. Good fortune, good will, it's like being in love with everyone. That heaven feeling... it's not of this world!" There was wonder in his voice.

How pleasant to have a friend to visit and drink hot tea with, a place to feel welcome in, just a block from Haight Street. With background music ranging from classic rock to Beethoven, Rainbow freely talks about God. His conversation is not boring. It refreshes me to enter the Magic Theatre, where there is Heaven like he said. Rainbow has done so much for me, aside from letting me crash there when he can. After Jubah introduced me to him he introduced me to Diamond Dave and Mutiny Radio, which in turn led to getting to meet other dynamic people. I feel energized by his buoyant outlook and deep insights.

He said, "The ocean's getting more and more turbulent. I'm holding onto the good Lord's lotus feet for dear life. That's the world I want to live in, the world Jesus talks about, the world the Buddha talks about, the world that Krishna talks about." He told about how at a Rainbow Gathering, in the center of the big circle which 20,000 or more people make, holding hands on the Fourth of July, he'd heard the Earth crying. He also had started crying. "All I could say was, 'I'm sorry! I'm sorry!'"

A TEN-WHEELER

It takes up two whole spaces of the parking meters at Haight and Shrader, even without a container loaded on the back. It's almost as tall as some of the buildings, with big double wheels and a sleeping compartment in the cab. It's visibly aging and road-worn but still full of power, like the proud owner who stands beside it. He said it's called a Cummings Road Tractor, a 400-deisel ten-wheeler.

Over his long loose hair and greying blond beard, he wears a brimmed leather hat that has bent to fit the shape of his head. It has a light on it sort of like miners wear. He wears leather leggings and a leather loincloth he made himself, black leather gloves without fingers, a dark shirt of olive drab long underwear, and he goes barefoot. His feet look like he's walked hundreds of miles. He said his name is "Dago" but they also call him "Leather Man."

"I'm a mechanic," he said, which is pretty obvious. On his wide toolbelt he has three pairs of Vice Grips, a tape measure, a key chain, a flashlight, and a "Micra" knife that's like a Swiss army knife, with lots of tools on it. He wears armbands of two-inch black Velcro to which are attached 110 and 117-volt testers and some needle-nose pliers. A pouch is clasped to his belt with a piece of an 1860's gun.

As incongruous as his big rig looks on the miniaturized streets of the Haight, it turns out this is his regular parking space on Sundays when the meters are turned off. He lives in the truck (who would have something that big to park in San Francisco, unless they lived in it?) An old timer in the neighborhood, he rebuilt the kitchen at the ChaChaCha club across the street back in the day. 👁️🔺🍸🍽️🍴   He rattled off a few big names of famous people he knew. He said, "Deep down inside everybody has morals. 😊🎓   They know what's good or bad." He said we should agree with the universe. "We're in denial," he said. 🙉🙈🙊💤

At the log I met an intelligent and alert young man with a multicolored paisley tattoo on his cheek. He talked to me with such excitement about his many ideas to save the planet that he could hardly catch his breath. ✊   He has "REBEL" tattooed on his neck, which could be interpreted as either a name or a verb telling people to rebel. On his fingers there are tattooed letters that spell, "SELF MADE." He wore a tie-dyed T-shirt with rainbow bears riding a train, and a patch of Jerry Garcia's hand with a lightning bolt inside it. Jerry Garcia's middle finger was missing because he'd lost it cutting wood. It was amazing that he'd played guitar so well with it anyway. 🎸🎵🎶🖖

STEEL-JAWED LIABILITY LAWS

He said something so nice to me as he walked by on Haight Street one night. He said "Please stay with us. We're glad you're here. The family needs you." Then he pressed a handful of something nice to smoke into my hand and walked quickly on without waiting for a "thank you." 🖤 🎁   I noticed two tiny braids in his beard, his red hair contrasting with a beautiful blue and purple tie-dyed hoodie. His name is "Red." He wears a necklace with a shell cut in half in a cross-section, with small turquoise pebbles inside each compartment of the shell. It's lacquered and looks like the kind of jewelry made with luminous butterfly wings under glass. 🦋

He and his cute little golden dog, "Kitty," were in regular attendance at the log. A Pomeranian/Chihuahua mix, he said he'd had her for twelve years, had watched her being born.  One day the little dog wasn't there. After the usual greetings and conversation, he asked me shyly if I'd do him a favor. He asked if I could help him get "Kitty" out of the pound. 🆘 🚶 🏚 🐕

Some lady had gotten his dog taken away from him on purpose, calling the authorities and saying falsely that he didn't take good enough care of her. I realized that there are cruel people out there who deliberately make the homeless and their pets suffer for no good reason. Everyone at the log swore that he treated that dog like his precious child. They couldn't imagine him ever doing anything to hurt her. The pound wouldn't give him his dog back, because he was homeless and didn't have the proper paperwork. 👜 🔱 👊 🚕 💇 😱

At first it seemed like it was going to be easy and I immediately agreed, having a special grudge against people or policies that take away people's dogs. He said he had the money necessary to bail her out. It made sense that if I showed up to adopt the dog all dressed up, in my own vehicle and with a drivers' license with a home address on it, they would let me have her. That was not the case. Before going down there I called to find out what the requirements were. ☎ You had to have either something that showed you owned a house, or a lease agreement saying your landlord would let you have a dog. I had neither.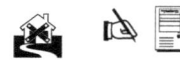

I went down there anyway, to see if the dog was there. She wasn't in the room with small, adoptable dogs, but a few days later I found her on their website. My efforts and his friends' efforts to find someone with a mortgage or a dog-friendly lease who was willing to do it, were futile.

I kept giving "Red" updates and at first, he was very excited and hopeful. When I showed him the picture of her little greying head on the website, he said, "That's my dog!" But after a while I realized that I should keep my plans to myself. It hurt him to think that he might get his dear little Kitty back, when he didn't feel it was likely to happen. He let me know this when he said with a heartbreakingly sad look, "I've pretty much gotten used to the idea of not having her." I realized that every time I mentioned her tore him up.  I plan to go down there again, hoping for a miracle. Is it possible that the steel-jawed liability laws might bend because she's been there so long? I doubt it.

As Red's friends worried that he was upset about his dog, someone handed me a poem. I quickly read it and slipped it into my pocket, and don't remember who gave it to me. It's only signed with a peace sign:

    RED

You are here, right now.
    You are surrounded by the spaciousness of a synagogue.
You live with the soaring arches and cavernous crypts of a cathedral.
    You are followed by holy words, blooming on walls of a mosque.
Wherever you go, there is no escaping Truth.
    The goddess is He. The holy man is She. You are the temple of One.

"Guard with jealous attention the public liberty. Suspect every one who approaches that jewel." Patrick Henry

YOU CAN'T BEAT HATE WITH HATE

A group of people sat on the edge of a planter behind McDonald's. A guy with steam punk glasses and a black top hat with pins said, "You can't beat hate with hate. The only thing in that book (the Bible) that makes sense is, 'love your neighbor as yourself.' Respect is the most important thing."

A man who'd been at the Standing Rock demonstrations against the Dakota pipeline told about how the feds sprayed water cannons at the demonstrators in freezing temperatures and shot at them with rubber bullets. He said they were tearing down shelters and setting dogs on people, and that a girl almost lost her arm from a concussion grenade.

Walking up the street I ran into a young man. He said, "I showed your poem to my friend ("Generation X"). He said it's the best poem he ever read and that it changed his life." Near the tie-dye emporium I met Cosmic Charlie, an older gentleman pulling a small cart. I think he has a home but likes to come out here sometimes and "live the life." His black leather jacket and other belongings are clean and in good shape. He is reputed to know big shots in publishing and said he could help me publish this book.

On Haight Street some of the big red painted hearts have names written in them, mostly of famous people like Jerry Garcia and Janis Joplin. People thought enough of Cosmic Charlie to give him his own sidewalk heart with his name on it. It's a little like having a star on the Hollywood Walk of Fame. He invited me to tour with the Grateful Dead and I unfortunately declined, unaware that he actually *was* friends with them.

"Slavery is an abomination and must be loudly proclaimed as such."
Thomas Jefferson

Note: All these things were said by Jesus (from KJV), though not in the same order. The few words in parentheses were added.

God's Message to Treehuggers and Peacemakers:

LAMBS AMONG WOLVES

The harvest (of Democrats?) truly is plenteous, but **the labourers are few:** pray ye therefore the Lord of the harvest, that he would **send forth labourers** into his harvest (of better laws). Go your ways: behold, **I send you forth as lambs among wolves.** (Matt. 9:37-38)(Lk. 10:3) **Be ye therefore wise as serpents, and harmless as doves.** (Matt. 10:16)

And **when they bring you unto magistrates**, and powers, take ye no thought how or what ye shall say: for **the Holy Ghost shall teach you in the same hour what ye ought to say.** (Lk. 12:11-12)

Settle it therefore in your hearts, not to meditate before what ye shall answer: for **I WILL GIVE YOU A MOUTH AND WISDOM, WHICH**   **ALL YOUR ADVERSARIES SHALL NOT BE ABLE TO GAINSAY OR RESIST.**

Ye are the light of the world. !!

A city that is set on a hill cannot be hid. Neither do men light a candle, and put it under a bushel, but on a candlestick; and it giveth light to all that are in the house. **Let your light so shine before men,**

that they may see your good works, and glorify your Father in heaven.

(Luke 21:14-15)(Matthew 5:14-16)

HE THAT RECEIVETH YOU RECEIVETH ME;
    AND HE THAT DESPISETH YOU DESPISETH ME;

and he that despiseth me despiseth him that sent me. (Luke 10:16)

For **it is not ye that speak, but the Spirit of your Father which speaketh in you.**

Say unto them, "The kingdom of God is come nigh unto you."

And as ye go, preach, saying, **"The kingdom of heaven is at hand."**

Freely ye have received, freely give. (Matthew 10:20, 7-8)

Judge not according to appearance, but judge righteous judgment.

(Jn. 7:24)   **Have faith in God.** (Mark 11:22)

If ye continue in my word (peace, love, mercy, truth)

    then are ye my disciples indeed. (John 8:31)

Thou shalt love the Lord thy God with all thy heart, and with all thy soul,

and with all thy strength, and with all thy mind;   ♥   🏋   🧠   × <u>100</u>

and thy neighbor as thyself. (Lk. 10;27)   **These things have I spoken unto you,**

    that in me ye might have peace. (Jn 16:33)

JESUS DIDN'T TEACH: that all are born in sin, the Inquisition, excommunication (shunning,) slaves and women "obey in all things," Adam and Eve, gays and idolaters are "worthy of death," antisemitism, shame of the body, hell, tithing, having to go to church, the Divine Right of Kings, that the Bible was perfect, or that he created the world. Paul the Apostle and OTHERS ADDED those, plus "obey every ordinance of man," "let the unjust be unjust still," that you have to believe or be damned, that you can "take up serpents" and drink poison, and that it's not what you do that counts, but what you believe in. Red letters in the Revelation are the writer's vision or dream and don't teach what Jesus taught, and have been killing people since the ink was dry. The Prince of Peace taught kindness, brotherly love, and Heaven on Earth.

GRATEFUL DEAD JESUS FREAKS

As I walked down Haight toward Ashbury, a young man stopped me and said he wanted to meet me because of the way I was dressed. It wasn't the first time my flowing tie-dyed clothes had attracted attention. When this happens, I realize it's what the clothes represent that people are interested in. When they say they like my clothes or some part of my costume, they're often trying to say they like what the Sixties stand for.

The conversation soon turned to God and politics. For a young person he knew a remarkable amount about history and government, even out here living on the street. He didn't seem homeless with his clean clothes and neat haircut, looked more like an Asian college student taking a break between classes. It turns out he's out here by choice, doesn't feel comfortable sleeping indoors. His name is Tom but they call him "The Ice Cream Kid." 🍦   We talked on the crowded sidewalk as crowds went by, then he led me around the corner to meet his friends.

There I met Buck Wild, who's also house-free but doesn't look it. He has an attractive wide-brimmed white hat that makes him look like a jungle explorer,  sunglasses, and a neat red beard. He said he survived the streets "By the grace of God." He said "I've slept in penthouse suites and on cardboard, and the good Lord helped me through the kindness of homeless people. I kind of like having nothing because when I have nothing, I have everything." He talked about the higher consciousness of the Summer of Love. "It takes us all to make us whole. I have enough heart for everyone. Even if there weren't any heart, we have enough heart for all."

He said that at a Grateful Dead show he was inspired when he saw a dancer, then later he became the dancer and danced the same dance for someone else. He said, "What turned me on to Jesus was that I went to the Rainbow Gathering, saw people helping people, kindness in action. I saw the light of kindness and the teaching of Jesus, kindness and love, compassion, the fruits of the spirit. Jerry Garcia and the Grateful Dead brought me to Jesus like no church could ever do."

The Ice Cream Kid said, "I too am a Grateful Dead Jesus freak."

LOVE THY NEIGHBOR

On Oak Street next to the Panhandle there are great parking places close to a park rest room, if your vehicle is under seven feet tall. Signs have been posted that those over seven feet can't park there between midnight and 6 AM. That's how they got rid of some hippie bus villages that must've flourished there. Across the street are some of the most gorgeous row houses, and Haight Street is just two blocks away.

A lot of people live there surreptitiously in their vehicles, which is illegal. The law, though not much enforced here at this time, says they could get a thousand-dollar fine or six months in jail. It's legal to sleep on the ice-cold hard sidewalk between 11 pm and 7 am, but not in your comfortable car.

During the day there are small communities happening on the grassy areas of the Panhandle. As I walked by, I saw a guy trying to fix his motorcycle, a tarp over him and the bike, also hiding any tools. He didn't look up, scared of police. Fixing vehicles on the street is another thing that's illegal for the poor. (Where else, if they have no home or driveway?)

A homeless man on Oak Street sat on his nest of blankets on the sidewalk. As I walked by, we started a conversation and I read him some poetry. He's an artist and had several canvases leaning against the opposite wall and propped against a stroller packed with his possessions. These included a cardboard sign that read, "Lost, Tired and Hungry." He liked the poems and gifted me a beautiful ring that he'd found. I gave him a crystal that someone had given me. The ring is of a timeless design, has a single turquoise stone that matches my tie-dyes,

On Haight Street that night about a dozen people stood around or sat on the sidewalk with their many dogs and backpacks, not very concerned about there being "too many hippies" since there didn't seem to be any police around. There was a very pretty girl named Abbi who looked like a movie star. She was dressed stylishly in black, which highlighted the luminousness of her face. She had a crystal and shell necklace with a big flat piece of abalone. "There is no immediate now," she said. "The immediate now is relative." ⌛ ⌚ ⏱ ⏰ 🌐 ??

"Parking Lot" was there and I actually walked all the way back to Oak Street to get my computer to read him what I had written about him. He said that after all the bad things people said about people like him, what I had written brought him to tears. I continued to read to the people in the dark on the sidewalk except for the light from the computer. Someone arranged for me to sit on one backpack and place the computer on another. I was grateful, since when you sit on a sidewalk you never know what's been on it. 🎒 👓 💻 🔦📖

Pretty Tony was there, the guy with the hat with a sword crossed with a long-stemmed rose, who'd said he knew more good people than bad. 🌹 His curly blond hair had gotten longer since I'd met him near Hippie Hill. His friend said, "You wanna hear a poem? Get ready to cry!" Though both were clearly masculine, they both teared up when I read "Generation X." "You're describing my life!" one said.

Nighttime is when you're supposed to be afraid to go out and hang out with weird-looking people, but I find delight in going where some angels might fear to tread. What I get there is not muggers and rapists, but a large helping of love from the strangers we're supposed to fear. A guy I didn't remember seeing before ran up to me and gave me a big hug. "I want to thank you for being who you are," he said, "for dressing up the way you do and for being part of our family." ≥ ❤ ≤

He could've said the same thing to lots of the people in the group or in the park. He's tall and was neatly dressed, has dark blond hair, a medium beard, and a baseball cap full of pins. "My family healed my heart and soul," he said, pointing to the random crew assembled there. "I get to feel love and joy and emotion because of my family."

👥👤👨‍👩‍👧 = 😊 💔 ☆ → 💕 🤸

The green and pink lights wound around the big trees made the place look so beautiful at night. I saw "Parking Lot" flying down the middle of the now-empty street on his skateboard. He seemed to have so much energy that I imagined a trail of sparkles shooting off of him as he glided by. Walking along Shrader I saw a car with "Love Thy Neighbor" written on its window in the dust.

UNSTOPPABLE

As the 420 celebration at Golden Gate Park continued there were actually more people, not less. The ten thousand didn't seem to mind the cold and a rising wind. Maybe it was because they stood so close together that they didn't feel it. Certainly, the drummers were surrounded by a wall of people that kept the gusts away from them. They generally don't worry much about cold, warmed by their constant motion. The drummers were crowded together even more than they would've been by the packed crowd because today, on 420, there were more drums than at other times.

So many drums together on this special day made a thundering sound. Behind each drummer's hands was the conviction of strong beliefs shared by most of the crowd, about the capabilities of man. They think that people really are as good as Jesus said, that they have a right and an ability to live in peace and harmony, and that they all could be Buddhas and Christs. It's hard to describe how it felt to see so many of these people in one place, walking by staring at the drums, wondering what it all means.

The drums were in synch, even the extra dozen drums that had showed up that day. They were picking up energy from the crowd so close to them, almost literally breathing on them. Some kind of communication seemed to be taking place between the people walking by and the drummers at their posts. The hopes and dreams of young and old seemed to be in those drums, the cry for freedom.

The drums were now louder than the crowd, louder than the hawkers. On and on they pounded, perfectly synchronized, so that they sounded like a machine that could fix the world. I felt the power of these people. A mighty rhythm took the drums to a new level. They sounded like a locomotive, unstoppable.

☆✦ 🚂🚃🚃🚃💨 ☆✦

LET'S TAKE ONE STEP TOGETHER: At the giant Rainbow Gatherings in the wilderness people yell "WE LOVE YOU!" repeatedly on one side of the camp and others answer back, "WE

LOVE YOU TOO!" Let's do the same thing out our windows at sunset on Saturdays, so that the Voice of the People can be heard! We could also play drums for half an hour at sunset on Saturdays at a window. Visit with or meet neighbors! WE NEED ALL OF US! (right + left)

Poems may be reprinted and shared by homeless for donations they can keep.
TELL TEN TO TELL TEN TO VOTE DEMOCRAT!   REGISTER 100 DEMOCRATS!
(https://www.usa.gov/register-to-vote)   (vote.gov) (rockthevote.org)
Democrats against forced mandates and other oppressive liability laws.
BILL OF RIGHTS   GOLDEN RULE   peacedrums.org   UNITE!

Democrat

STREET LOVE FOR EVERYBODY

At the other log I met Kicking Raven, another gypsy king. His other name is Atreyu. He's forty but looks much younger. He has a half-shaved head and a cool black leather vest with pins and emblems all over it. They include the star of the Indian Police of which he is a member, and a large patch of the Two Feathers Nation. I saw a Flower of Life patch, two vintage buttons for train riders, and a flying saucer patch. There were no skulls. He said that all his clothes had been given to him. "All these things came from people who meant a lot to me. I wouldn't wear them otherwise."

He said that raccoons stole his pizza in the middle of the night. He'd put it right next to his head so they wouldn't get it. It seems that Kicking Raven is one of those who like to sleep outside without the encumbrance of a tent. He must be one of the "tent-free." He woke up to a big raccoon standing up on his hind legs and hissing at him loudly, right in his face. He said the raccoon was saying, "This pizza is MINE!"

The raccoon took the pizza but then brought back the bag and the paper plate when he was done and put the bag right next to his victim's head where it was before, just to show him. "Vindictive little fellow," Kicking Raven said. 🤔 🍽️ 🐾 ?? He told me about some puppies that he and some friends had left alone in a motel room for a couple of hours. They'd gotten their revenge by shitting all over the beds and walking through it, especially on the pillows. "They knew that's where we put our heads." ⏰ 🐕 🐾 🛏️ 🐾 💩 🐕🧹

Like many on the road, he said that he'd grown up in foster homes without a family. One time his "crew," his group of travelling friends, decided to form their own family. They planned to get together for holidays and everything. 🚶🐕 🎄🎅🔔🎁🥂🎒❤️ 🚶🐐

He builds things, but not for money. 💰 OK FREE "I just want to give people what they need and what they deserve. My whole life has been devoted to helping everybody besides myself. They come first. I'll do anything for my family" (meaning the human race.) He said, "If I see something unjust or someone being mistreated, I'll do everything in my power to help them. I've got street love for everybody."

FIFTEEN-HUNDRED DOLLARS TO GET HER DOG BACK

Ashley told me she's had her dog taken away by police six times and has paid a total of **$1500.** to get it back. 💰🐾 🏃 She was a foster child, and her dog is her only family. The medium-sized short-haired gold dog lay at her feet. It has deep brown eyes and a curved tail, some greying under the snout and a little white on chest and paws. It has soft velvety ears of a darker brown. 🐕 🎒

Ashley is the girl who'd run up to me and said she tells her friends about my writing. 📖 🗣 She proceeded to tell me how she lost her dog so many times, an all-too-familiar story.

The most recent one happened in Mendocino County. A friend was taking care of her dog for a few days, someone who'd known the dog since it was a puppy. That person got arrested. A mutual friend was there when it happened and was willing to take the dog so it wouldn't be taken away, but (due to overreaching liability laws) the cop couldn't let him without written permission from the owner. 👐 🕺 🚓 🐕 → 🏛

Ashley didn't know this was happening for six days. By the time she found out, the dog had been in there ten days and it cost her **$700** to get it out. ⏰ × 🔟 = 💰💰💸 Another time in Mendocino County she was arrested for unlawful camping, and they took her dog.

🏛 ← 🐕 🚓 🕺 🌳 ⛺ 🌲 💔

Another time, in Sacramento, she had a tug-of-war with a police officer with her dog's leash. Ashley had just broken up a fight and everything was OK, and she was thanking the police officers who'd arrived. All of a sudden, a woman police officer grabbed her dog's leash to take the dog away. 🤼 Ashley wouldn't let go of the leash and was arrested. She later had to pay **$80.** 💸 to get the dog back. It was very fortunate that she happened to have the dog's papers and vaccinations with her, that they hadn't been lost, stolen or confiscated on the road. Without them she wouldn't have been able to get her dog back. (liability laws) 🔱

📄📋🆗 → 🏛 → 🐕 🚶 💕

Another time she got arrested for not getting out of a tent fast enough because she had a busted ankle. 🌲 ⛰ 🚶 With some others she'd limped into the remote campsite a quarter of a mile from the street, not expecting to be rudely awakened in the middle of the night by officials. She told them her ankle was messed up and asked for a minute, but they wouldn't give it to her. A friend tried to help. Both got arrested and the dog taken.

Another time it was for trying to use a bathroom at a restaurant. An employee had actually gone inside the bathroom stall and pulled her out by the hair to the sidewalk, where she was arrested and her dog taken.

She stroked the dog's velvety ears. She said it had been taken from her twice for camping, twice for trying to stop a fight, and a couple of times just for being in the wrong place at the wrong time. She said, "They never give you back your leash and collar. My dog had a rad collar."

NIGHTMARE

As we sat on some steps near the Horseshoe, Ashley and some others told me a gut-wrenching story about something that happened a few years ago.

When officials were trying to pass the "No Sit and Lie Law," they dealt with opposition from the Homeless Coalition by making promises they didn't keep. The hippies were told that they would be able to sit and lie on the sidewalk all they wanted, and that the Homeless Coalition would pay for any tickets they got. Pretty soon the streets became life-filled again, with music and happy groups of people.

They say it was a set-up. All of a sudden, officials turned around and started arresting everybody and giving them tickets for camping, panhandling, drinking, and sitting down on the sidewalk. No organization was able to step up and help them. Most of the officers were just doing their job and probably didn't like it. But there were a few who seemed to enjoy it. 🚬 → 📄🗒️🦇 ▲ → 📄🗒️🦇 🎷 → 📄🗒️🦇

One particular officer had a bad reputation. He was the same one who'd been giving people drinking tickets, and he'd broken a guitar over a guy's head after telling him to shut up. 🎸😵 But he had not yet reached the lowest point in his career, when he shot a dog in front of the children's playground in Panhandle Park. Later the department transferred him because some residents complained about his shooting the dog in front of kids.

This is how it happened. Richie had a beautiful black medium-sized dog with dark brown eyes, named "Nightmare." ☾ His girlfriend, Amber, had a dog named "Daydream." ☼ With some other people they set up on the grass on the Panhandle, a narrow strip of park between Oak Street and Fell, where the Grateful Dead used to play free concerts.

Two officers arrived, a woman and this officer, and started handing out tickets for panhandling and drinking. They told people to tie up all the dogs to a pole. Nightmare didn't have his leash, so the officer just looped another dog's leash through his collar. Though the two dogs had always been like brothers, they were freaked out at being stuck against each other like that, and at all the commotion, and they started fighting.

The woman police officer tried to help, got Richie out of the cop car, and started to undo the handcuffs so he could separate the dogs. 👣 The other officer ordered her to put the handcuffs back on and to put him back in the car. Then he shot his gun two times into the tangle of fighting dogs. 👨‍👩‍👧‍👦 👨‍👩‍👧 🧍🧍 🕺 🐕 🏃‍♂️💨

Nightmare was shot twice in the chest. Richie was screaming in the cop car, fighting to get to the dog. The dog was screaming. People were throwing up. It took eight minutes for the dog to bleed out. Richie watched the whole thing from the cop car, then was taken to jail. He probably also lost all his stuff.

A year later Richie hung himself in Golden Gate Park. He'd been very depressed since it happened, had never really gotten over it. One evening he and a group of friends were walking through the park to go camp when they noticed that he wasn't with them anymore. Later that night a group went looking for him. They found him, where he'd hung himself from a tree near the Japanese Gardens.

Amber was devastated by his death. I looked over and noticed that Ashley, who'd been telling the story, was crying.

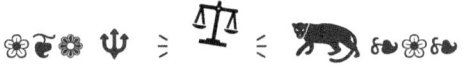

CORPORATIONS

You are not human but have all the rights a person has, without the heart.

    Like bulldozers you tear into the people's lives without regard.

You make the laws and tailor them to your own ends,

    stealing from people everything from rain forests to family life.

There is no conscience in the policies that you install,

    and laws you make prevent others from using theirs.

Your lust for profit sucks vitality out of this nation and the world the way a vampire sucks blood.

What dark cabal made you, what evil men in smoke-filled rooms

wearing those top hats made of beaver pelts?

How grand they thought they were in their fine suits

Built to Last

made by exhausted factory children going blind.

How good they thought they were, the sons of

witch-hunters and slaveholders,

as they ordered everyone's lives, decided the Earth's fate.

It was of no serious concern to them that resources w3ould be destroyed;

the scriptures which they swore upon said that the world would end.

They liked that part or any scripture that condemned mankind,

or said that he must burn in Hell or live by the sweat of his brow.

They jumped with glee reading where it said to obey the kings.

They sighed with joy when Paul told slaves their masters to obey.

What Jesus taught inside their Bibles went unread, the pages new.

The parts that said people should slave away were worn to shreds.

They dumped the passages about helping the poor

and anything about the Golden Rule or cancelling the debts.

Volume on volume, "new translations" of the holy writ

      removed further and further what Jesus had said.

The laws also departed from the Bill of Rights,

      taking back from the people things the Founding Fathers gave.

With subtlety that rivaled Eden's snake they conjured awful laws 🐍

      that gave them more power than mandarins had held.

To keep the people busy they devised an artificial market crash and war,

      took all their stuff and threw them on the street.

The corporations bought the fields the Oakies left

      and all the bankrupt farms and businesses of pioneers.

They bought also mineral reserves and everything the people owned,

      with deep pockets and huge discounts others couldn't get.

First thing you know they owned just everything in sight,

      including the people themselves with all that debt.

Unfair advantage of the big and strong but not-that-smart

      has led to the demise of species many times before.

Bad laws gave them ungodly power over people's lives

      as they created narrow visions of the future of mankind,

to make men live like robots and be starving or obese,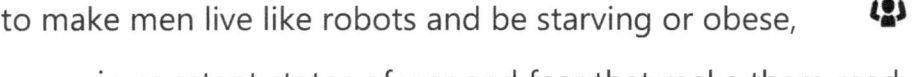

    in constant states of war and fear that make them ready to obey.

TV makes people so afraid they can't walk down the hall at night to pee

    or go outside to get the mail.

This makes them more willing to vote approval for new corporate jails

    and also more prepared to be in them themselves.

Now corporations plan to unleash the nightmare Orwell feared

    and perhaps greater suffering than the world has known.

All just for money, such a stupid thing, and to be bigger than the rest.

    What a sad reason to destroy the Earth, to throw away so much.

This nation's promise is worth too much, Americans are too good,

    to be a part of the debauch history will judge.

We must REPEAL, REPEAL the foul laws that were made,

    replacing them with fair laws that are civilized.

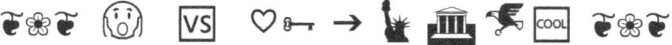

LET'S TAKE ONE STEP TOGETHER: At the giant Rainbow Gatherings in the wilderness people yell "WE LOVE YOU!" repeatedly on one side of the camp and others answer back, "WE LOVE YOU TOO!" Let's do the same thing out our windows at sunset on Saturdays, so that the Voice of the People can be heard! We could also play drums for half an hour at sunset on Saturdays at a window. Visit with or meet neighbors! WE NEED ALL OF US! (right + left)

Poems may be reprinted and shared by homeless for donations they can keep.
TELL TEN TO TELL TEN TO VOTE DEMOCRAT!   REGISTER 100 DEMOCRATS!
(https://www.usa.gov/register-to-vote)   (vote.gov) (rockthevote.org)
Democrats against forced mandates and other oppressive liability laws.

BILL OF RIGHTS   GOLDEN RULE   peacedrums.org   UNITE!

CAN'T HELP BEING GOOD

A young couple sat on a blanket on the sunny grassy area near the Horseshoe. The girl said, "It's easier to be good than bad." Flying in the face of almost every theology, she said "Most people can't help being good." They'd just lost a lot of their stuff but didn't seem too concerned about it. They looked at each other with love. He said, "She completes me."

Her family didn't approve. He told of his dream of buying 200 acres in Missouri and making a Peace Village for everyone. He was sewing, making a black leather loincloth with blue lining. She showed me the fashion drawings she carried in a large notebook in her backpack. There were period styles, elaborate corsets, flowing skirts, and also futuristic designs. We talked about spiritual things and how to fix the world. She said, "Whatever different thing you do, makes people resilient. Whatever people do to increase their consciousness makes the world better."

A guy in a Grateful Dead t-shirt wore a wristband that said, "Thank God I'm Grateful." Another guy in a black top hat said, "The Great Spirit will take care of you if you're doing the right thing."

HAZARDOUS CONDIMENTS

Some people want to take eating the right thing a step further and be mindful of the awful way factory farm animals are treated. With all the times I've mentioned and advertised McDonald's, I owe it to a vegan friend of mine to write a word about this issue. This is not a guilt trip; corporations should change how they treat animals.

Scrubbed techies Elijah and his friend Joshua dine at McDonald's but they don't eat any of the food for sale there. They buy it across the street at Whole Foods and carry it over. Even the water they drink doesn't come from McDonald's. They bring it with them in special cartons. I bring my computer and Elijah helps me with my web site while they both peruse the room for girls they'd like to meet. At this they have some success since they are both attractive and aren't homeless.

There are serious health concerns about eating the poisoned products of corporations. With their great political and financial power, huge companies have tweaked our laws protecting the public's health until they don't apply to them. Authorities move in if a lady sells tamales from a grocery cart, but they look the other way as corporations put toxic chemicals in all we eat, make GMO's that could destroy the Earth's ecosystems, kill the bees 🐝 with pesticides, and package everything with plastic that gives us cancer.

The meat we eat from grocery stores comes from animals so packed together that they can't move and must spend their lives standing in their own fecal matter. Cows are pumped with antibiotics to limit the amount of pus in the milk from their infected, bleeding udders. Baby chicks have their beaks cut off so they won't peck each other to death, packed in crates as tightly-crowded as in the Nazi boxcars with victims going to the concentration camps.

Cattle are infused with female hormones to make them fatter, lowering our sperm counts. Then they're hung upside-down by their feet from a hellish contraption that moves along slowly with endless rows of terrified, tortured animals in line to have their throats slit. The video didn't say how long they have to hang there like that. They're supposed to be made unconscious first with a stun gun, but for many of them it doesn't work. All their terror and agony, in the form of adrenalin, is in every bite of the burger we eat. Also, pregnant pigs are kept in "gestation crates" where they can't move.

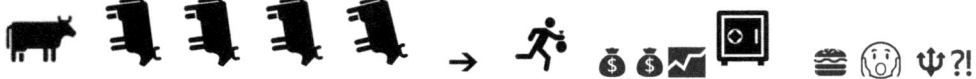

As if that wasn't bad enough, it turns out that workers at some slaughterhouses and meat packing plants are denied bathroom breaks and are advised to wear diapers while they work, so the line won't be slowed down. I suspect that this one might be another offensive, ineffective and overreaching liability rule. Do insurers think that keeping the employees from going to the bathroom and making them sit in diapers might make the meat "safer" from contamination in case they forget to wash their hands?

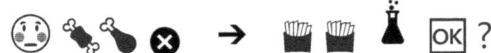

When I saw Elijah enter McDonald's, I quickly went up to the counter and changed my McNuggets order to two orders of French fries. The fries were made with GMO potatoes, fried in cancer-producing overheated oil, and sprinkled with heart-killing salt, but they didn't involve torturing animals. They didn't taste very good either and were not that hot, barely palatable except for the chemical cocktail in the dipping sauce.

As I started to try to stuff these down Elijah made a request. I was pleasantly surprised that a young man who looks so worldly-wise would ask that we pray and give thanks at the meal.

A NUDGE FROM GOD

Night life is something that's increasingly rare in our society. A generation back, before black op mass shootings and insurance laws were put in place limiting every single thing we do, there were often people "loitering" at night on the streets of cities, talking and laughing and having fun. Now most of that has been denied, but here on the Haight, that human interaction is still active.

The house-free are not allowed to sit on the sidewalk and have to remain standing all day. At eleven o'clock at night, the rule changes and they're allowed to sit down all they want without fear of getting a hefty fine. At that time the businesses are closed, most of the tourists are gone, and authorities are less intense about enforcing police state regulations that have made it illegal for people to gather on their own streets. That's when the party begins.

All up and down the street there are groups of people talking excitedly or making music. Some bring portable amps and electric guitars. There's less concern about noise on the now almost-empty streets. The lights from a few businesses that are still open make the asphalt of the street seem to glow in many colors. Some of the young people there also appear to glow in sparkly clothes, sailing magically down the street on their skateboards, illuminated by thousands of tiny green and magenta lights wound around the trees.

I met Dirtweasel, whose bright rainbow tie-dyed t-shirt attracted my attention. He expressed the nearly religious way he felt about his skateboard. He said, "My skateboard saved me. It's amazing how just a piece of wood, some plastic wheels and some bearings, can have the ability to transform your life."

He said the skateboarders are a brotherhood, like a tribe, who recognize each other without a word being said, and who watch each other's backs. He said he got everything from skateboarding, his passion in life, his community, his liberty. He knew which kind of plastic the wheels were made of. and named off all the different kinds of wheels and what they were good for. He said, "when I'm on my skateboard, the world is open to me. I don't need much money and I can go wherever I want."

The young people on the street joke with the remaining passerby. "Hey you dropped your smile" one calls out. 👁 The funniest cardboard sign I've seen said, "Donations for DNA Test - Girlfriend May Be Sister!!! Please Spare $!"

I met a pretty girl named Pixie who had magenta eye shadow with glitter, a magenta shirt, lipstick and jewelry. I overheard that she'd just lost all her stuff. She needed clothes and a tent, which by coincidence I happened to have in the truck. The tent had a broken zipper, and the door would need safety pins unless she could fix it. She assured me that she and her friends knew how to fix tent zippers. ⛺ + 👗👒👖👕

The night life and community that's been so much denied in our lives is happening in full force on Haight Street, where big red hearts still line the sidewalks where people stand or sit. ❤❤❤ Music echoes down the carless street that's lit up with colored light reflections.

Near Gus's Haight Street Market a random guy I didn't even recognize walked up to me, called me "Mamma" and said the most wonderful thing. I was feeling kind of down, which he couldn't have known. He said, "You can know you always have a place here with us. The family needs you." If I never make any money for writing these books, I've already been paid.

A guy named "Clutch" in a blue tie-dyed hoodie said he knows "something like God" is real. He told a story. He was crossing the street, and his friends who were behind him called for him to come back to where they were. He heard an audible voice that said "No, just keep walking." He actually felt a nudge in the middle of his back pushing him forward away from the street. On his third stride a fast driver's front tire bumped his heel. He's sure he would've been killed or seriously hurt if he'd listened to his friends and tried to go back across the street.

PURITANS IV: God's Message About Leaders of Extremist Right-Wing Churches (Not the actual Puritans, or truth-seekers and devoted pastors misinformed by dangerous doctrines.)

The megachurches' passion for religion is misplaced,

> away from all the true concerns of daily life.

The laws some legislators make treat human beings like specks of dirt,

> forfeiting cars of working poor for things like dumping trash.

Police stings on TV entrap those Jesus loved,

> put them in cages to make profits for the corporate Beast.

The votes for right-wing policies have sentenced galley slaves for petty crimes and smiled kindly at those who poison all with toxic crap.

God likes the coarsely-spoken truth

      much more than fine words telling lies.

The cunning doctrines of religionists

      make people look down on the poor and how they talk.

But they condone taking God's name in vain

      to teach warmongering dogmas causing genocides.

They say "God is a man of war" to justify their deeds

      then drop millions of tons of bombs on little kids.

God is at home in hobo jungles amid grocery carts,

      more than on gold and purple chairs with televangelists.

God is at ease with those who drink cheap wine and live on Cup-a-Noodle,

      who shiver under bridges and in doorways and in parks.

The Holy One is not so comfortable with people having tea and cake

      while stepping on poor people's throats.

So many've thought themselves so good because of being clean

      compared to those whose toil and sweat prepared their bread.

Those who hunt the helpless addict to destroy his life.

    should look at their own ghastly crimes of usury and greed.

The speck that's in your brother's eye is small concern to God

    compared to the atrocities that theologians do.

Throughout history they've been the ones

    to recommend harsh penalties for tiny crimes.

It's they who've given kings and emperors their leave

    to ravage villages with war, killing man, woman, and child.

Some preachers almost always teach the "Fall of Man" and the world's end,

    violent events that bring the worst out of those who presume to rule.

Paul's words also divide the rest of humankind from the "elect,"

    and guarantee that blood will flow on doctrinal points.

All in between seems pointless or just less convenient to the goal

    of getting tithes and seeming better than everyone else.

They're willing to destroy the world to prove John's prophecies are true

    and to unleash unfathomed suffering on all living things.

JESUS DIDN'T TEACH: that all are born in sin, the Inquisition, excommunication, slaves and women "obey in all things," Adam and Eve, idolaters and gays are "worthy of death," anti-Semitism, shame of the body, hell, tithing, having to go to church, the Divine Right of Kings, that the Bible was perfect, or that he created the world. Paul the Apostle and OTHERS ADDED those, plus "obey every ordinance of man," "let the unjust be unjust still," that you have to believe or be damned, that you can "take up serpents" and drink poison, and that it's not what you do that counts, but what you believe in. Red letters in the book of Revelation are the writer's vision or dream and don't teach what Jesus taught, and have been killing people since the ink was dry. The Prince of Peace taught kindness, brotherly love, and Heaven on Earth.

THE POOR

Possibly the first name given to one of the earliest congregations of Jesus followers was "Ebionites," which translated means "The Poor." What better words could there be about what Jesus really taught? What better way to point out those he loved the most, the humble of the Earth who manage to hold onto their humanity, and are much more fun to hang out with than the princes of religion?

It was not some sort of organized asceticism that caused these people to be called by that name. Unlike later religious orders who mandated weird rules bordering on the morbid, there was no deliberate attempt at self-denial. There were those who were rich in resources but wanted more than that, who actually enjoyed having less stuff and being less worried about it.

But most of those who followed Jesus were actually poor to begin with, like most people on the planet today, in the service of kings and businesses. They loved Jesus because he loved them. They made up the greater part of the raucous crowds that followed him through the towns and across the fields.

He spoke their language, about everyday things that most of us are concerned about. His stories were about relationships, making a living, touching the sublime. He spoke to the heart of the people, showing them a sacred space where all beings are connected. When he said, "whatever you've done unto the least of these you've done it unto me," he was referring to the connection between people, something that some have experienced who've seen the veil lifted 🗝 that separates humanity.

At Golden Gate Park and on the Haight, the poor whom Jesus so admired certainly reside. Their appetite for God is unmatched. Their experience of Heaven, here and now, has become rare in the rest of society. Like the Ebionites, they can appreciate the advantages of having less stuff. The world might think many of them are nuts because they actually "take no thought for the morrow, what ye shall eat and what ye shall wear." Even though some of them wouldn't call themselves religious, they seem to bank on the sense that their Father in Heaven knows what they need before they ask. ✨ 🎁 🎁 🎁 ✨

Because of their hard, tentative lives, their currency is different than that of most people. They value wisdom and experience as much as comfort and ease. They value adventure as much as security. Like the poor everywhere, they have other goals besides mere survival. Many of them try to follow the path of the Buddha, or of Christ, or of the freedom fighters who made the American Revolution. Jesus was about inner and outer liberation. That's why he said the meek would inherit the Earth.

TO BE HUMAN YOU HAVE TO BE HUMANE

It was very cold and I'd spent all day on the Haight, had danced to music on the corner of Haight and Ashbury to keep warm. ❄ Nighttime interactions were fun except that my feet started to feel frostbitten like when I lived in Alaska. With all the distractions, I didn't notice it until realizing that I could barely walk. Still I stayed. I went into Amal's Deli to warm up. There I learned how to warm my hands by placing them around the heated soup containers on the counter.

I heard Amal advise a young man not to put hot sauce on his food because it wasn't good for his cold. She called him by name, Matthew, and seemed to care about him the way a relative would. I knew she cared about dozens of the young people that way.

At Amal's you never know who you'll make friends with, from street people to police officers to celebrities. I ran into Ron Greco, a rock musician with seven albums. He has that rock star look, with black clothes and a mullet haircut. His latest album is called "Blues in the Haight."

Outside the door I met Bird, an older man in a wheelchair. Because of a medical condition he's not as good looking as he once was, and his clothes are not as clean as they could be. Yet Amal lets him stay there, as long as he doesn't block the entrance. I found out he's a "seminal theologian," a musician and poet with published works. In the excitement of the conversation, I didn't notice that we were both right in front of the doorway. Amal came out and scolded him for it and he moved a little further from the door. Later when I asked her why she lets him stay she said, "because I love him."

A variety of people gravitate around the store, like stray cats or dogs that keep coming back when you keep feeding them because you don't want them to starve. These are more hungry for the love she gives them than for any scraps of food.

On the sidewalk I heard live piano music coming from a white van with the side door open. "Mr. Brandy" transports a full upright piano in his van, which also doubles as his home. There's no clutter in the van, very neat, like a room. There's something about it that feels like a cocktail lounge, with boas hanging in clusters on the wall, a sparkly gold material background, and also red and orange silk draperies around the base of the piano. His very accomplished piano playing adds life to the street. People put money in his donation bucket.

He wears sunglasses, a nice jacket, and a fedora. 👓 You can tell he's a sharp dresser. Despite his medium-length greying hair, there's something very youthful about him. I saw his clothes hung up neatly on a rod across the back of the van, hanging down onto his bed area underneath. I guess it doesn't bother him to have the clothes hanging over him as he sleeps.

Despite the cold I remained to visit on street corners with clusters of young people who likewise ignored Arctic-like weather conditions. One of them had only a thin sweater but seemed just fine. I asked him why the street kids seem so seldom sick. He said he thought that when you live outside in the elements, your immune system goes into overdrive.

A guy told some jokes: "French fries weren't first cooked in France. 🍟 They were cooked in grease." And "I'd tell you a joke about pizza but it's a little cheesy." 🍕🍕 Plus "A mushroom walked into a bar. The bartender said, 'We don't serve your kind.' The mushroom said, 'Why not? 3I'm a fun guy.'"

I met "BamBam," who looks just like a Viking. His hair is mostly shaved off, except for a strip about four inches wide from his forehead to the back of his head, ending in a small ponytail. His beard of reddish curls and his well-worn road gear also suggest an exotic other-time quality. He looks like somebody who's about to sack Rome but instead he said, "I have an ingrained belief that if you always give everything you have, you will never go without. By doing that I can change the world one person at a time."

His t-shirt told about the legend of the Grateful Dead. The story is: a man came upon a group of people abusing a corpse because the deceased hadn't had money for his burial or to pay his debts. The traveler paid for the man's burial with his only money. Later he met a stranger who brought him lots of good fortune, including making him rich. The stranger then revealed himself to be the man who had died. He was The Grateful Dead. That's how skulls and skeletons came to be on hippies' t-shirts.

"BamBam," gave himself the name of the baby cartoon character in "The Flintstones." There's another thing that makes him look like a vision from another time. It's a long fur-lined vest with a wide fur collar almost like a cape, totally Stone Age fashion. I assumed that the unusual fur collar was made of ordinary sheepskin, but he said it was actually skin from a ram his dog Titus had killed.

Before anyone could stop the dog, he'd grabbed the ram by the back of the neck and then finished him off by biting his jugular. BamBam and his friends had then butchered and eaten it in the course of several days, making stew out of it because it was so tough. The golden boxer at his feet looked as strong as a lion and almost as big, capable of bringing down a ram.

With BamBam I met Cave Man, equally wild-looking. He's tall and animated and his long curly black hair radiates out in a way that seems to express an electric energy he has. He has the vitality of a real pirate or maybe an actual cave man. He surprised me when he spoke. Despite his rugged look and that some people might run from him on the street, he said, "To be human you have to be humane."

A STATE OF SUSPENDED HOPE

I ran into Dago, who has the ten-wheeler truck. As I admired all the tools he wears attached to his clothes, we had a great conversation while I was double-parked with my window open. He takes pride in being able to build and fix things for people. It turns out that the light he wears on his leather hat is for working in attics where it's dark. He said he has many names, including Running Bear, Little Jesus, and Mad Max. He said, "I talk this moral stuff." He said about life, "This is all God, every little molecule. It's the university of morals."

At Monday pancakes in the park I met Davy Jones, intelligence and kindness in his deep blue eyes. He said the reason he was called that was because he had broken so many bones. He told a story: He and his dad got stuck on a ski lift and had to jump off and he was injured, breaking many bones. The ski lift had closed, and no-one knew where they were. He and his dad spent the night in a snow cave, where he said he died several times. He described being "crucified" when they lifted him out and tied him to a rescue stretcher. That's why he's called "Davy Jones," because he cheated death. He's been in car and motorcycle accidents too.

His dog is called a "Pharaoh Hound" though not the same kind of dog the pharaohs had, although she resembles them when it comes to her tall, wide velvety ears. She's medium-sized with golden-colored short hair.

Her ears are the reason he has her. "Ginger" is actually a very fancy dog from a breeder but one of her ears doesn't stand up as required by standards for a show dog. The Breeder couldn't get much for her, so he'd gifted her to Davy Jones. About the condition of the world, he said he was "In a state of suspended hope." 🌐 ✌️

On Haight Street I ran into "Orange" and some of his friends. I enjoyed a conversation with Panda. I met Scotty Don't, tall and charismatic, with medium-length brown hair and a thoughtful face. Living kind of a rough existence, he said he wasn't sure if he was a hippie. I said maybe he's a hybrid between a hippie and a street kid. I also met Dallas, who has a wonderful smile, and his black dog named Sugary. It's a perfect name because the black fur around the dog's mouth has sprinkles of white hair that make it look like he just put his nose in a sugar bowl.

One young man named Josh wore pants made of square patches like those in a patchwork quilt, a now-rare 60's style. The patches looked like they were sewn together by hand. He carried a mandolin. His dog is named "Balto," after a famous sled dog who saved Nome, Alaska in 1925 by bringing antitoxin 600 miles during a blizzard for a diphtheria epidemic.

NOT BORED WITH BLISS

At the Magic Theatre Rainbow answered the phone: "Still hoping for peace!" 🪔 🥠 🦴 🍀 ☮️ We went to a pizza place where I did my part to support the arts and keep him from starvation. 🍕 🍕 He said, "I want to get as close to God as I can get, intimate with God. 💔 🙇 God appreciates being appreciated." He said that all the great masters are talking about the same thing. "When you surrender to the infinite, you're pliable. You can work with it, be more flexible. I'm trying to do God's will. That's all I want. All I want is for it to be right. I don't wanna learn any more harsh lessons." 🍎📊❗

He said, "I'm a drop in the ocean. The drop is in the ocean, but the ocean is in the drop. 🐾💧 We are water. When we open up and let in the light, there are rainbows. We become a rainbow. 🌈 One plus one is one!" He said, "I believe the ultimate thing is love. If everybody is love, that's the thing that's gonna substantiate the whole planet!

"I want to live in a world that works. War doesn't work, hatred doesn't work, so let's try something different. Let's try getting along. Let's try getting to know each other. The idea is to move forward. Within your own heart is a universe. It's not about me. It's more about us. Every atom in your body is buzzing. All we need to know is how to get peace of mind, how to be happy, how to experience bliss."

He said, "I feel like everything I see and everywhere I go is already sacred. I'd never get bored with bliss." He added. "As long as your karma doesn't run over your dogma, you'll be ok." 🐕🚗💨

At the park Wendy Whimsey in her bowler hat was dancing in a relaxed, distracted manner, wearing a long purple coat of shimmering material. As she moved gracefully she trailed two purple scarves in the air, while at the same time enjoying a sweet roll from the food pantry. The next time I went to the park she was gone, to parts unknown, but I was assured that she would someday appear again. There was a chalk drawing at the log: a pastel lightning bolt like panels of stained glass. I took a picture of it before the rain could wash it away. ✏️📷

THE HAIGHT STREET PUMPKIN

The San Francisco Summer of September and October has a very special thing about it. I am told that photographers like to show up during that time because of a spectacular light that occurs at sunset when the sun is in a direct line with Haight Street. As if built by the designers of Stonehenge or the Pyramids as a kind of calendar, the street is aligned with the rays of the setting sun, which touch everything with a golden light. This happens during the best and warmest time of the year, around Halloween, when normally lots of "travelers" are there.

A tall young man with lots of blond curls, whose name is "Chance" walked up holding a big pumpkin he'd found on top of a trash can. It was rotten in just one area on the bottom, which we cut out. A guy carved it who said he was a cook, and he did a really good job. I requested that it have a happy face to show the world about this place. The face he made was downright jubilant, with a wide smile and happy eyebrows. Then someone put a joint in its mouth. It was the Haight Street Pumpkin.

Across the street was The Burger Urge, which displayed over the front door, about twenty feet up in the air, a huge plastic hamburger prop. Chance decided that he wanted to climb up there and place the pumpkin on top of the bun. I didn't see any easy way for him to get up there and he could fall to the concrete below. He didn't mind the risk if it would make a statement.

But then we all thought of something. The pumpkin could fall on somebody's head. It was a liability issue, and the business owner would have to find a way to get up there and take it down. Putting it there would not be doing unto others as you would have them do unto you, so they decided against it. The pumpkin ended up on display at Amal's Deli.

THE LIGHT IN THEIR EYES

It's hard to understand how people living such hard lives can seem so much happier than most other people I know. Among the nomads of Golden Gate Park and on the Haight, there is smile after smile, and person after person with a beautiful light in their eyes. 😊   What could it be that makes them that way, after sleeping in the rain, getting harassed daily by authorities, being looked down on by gentrifiers?   ⋛👁⋚ 🤸 [FREE]

Their eyes are alive, their faces are alive, and their minds really seem to be alive. ⋛🧠⋚   They don't waste time talking about stupid stuff like movie stars. They don't stare at tablets. 📴   Instead they look at each other, talk to each other and to other people. Their interactions with tourists and other passerby usually include compliments and questions like "how's your day going?" Without the never-ending demands of jobs and debt slavery, they seem to have time to listen to other people, to care about them. 🕸 ⏰ [OK]   Without the constant din of media lies and brainwashing, they seem like real live, natural human beings.

There are many who believe, myself included, that the media deliberately attempts to disrupt us and dumb us down. The girls with boy voices, boys with girl voices, endless stories of betrayal and mayhem, do something to us. They make us afraid of each other, afraid of ourselves, afraid to go outside. Children's cartoons with sex organs imbedded in them, and themes with terrifying monsters which menace and chase the characters until the last minute of a cartoon, do something to the children.

Totalitarians have learned from their psychologists that if they can disrupt and disengage the basic social strategies that have always before helped humans to survive, they can gain unprecedented power over us. Put that together with the horrendous machinery of their computerized surveillance, the prison system, and things like geoengineering and secret biological warfare against their own people, and hello, you've got a galloping totalitarian police state. It's already here and we're faced with having to find a way to put a stop to it.

Peons and sex kittens, and people who think they're dysfunctional, don't fight back very well against corporate police states. People who think their adversary is the opposing football team, or some terrible flaw or sin within themselves, might not notice the big monster lurking nearby. False religion and out-of-control unregulated capitalism have teamed up to bring to life the prophecies of doom that John of Patmos wrote in Revelation while in his "trance."

Nobody even really knows who he was, and his book was almost not included in the Bible. There's nothing in his book that Jesus taught. It's full of vindictive and vague accusations, giving power to bullies for the last two thousand years. It's a source of those scary quotes about eternal torment in a lake of fire. In the religious tracts we receive and in the rantings of TV preachers, these quotes are often sandwiched between a couple things Jesus actually is claimed to have said, fooling people into thinking they came from him. I call this a "Jesus Sandwich." 🍔

John of Patmos, from information gained while he was "in the spirit," claims that Jesus will return dressed in "a vestment dipped in blood," 👕 and that he will oversee a slaughter in which there will be blood as high as a horse's bridle for two hundred miles. 🗡️ 🌊 🐎 A small cabal of incredibly wealthy entities is getting ready to make John's ugly prophecies come true for profit and power. The "Four Horsemen of the Apocalypse," war, famine, pestilence and death, are none other than the corporations.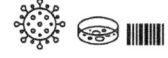

Sometimes I need to get out to the park and look into the faces of the house-free, in order to regain a grip on normalcy. The media bombards us with artificial role models of psychokillers and bratty kids. The news frightens us with mass shootings, some of which might be black ops designed to build new prisons and put up more cameras. Brilliant psychiatrists, some of them former Nazis, have used their minds to find ways to break the bonds between husbands and wives, children and parents, neighbors and friends. Their research has been applied to us through the media until a lot of us don't know if we're coming or going, which makes us easier to control. 🤖⛓️😱⛓️??

Out at the park, near the log beside the pond, people talk to each other in a real way. They look at each other in the face. The women wear flowing clothes instead of the sexualized tight clothing sold at malls. The men are confident and strong. You can tell they do their own thinking and that they could build a cabin with their bare hands 🛖 if they had to. The many marriages I've seen out there seem secure and happy. I've seen guys get in fights but not couples. ₹💑₹

That light in their eyes refreshes me, uplifts me to hopeful thoughts. I know it's a light that's inside every human being, even when dimmed by oppression, exhaustion and confusion. I believe it's the actual light of God, the thing Jesus was talking about when he said, "The Kingdom of

Heaven is within you."

TRAINHOPPERS AND GUTTERPUNKS

The "San Francisco Summer," September and October, is past. Many nomads like to be here during that time, in a kind of family reunion. For most of the rest of the year, an arctic wind often blows through the park. When rains come, many travel to dry locations. Like one of them said, "Why let the birds be smarter than you?"

Now they were going off in different directions, making promises to maybe be back again in a few months. To my surprise many of them were not going to warmer climates but were attempting to travel to freezing-cold New York to attend a Grateful Dead show on November 12th. They said they were "going on tour," which meant that they planned to travel all around the country, illegally hitch-hiking and trainhopping, to go to all the band's shows.

Many of them don't even attend the shows when they get there, since they can't afford the tickets. They just hang out on the parking lots around the shows, where they can see their friends and still hear the music. I think that's how their nomadic way of life began originally. Jesus taught humility, but these people take it to a whole new level. They call themselves gutterpunks, gutters, crusties, dirty kids, scumf-cks and road dogs. Those who go "on tour" call themselves toursluts.

By the way, these names are not a reference to a3ny lack of morality (or cleanliness). I've found these people to be as careful about what they do and what they believe in, as other people. They apply the Golden Rule Test when making decisions. Those who still have cars are called rubbertramps. Those who ride trains are called trainhoppers. They sometimes ride on a "suicide porch," an open balcony on the back of a train car with a hole in the floor through which they could fall on the tracks.

I worried about the safety and comfort of those who would be riding trains with no bottom, which must expose them to incredible wind chill factors in rain or snow. They would have no refuge or safety except in each other, often not knowing where they would sleep or what they would eat. In many unfamiliar places they could lose everything at any time, including their dogs.

Most of these children grew up in foster homes, but some came from comfortable middle-class backgrounds, never expecting or imagining anything like this. When they were born there were still jobs, some apartments were still priced so normal people could afford them, and you could hope to go to college without a lifetime of debt. Through no fault of their own, all that has changed. Some of these are children whose parents treasured and pampered them, fed them healthy food, bought them the latest styles, had great hopes for them. Now many of the parents are living in their cars.

For all their hardships I've rarely heard the kids complain. They seem to take pride in how tough they are, in having declared their independence from the rat race. Liberty is their great treasure. Even when they lose everything, they hold their heads up high because they still have that.

RESONATING WITH THE HOLY

That day I was hurrying to the drum circle and didn't have time to stop by, but when I looked over toward the log across the pond, I saw something I hadn't seen since I could remember: the log was empty. Not a single person was sitting there, no leashed dogs or backpacks. Where all that rich life had been, that rare and precious community, there was now only landscaping. As it turned out, that's exactly what the makers of a new rule had in mind.

I hurried on my way but thought it was very strange. Maybe the sprinklers had been turned on or something. But the next day when I went eagerly to the log, anxious to see my wonderful group of friends, it was weirdly empty again. The sunbeams from the tall trees were falling on it in a surreal and beautiful way, the sprinklers had not been turned on, but there were no people there.

I knew that some of my house-free friends had said that they were "going on the road," some planning to make it all the way to a Grateful Dead concert in New York in November. Was it possible that so many had left that the log was empty? I didn't think so. I went across the way to where there were some people, though not the same ones who'd sat on the log on the hill above the pond. They were not sitting up comfortably on the logs near the tunnel like they usually were. Instead, they sprawled awkwardly on dirt embankments with their dogs.

I asked them what happened and that's when I found out. They'd been told it was now illegal to sit on the logs. It hurt to hear it and I didn't want to believe it. Hippies have been sitting on those logs since before the Summer of Love, for over half a century. This park, where historical events that are sacred to us took place, has for us some of the elements of ancestral land, if only because we love it. There are many who know every tree, every glade, every bush in this park.

I felt outrage that again something that belonged to the people had apparently been privatized. I was told by those sitting on the ground that they'd heard the art museum "owned" the logs and had designated them as "landscaping" that people weren't allowed to sit on. They'd heard that some people had already gotten tickets. 🌀 The art museum wanted the park to be more "family-friendly."

👔💼📢📄 → 👨‍👩‍👧‍👦 = ⛪🎩 → 🗑️

That's how fast even something resonating with the holy can be shut down, like these gatherings of people around the logs. These young people were setting in motion the very forces of life, just being people, just being free, just talking about the things they talked about while sitting on the logs, and hoping in the way that only young people can hope. As Jesus taught, whatever you do to these young people, you do it unto God. God is being told He can't sit on the logs. 🌀

It was jarring that so many of my friends had left so suddenly. The people sitting on the embankments assured me that those who'd gone travelling would be back sooner or later. I'd seen it before, made friends with groups of people only to have them disappear in a couple of weeks.

Here again there was conversation and laughter, and even music from a guitar. They were in high spirits, not dwelling on misfortune. There was something so strong about them, so reassuring. They were carrying on the work of keeping the life forces going, of preserving things that are real, teaching peace. 🍎❗ ☮️ 🕊️ Sitting on the ground, one said he even felt stronger than before, connected to the power of the Earth.

🌱🌸🌱🌸 ▌║▌ 🦁 ⚖️ 🌿🌸🌿🌸

WITCH HUNTS

When they make plants illegal, it doesn't look good for our liberties.

During the massive number of witch and heresy trials from the 1100's to the 1700's, millions of people lost their lives, most of them women. It wasn't dancing with the devil that most of them were accused of. The majority were convicted of using medicinal plants to heal people. Midwives were rounded up and executed with gruesome deaths. Theologians said midwives interfered with God's will by relieving women of pain, which was Eve's punishment. The Inquisition was also against abortion and contraception... sound familiar?

Authorities forbade all healing by women, under threat of death. This led to a male doctor monopoly, although women had mostly been the ones to take care of their family's health since the beginning of time. People blamed witches, not the state, for their troubles like the Black Plague, their poverty, and so on. Many if not most of the proceedings were spurred by greed. The accused's property was "forfeited" to the Church, with the accuser getting a large cut. Feuds over land ownership were often at play, including in the Salem witch trials.

Now in our lifetime plants have again been made illegal for the people to use. The "Drug War" began as a strategy to elect Richard Nixon, now implicated in the murder of J. F. K. In a legal policy similar to an evil spell, the harsh penalties silenced whole generations of pot-smoking peacemakers. Again, people are prevented from healing and medicating themselves, making them reliant on big pharma for everything. Pot may be legal in some states, but it's still highly illegal under federal law, and there are still people languishing in prison for it with twenty-five-year sentences. It bothers me that they were charged with "possession," and that their property was "forfeited," just like at witch trials.

Among the nomads some girls like to emulate the women healers of old, wearing dreadlocks and becoming experts on healing with herbs or crystals. A few of them like to be a little more "edgy," wearing for   decoration emblems that not only set them off as different, but which ignite the prejudices of ideologues and others. Let's be aware that some people out there are not making their judgments under normal conditions. They've been brainwashed by media to fear others.

One pretty girl named Kat had a collection of buttons on the black leather jacket she wore. She had one that said, "Hail Satan." It's a sort of protest about how badly churches have treated people. Some of the youth even think that they are reincarnations of those who were slaughtered in the great witch hunts. Most don't attach any big meaning to these symbols, but just think they're "cool."

My motherly instincts aroused, I told her that I thought wearing it put her at risk of being hassled by the police, and that it made people hate hippies. Like I had guessed, it wasn't something that she was into. Someone had given her the button. I asked jokingly if she would notice if I took the button off (while she was wearing it) and put it somewhere else on her jacket, for instance behind the lapel. To my great delight she removed the button and pinned it there where it would never be seen.

OUR TWO-SPIRIT BROTHERS AND SISTERS

I'm hoping that the following information will give Biblical ammunition to people being accused of things Jesus never mentioned, and that are barely mentioned in the Old Testament. Jesus taught nothing about homosexuality. The closest he comes to mentioning two-spirit people is this sweet scripture:

He said unto them, "All men cannot receive this saying, save they to whom it is given. There are **SOME EUNUCHS** (castrated men), **WHICH WERE SO BORN** from their mother's womb: and there are **SOME** eunuchs, which **WERE MADE EUNUCHS OF MEN**: and **THERE BE EUNUCHS, WHICH HAVE MADE THEMSELVES EUNUCHS FOR THE KINGDOM OF HEAVEN'S SAKE**. He that is able to receive it, let him receive it." (Matthew 19:1)

The Old Testament also has something nice to say: **NEITHER LET THE EUNUCH** (castrated man) **SAY, "BEHOLD, I AM A DRY TREE."** For thus saith the Lord **UNTO THE EUNUCHS THAT** keep my Sabbaths, and **CHOOSE THE THINGS THAT PLEASE ME** (kindness), and take hold of my covenant; **EVEN UNTO THEM WILL I GIVE IN MINE HOUSE** and within my walls **A PLACE AND A NAME BETTER THAN OF SONS AND DAUGHTERS**: I will give them an everlasting name that shall not be cut off. (Isaiah 56:3-5)

There are two scriptures used against gays in the Old Testament: **(Leviticus 19:20): "You shall not lie with a male as with a woman; it is an abomination,"** and Leviticus 20:13: **"If a man lies with a male as with a woman, both of them have committed an abomination; they shall surely be put to death; their blood is upon them."**

Scriptures just previous to that talk about people worshipping images of animals, which makes it sound like they're talking about people in their past, possibly Egypt. A noted theologian wrote, "<u>**No Christians think we should follow (Leviticus) today.**</u>" (Sam Allberry, who wrote "Is God Anti-Gay?") That may be because it contains weird prohibitions, and prescribes death for a whole bunch of things, including sex with a menstruating woman.

There are four places about this in the New Testament, none of them from Jesus. They are **(Romans 1:26-32)**, **(I Corinthians 6:9-10)** by Paul, who never met Jesus. Nobody knows who wrote **(I Timothy 1:8-10)**, and **(Jude 1:7-8)**.   None of the four are from Jesus, and they are surrounded by poisonous scriptures telling people to obey rulers.

Thomas Jefferson and most of our country's founders were Enlightenment thinkers who believed that the writings of Paul in the New Testament didn't match Jesus. Jefferson didn't include any of them in his Jefferson Bible. I strongly believe that putting aside Paul's doctrines for a second is necessary to find out what Jesus really taught.

(Romans 1:24-32): Wherefore **God also gave them up to uncleanness through the lusts of their own hearts, to dishonour their own bodies between themselves**...who changed the truth of God into a lie, and **worshipped and served the creature** more than the Creator, who is blessed forever. Amen. For this cause **God gave them up unto vile affections: for even their women did change the natural use into that which is against nature: And likewise also the men, leaving the natural use of the woman, burned in their lust one toward another; men with men working that which is unseemly**... God gave them over to **a reprobate mind**, to do those things which are not convenient. Being filled with all unrighteousness, fornication, wickedness, covetousness, maliciousness; full of envy, murder, debate, deceit, malignity whisperers, Backbiters, haters of God, despiteful, proud, boasters, inventors of evil things, disobedient to parents, Without understanding, covenant breakers, **without natural affection**, implacable, unmerciful: Who knowing the judgment of God, **they which commit such things are worthy of death, not only do the same, but have pleasure in them that do them.**

What a long list of people worthy of death! The scripture right before all this **seems to indicate that Paul was referring to their Pagan or Egyptian neighbors**, who "changed the glory of the uncorruptible God into an image made like corruptible man, and to birds, and fourfooted beasts, and creeping things." (Romans 1:23)

(I Corinthians 6:9-10): Know ye not that the unrighteous shall not inherit the kingdom of God? Be not deceived: neither fornicators, nor idolaters, nor adulterers, nor **effeminate,** nor **abusers of themselves with mankind**.

(That's where the term "self-abuse" comes from, and it doesn't even say that.)

(I Timothy 9-10): Knowing this, that the law is not made for a righteous man, but for the lawless and disobedient, for the ungodly and for sinners, for unholy and profane, for murderers of fathers, and murderers of mothers, for manslayers, For whoremongers, **for them that defile themselves with mankind**, for menstealers, for liars, for perjured persons, and if there be any other thing that is contrary to sound doctrine.

The chapter ends with this mystery theologian condemning two men, whom he names in his holy book, "whom I have delivered unto Satan." In the next two chapters, women are told to be quiet and slaves to obey.

(Jude 7-8): Even as Sodom and Gomorrah, and the cities about them in like manner, giving themselves over to fornication, and **going after strange flesh**, are set forth for an example, suffering the vengeance of eternal fire. Likewise also these filthy dreamers **defile the flesh**, despise dominion, and **speak evil of dignities**.

In the Old Testament, homosexuality is not among the list of sins God is punishing Sodom and Gomorrah for. For a more detailed study of all these scriptures, including comparisons of different versions through the ages, please visit my website, peacedrums.org.

I tried to compare what it says in different modern Bible versions and ended up swimming in a sea of acronyms, with a dull headache: NWT, LSV, ASV, ESV, NIV, NASB, MLV, NLT, NKJV, NCV, GW, HCSB, NRSV, NirV and LEB, to name a few. I studied ancient Bibles and the earliest writings, Mancion in 144 A.D. and Codex Sinaiticus in 200 A.D. For those who may not know, the Old Testament is material written before Jesus, and the New Testament is after Jesus. The number before the colon is the chapter, and the one after it is the verse.

The accusations seemed at first to be aimed at specific people in the past (the Old Testament mentions those who worshipped images of animals,) and later, in the New Testament, to many more categories of people, and in the present. Some translations said you should kill the offenders and also those who approve of them, and others said you should kill only those who do those things and also approve of them. None of this is from Jesus.

EXPLOITED ON BOTH SIDES OF THE AISLE

All things considered, I believe that even though God may not have a big problem with transgender issues, conservative religious people do. Their giant voting block has used this issue to swing elections to big business since Nixon. This topic being in the forefront at election time has always galvanized church-going Republicans to show up in droves to defeat "liberal" Democrats and save the unborn. The pro-big business police state policies enacted by those they elect this way, usually without their real consent, have never been good for the majority of Americans.

Transgender people I know are not heavily invested in telling little kids they can change their gender, with bully laws that will get teachers fired and make schools lose federal funding and go bankrupt. I am personally opposed to these laws. These kinds of policies definitely make some people hate gays and think they're from Satan, instead of having the opposite effect. Powerful financial interests, traditionally aligned with the

Republican Party, use the good intentions of both sides to get the power and control over us that they want. They use both the liberals' wish to protect everybody, and the conservatives' wish to follow their religion, to screw us all.

At this crucial moment in history, it's more important than ever that we find ways to unite. Enlisting the power of the state to enforce what should be personal decisions, violently drives us apart. As we stand on the brink of a totalitarian plutocracy, we should be repealing corporate personhood, instead of re-arranging the deck chairs on the Titanic.

HOPE AMERICA II: SPACIOUS MINDS

"Smile on your brother!" heroes sang,

    and Peace Drums made the happiest sound,

by making hope for the oppressed

    and also for the plants and animals bulldozers tread.

"Everybody get together right now!" is what forefathers said,

    when they dreamed of a place where all could live in peace.

The sins of slavery and of Native genocide did stain those hopes,

    but tears of Lady Liberty joined those on trails of tears.

Built to Last

It wasn't even simple greed or cruel tyrants

    that could rape such a bright hope.

Secret societies from ancient times, perhaps from Egypt's mystic eye, were perhaps waiting at the New World's shores

to kill the holy child as soon as it was born,

    installing the same tyrannies that bent the forebear's necks.

In dark silk robes in basements it's said they performed weird rites

    invoking gods of Egypt to retain their wealth.

Some people say they're meeting even now

    in hidden halls which big stone lions guard.

They say the pyramid that's on the dollar bill, with the eye on top,

    is a reference to their dead god.

They say the Obelisk in Washington, a monument from Egypt's past,

    was brought here with idolatry to help Insiders rule the world.

They say that Ronald Reagan, called the Sun God on his funeral day, ☼

    changed inaugural plans to face the Obelisk in a construction zone.

In any case, bullies don't need secret societies to do their tasks.

    Computers can do well enough, and debt, and jails for all.

The torture chamber isn't needed when the state can take your child,

    or give you lifetimes in a cage for things that didn't used to be a crime.

People are easy to control when they are always sick and scared.

    They don't have time to think about what's going on.

Between TV, fast food and their three jobs

    they're bound to always have something that hurts.

Nevertheless, so many try their very best,

    registering voters and recycling everything they use.

People around us from all walks of life, both rich and poor,

    discuss the Way of Peace more than they discuss sports.

Some with long hair and some without, they talk about how to do right,

    how to love enemies and be like Christ.

The hidden mikes looking for drugs don't seem to hear this

                                        wondrous speech,

    but God hears it and finds in it a renewed hope for man.

America the beautiful for spacious minds that think new thoughts,

    trying to fix the misery that has plagued the world

since pharaohs, emperors and kings trod on people's backs

    and built vast monuments cemented with men's blood.

Our journey's not been perfect or without some greedy traitors' touch.

Still in this pioneer heart is Liberty, both for ourselves and others too.
Even while the monopolists made factory children slave,
> protestors filled the streets demanding just laws and a living wage.

This is where Peace Flags waved at Woodstock and at Monterey,
> where sons of rich men joined with those of lesser means

to say they dreamed about a world with no more war, no more bad deals,
> where people's sweat and blood and tears are not traded

for higher stocks. In this great land, even the wealthy want a change,
> not satisfied with messes made eons before their birth.

They too can't stand to watch the people starve and the rain forests fall,
> all on the Web for us to see each day.

There is a hope expressed in whispers around coffee tables and
> in old rock songs that people are still listening to.

The dream of brotherhood of which they sing
> is a thing greater than time can erase or TV brainwashing corrupt.

It is the dream that Jesus had, and all great dreamers through all time.
> It is that people care enough about each other to repair what's wrong.

This seems to be the only really good reason we have
> to think that we can fix this mess and carry on.

LET'S TAKE ONE STEP TOGETHER: At the giant Rainbow Gatherings in the wilderness people yell "WE LOVE YOU!" repeatedly on one side of the camp and others answer back, "WE LOVE YOU TOO!" Let's do the same thing out our windows at sunset on Saturdays, so that the Voice of the People can be heard! We could also play drums for half an hour at sunset on Saturdays at a window. Visit with or meet neighbors the first Saturday of the month.
WE NEED ALL OF US! (right + left)

Poems may be reprinted and shared by homeless for donations they can keep.
TELL TEN TO TELL TEN TO VOTE!   REGISTER 100 VOTERS!
(https://www.usa.gov/register-to-vote)   (vote.gov) (rockthevote.org)
Democrats against forced mandates and other oppressive liability laws.
BILL OF RIGHTS   GOLDEN RULE   peacedrums.org   UNITE!

"The abolition of domestic slavery is the great object of desire in those colonies." "Nothing is more clearly written in the book of fate than that these people are to be free." Thomas Jefferson

Non-cooperation with evil is a sacred duty. Ghandi

"NOBODY'S A BAD PERSON"

    In the morning I sat on the ledge at the park by myself and cried, seeing a vision of all the displaced people of the Earth, from Nazi victims to urban car dwellers. I imagined how it must feel for those who returned home and sat on the same places they'd sat on with their loved ones, who were now gone. This small concrete ledge had been filled with people every day, with people all around who were now nowhere to be seen. 💔 Suddenly I realized that something else was missing.

    I'd noticed earlier walking by that when I'd looked in that direction, not only were there no people there, but I couldn't see the log itself. Maybe I was just looking from the wrong angle and the log was obscured by the land or bushes. That was wrong. The big log that had been above the ledge, where gypsy kings, pirates and vagabonds had sat enthroned, had been removed.

Heartsick I moved away from the area, but then came back when I saw some people there. Lena was there, the girl with beautiful long blond hair who'd first invited me to sit there. She told me it was true that they'd actually REMOVED THE LOG so that the hippies couldn't sit on it. She and a couple of her friends and I sat on the ledge that had been below the log and stared at some little orange flags stuck in the ground next to some plants and trees around the pond. Were they planning to make changes and start pulling things out? ⚑ ⚑ ⚑

Lena also wondered where everybody had gone. None of this stopped the usual banter about how everybody loved each other. Her friend Swags was wearing a Santa Claus hat. 🎅 Lena said about Swags: "This is my heart." She said to him, "I could say so many nice things about you." Then she said, to him and his friend, "Swags has a beautiful soul. Toshi, you have a beautiful soul too. Your friends are my friends."

Swags said, "I strive to be a very open-minded and free-spirited person. I love people and all their interactions. Nobody's a bad person."

FENCING OFF HEAVEN

On the stairway near the Horseshoe, I saw Pretty Tony and Cory. They told me that officials were planning to "re-do" the front of the park, change the pond, and put in a bunch of concrete with concessions. They assured me it was really true, that they'd heard it from gardeners and business owners. There would be unspecified work on the tunnel and the beautiful old bridge over it.

This part of the park was to be "renovated," fenced off for years. There were rumors that it could be fenced off in a couple of weeks, at the first of the year. ⏰ I cried. 💔 I was going on a trip and would return to find devastation. My friends would be gone, our paradise blocked off behind more clipped-together sections of silver chain link fence. They said even McDonald's was going to be torn down.

Postscript: they were at least partly wrong. They restored the 1889 bridge, and the pond is still intact over a year later. But rumors always swirl about changes threatening to be made in the park or on the Haight. Changes often lead to more restrictions. They were right about the McDonald's closing.

Tony and Cory and I were sitting on the stairs, next to another fenced-off portion that has signs reading "Area Closed for Renovations." It has pieces of silver chain link fence clipped together at odd angles around it. It looks like the barricade was put up hastily, temporarily, but it's been there for years. I was told that they did this to keep people from camping or urinating there. No "renovations" have taken place.

The part that's fenced off is one of the most beautiful places in the park. Although it's close to the street and also to the busy byway through the park, it seems strangely secluded, like a sacred spot. There are big oaks with curved, sun-dappled big thick trunks, soft grasses, and flowering bushes waving in the breeze. Two giant Eucalyptus are taller than anything anywhere around, the sun brilliant on their white trunks and on their branches reaching toward the sky.

I've always felt angry seeing the signs on the fence reading "No Trespassing – Trespassers Will be Prosecuted," but on this day I felt particularly resentful. It's these big companies that are trespassing on everything that's human or normal as they make money tearing down and rebuilding. It is investors who have no appreciation for this place and what it stands for.

Machines have fenced off Paradise and we can only peer at it through financial and theological fences. It seems to illustrate how Heaven is locked away from us in so many ways. The hippies sit on dirt embankments along the fence and lean against it. Someone punched a hole in the fence. Sometimes they let their dogs in there.

Soon afterwards the "renovation" would take place. The whole area would be bulldozed, the bare ground razed clean of vegetation. The most noticeable feature would become rows of wooden railings meant to keep people from sitting on the ground in the park. The logs we sat on would all be removed, and even the cement ledge people used to sit on across the pond. The vintage concrete bench at the Rainbow Stairs would be hacked off with jackhammers. The benches and tables of the "parklet" in front of Haight Grocery would be ripped out and hauled away.

In the beautiful place beyond the chain link fence, they would cut down several big trees. There would be no more mysterious shady places and grottos. What they would put under the few remaining trees seems the most violent of all. In an obvious strategy of hostile architecture, any place where people might sit in the shade under those trees would be completely covered with a layer of big rocks. Liability laws and gentrification would obliterate anyplace people might sit or gather and talk about their vanishing liberties. In another beautiful spot, a huge bush with gorgeous blue flowers was cut down, and two giant trees.

Cory and Tony told me about the renovations in the Horseshoe area in 1993, which used to be "a lot more wooded." They told me about the many bushes that used to be there, big 10x10 areas covered with bushes where people used to hollow out spaces and camp inside them. Then authorities shut down the bathroom in the area, and Food Not Bombs got arrested for feeding the homeless. Then the bulldozers moved in.

Pretty Tony said, "We're dirty kids. We adapt and survive."

Cory said, "WE'RE THE WARDENS OF THE HEART OF HIPPIE."

CHRISTMAS EVE

Late on Christmas Eve, after attending family gatherings, I went out to the Haight to be with my "street family." It was great to see that over a dozen people were clustered near a street corner. They were laughing and talking and making music. I pulled out my tambourine and danced with them. There were no special Christmas decorations on Haight Street, but the usual pink, green and magenta lights were all lit up.

I met Elecia, a beautiful girl wearing a long, flowered skirt and a rainbow beaded necklace. Her dark hair was in tiny braids, some of which fell over her face, which had mystic symbols painted with henna. She looked ancient and cosmic and wise. She said the Haight is "a God pocket of ascension." ↑ ↑

A car pulled up across the street and about three people got out and started carrying over bagful after bagful of individual prepared meals. The bags were the kind you get at fancy department stores, with little rolled handles. Best of all there were what must've been a dozen chocolate-pecan pies, boxed from a bakery. Everybody that wanted one got one. This would make a nice Christmas surprise for their tentmates.

The feeling in the group was very high, even on this dingy sidewalk on this not-so-warm night. People hugged each other and wished each other a merry Christmas. Three (very masculine) men put their arms around each others' shoulders and kept saying, "I love you bro!" Other people joined them and pretty soon there was a big knot of people on the street corner in a group hug, all telling each other that they loved each other. It may be an example of what Jesus had in mind when He said, "By this shall all men know that ye are my disciples, that ye have love one for another."

It was past eleven o'clock, so it was legal to sit on the sidewalk, so it was scary when the red, blue, and yellow lights of police approached and pulled up. Were they ordered to crack down on people for smoking or drinking or sleeping? There was alcohol there, but people didn't seem drunk. There was no reason for police to interfere. Two police officers got out of the cruiser. Were they going to arrest people?

I was already across the street, having made a quick exit as soon as I'd seen the lights. I go where angels fear to tread but I know when to get out of Dodge. Myself and several others peered from around a corner to see what would happen. Was there someone they were looking for? Would anyone go away in handcuffs?

Nobody was getting arrested and from this vantage point behind the corner, the body language of both parties seemed downright friendly. Finally, the police officers got back in the car and glided off, their flashing colored lights still illuminating the people and the Victorian row houses. I went over there to find out what had happened and got a big surprise. It turns out the cops had just stopped by to wish them a merry Christmas!

I was told a story about "The Stealie Cops," a pair of police officers who'd been transferred because they were too nice to the kids. One of them had actually worn a Deadhead sticker on his gun. The stylized "Lightning Skull" on Grateful Dead paraphernalia has a name, "Stealie," which is short for "Steal Your Face," the name of one of their albums.

The party continued but when it got too cold, Elecia and I sought refuge in the cab of my truck. We talked for a long time about spiritual stuff. She seemed like an old soul, was hungry for God. While we talked, we enjoyed the cake-like chocolate-pecan pie with no plates or utensils. It was so delicious we almost ate the whole thing. This was better than any pie I'd ever had at any Christmas party. Each mouthful had a gritty sugary feel, with finely-ground pecans and just the right amount of chocolate. The only thing that stopped me from eating more was the fear of making myself sick.

When it got late Elecia said goodnight and went out into the cold night. As she walked off toward the dark trees and bushes of Buena Vista Park, she seemed sublimely unconcerned about sleeping there on the ground in only a sleeping bag. She waved back at me with a happy smile.

"A free people claim their rights as derived from the laws of nature, and not as the gift of their chief magistrate." Thomas Jefferson

THE FIRE DANCER

The night of Christmas day it was pouring, and lots of people were at McDonald's. There was a little bit of a party atmosphere, though the house-free don't regard this as their favorite kind of weather. As usual they were making the best of it, happy just to be indoors until they would have to go out and find a place to sleep out there. A man named Al sat in a corner booth and played the guitar and sang beautifully. He knew so many pretty songs. The canned music that's usually on at McDonald's had been turned off. The food workers were letting the house-free stay longer than they were supposed to, and they weren't busting them for a few dogs hidden under tables.

Elecia was there. She'd lost most of her belongings earlier that day, when a friend who'd been watching her stuff had left it unattended. The beautiful flowered skirt was gone, and her sleeping bag and her ukulele. Typically, she was not upset about it.

Scott was there in his beautiful eighteenth-century velvet clothes, but with no shoes. He said he threw them away because they got wet and he couldn't carry them. I couldn't stand the thought that the gorgeous works of art he was wearing, and his two-hundred-dollar leather top hat with the roses on it, would get wet and ruined. So I got him a tarp that was in my truck (he had no blanket or sleeping bag), and also a disposable raincoat I had. Elecia actually gave him the shoes she was wearing. As she went off barefoot into the freezing rain, she said they didn't fit that well anyway.

On the last day before a trip I had to go on for a few weeks, I found it hard to leave the Haight. I needed to drive home before the fog hit, but found myself going one more block, then one more... On a corner there was a group of young house-free gathered, standing of course. They were just buzzing with talk about all the injustices in the world, but not their own privations. A young man said, distressed, "Some kid died to make the shoes I'm wearing."

Three dogs cavorted on top of my feet as I stood around in the cold wind listening to these amazing words. These people take the Golden Rule very seriously. It's not that they hope for a heavenly reward for being kind, or fear retribution if they're not. They are kind and care about other people because it feels good, because they can't help it. It's like it says, that "the law of God will be written in their hearts." Who would guess that these homeless on the corner could have a miraculous outlook? Soaking up the hope these people were giving me, it was hard to pull away.

I met Tia, who has short, neat turquoise dreadlocks. She's passionate and knowledgeable about politics. She has a luminescent silver Pitbull that's officially a "blue dog" because of the type of blue-grey fur he has. He wears a dog coat of blue and white Nordic designs, complete with a hood with a border that looks like fur. It looks really cool with his red harness and leash. He also wears an expensive-looking black leather collar with pink stitching, studded with white and pink large flat rhinestones. He has white paws and a white star design on his forehead.

From her backpack Tia took out what looked like a dog toy, a tennis ball on a string. She threw it a couple of times and the dog brought it back, but then they stopped playing. She started doing this incredible dance, twirling and spinning the tennis ball on the string. It was beautiful and graceful, a spontaneous free performance there on the Haight Street sidewalk. With amazing skill, she moved powerfully as she spun the tennis ball up and down and in every direction. It turns out she's a fire spinner and knows how to dance gracefully in the same way with dangerous flaming orbs. That might come in handy in the kind of world we live in.

JOSHUA TREE

The desert seems to have a special energy here between two earthquake faults. Peace drums are heard through ancient canyons filled with big Joshua trees. Their rhythms echo against the jagged hills, huge shelves of stone pushed up by a tremendous force eons ago. In this arid place things grow and bloom, with a resilience the drummers borrow. In the distance coyotes howl and sing with the drums.

Something happens here in the desert, where artists, writers and mystics reside. The place is full of art galleries and bookstores. The energetic search for truth and meaning is on the faces of their patrons, who dress in beautiful imported flowing clothes and other artful creations. They have poetry readings, political meetings, and frequent drum circles, which I attended often during my months there.

The reason I went there in the first place was to visit my friend Art Kunkin, the founder of the famous Los Angeles Free Press  (see next section). But the place and its charms, and the friends I met there, and wanting to help my fiend Art, enticed me to stay much longer than I'd planned. There is the weekly vegetarian potluck and drum session put on by Sunny and Deborah at the Beatnik Lounge, full of smart people with ideas about saving the world. Food Not Bombs also meets there, putting on a giant potluck once a month, also with drums and music.

I was invited to several remote places where drummers who are landowners have made inspiring areas where people can gather. Because of the tremendous heat of the day, events are usually in the evening. Powerful drum sessions take place there under the starry desert sky. The drummers drive many miles to get to them. Mikey has one in Sky Valley with a big lit-up heart on the gate to his place, which is called "Lovelight Ranch."   Abbie has get-togethers in her artfully decorated yard in Morongo Valley.   She put on a great party I attended with drumming, tons of homemade macaroni and cheese and delicious salad, and of course the honored guest, Arthur Kunkin. Danielle and her husband have amazing Bluegrass musician friends who come play music at their home once a month.

Economically, most people I've met here are not like the hippies I'm used to on Haight, though they express similar beliefs about peace and brotherhood. Most of them are college educated, own property, and wear gorgeous expensive hippie clothes hand-made and sold in local boutiques. Their cars are newer models, not beat up. Yet they have the same heart,

the same hopes, as the "house-free" out there on the streets.

Dee and her husband have created an amazing space where I heard the most serious Peace Drums. Amid swirls of white Christmas tree lights and flowing sparkly banners, a fire dancer and a girl dancing with glow-in-the-dark hoops made a spectacular display. The drums were wild and free, demanding liberty for all, expressing love for all. Beautiful Dee with eternal wisdom talked to me like an angel, as if she knew me.

Her sons had built a structure with only three walls and a roof, so that it's open on one side. Inside on a long wooden table there were two casseroles, one with meat and one without, and wine and fruit and cheese, all organic of course. The aroma of nature's most renewable resource was in the air. We seemed situated in a kind of elevated valley surrounded all the way around by volcanic hills. It felt like a dynamic power spot, where primal energies might help the drummers heal the world.

"It is well that the people of the nation do not understand our banking and monetary system, for if they did, I believe there would be a revolution tomorrow morning." Henry Ford

A RENAISSANCE MAN

The desert is a place where sages and philosophers like to hang out. Accordingly, that's where I visited my long-time friend Arthur Kunkin. He was the founder of the famous Los Angeles Free Press, which was the first independent alternative newspaper to come out in the Sixties, and the inspiration for the hundreds that came after it.

He's been personal friends with dozens if not hundreds of famous people. He was mentioned in Ken Kesey's book, "The Electric Kool-Aid Acid Test." He took acid with Timothy Leary, and the beat poet Allan Ginsburg used to crash on his couch. I also crashed on Arthur's couch at about the same time in the Seventies, probably the same couch.

More recently he studied the JFK assassination, living forever, Tibetan Buddhism, Alchemy, and "Mental Physics." He was a sought-after lecturer and his articles on deep spiritual knowledge are still published in many journals. He was incredibly active for someone ninety years old. It was no surprise that he was living in a spiritual community in the desert, where for eighteen years he'd been invited to live for free in a mobile home on the grounds. At one time he even ran the place, called the Institute of Mental Physics.

Walking into his home I was amazed by all the books. A lifetime of learning, of striving for truth and meaning, were on hundreds of shelves lining every available bit of wall. Shelves sagged with double rows of books on dozens of bookcases. Every corner and crevice of his home (and outbuildings) had stacks of books, some up to the ceiling. And these books looked like they'd been read. Pulling one out at random I'd find notes and thoughts he'd put down in the margins. Dozens of three-ring binders were each full of the transcripts of lectures he'd given on scholarly spiritual subjects. Whatever bit of wall space was left was taken up by framed public service and journalism awards.

There were also exotic statues from Tibet and other parts of the world, including an almost life-sized golden Buddha in a lotus position in the living room. 🧘 Moving books out of the way we sat on velvet wing chairs and talked about the thing he's most loved and remembered for, as an icon of the Sixties. From the beatnik era to the present, he knew the greats, was at key places at key moments. His role as a pioneering alternative journalist gave him entry into all the holy places of the Movement. 📓 = ⋛ 🔑 ⋚

He pulled out a large, worn black carrying case, the kind artists use to transport drawings or paintings. In it were the laminated copies of the front and back pages of each Free Press. The very first one had come out in May of 1964. There was a picture of the young Arthur, barely more than a teen, in his signature glasses and bushy hair that made him look like a turn-of-the-century revolutionary. He said he'd started the paper with only fifteen dollars. 👛 $15. → ⋛ 📰 ⋚

In the laminated pages I saw black and white pictures of a youthful Bob Dylan and Joan Baez, and their interviews with him. His paper was known for the unexpected and the brashly honest. He pulled out one of the front pages. "I got sued for twenty million dollars for this one," he mused. It was when he'd published all the names, addresses and phone numbers of all the undercover narcotics agents in the Los Angeles area. Three times his newspaper office was bombed, and he still doesn't know who did it. Two of the times the bomb actually went off and blew off the back door to the Free Press office. Another time, he stamped out three sticks of dynamite on the driveway. 💣 🧨 🧨 🧨

We walked in the desert at night in the light of a full moon, feeling a timeless connection with the Earth and all its people. It's not that I agreed with him on everything or shared all his interests that got me to drive over a hundred miles to see him. It's that he was one of those people who've

touched the pulse of history, maybe even influenced it some.
I'd like to be in that club.

    I stayed long enough to clean up his office, his house, his yard, and a junk-filled back house that someone could live in and care for him. A good friend of mine named Amy took care of him tenderly until he died peacefully in his bed about a year later, at the age of ninety-two. The church in Echo Park where they had his memorial was packed with some of the great social thinkers of our time.

THE RETURN

    Having been absent from San Francisco for six months I was impatient as I drove to the Haight. Anxiously I waited at each red light along Lincoln, heart pounding with anticipation. I negotiated the complex turns to reach the area, the only one like it in the world. When I'd left there, the kids had said to me, "Come back to us. The family needs you."
I couldn't wait to set my eyes on them.

    When I came back, everything had changed. Driving down Haight Street I noticed right away that there were not many nomads. The excited groups of youth that had stood at every corner were just not there. Was it because it was still cold outside? These seasonal travelers would know through their own grapevine that bitter winds still blew through the area. It was still only the first day of the "San Francisco Summer," September and October. Maybe when the weather got warmer my friends would show up. I could only spot a couple of the people I'd known before.

    The McDonald's had been closed as predicted and was all fenced off, including the parking lot. In the park I already knew that the log where the gypsy kings had sat had been removed, but to my horror I found that part of the area around the pond had been blocked off with a chain link fence. My heart hurt to see it. Even the Common Thread show at Mutiny Radio had now been cut back during my short absence, being on the air only two Fridays a month. 🎤

In what later became a routine, I drove up and down the length of Haight Street several times before deciding where to try to park. I wanted to scout out where there might be groups of youth, if any. I passed by slowly, searching the sidewalks and also peering down the side streets. 🔍 I saw only a couple of hippies almost all the way down Haight. Where there had been vibrant tableaus of the stuff dreams are made of, now there were empty streets except for a few housies and tourists who didn't look at each other as they passed. 💔

It was only at the intersection of Haight and Ashbury that things looked almost normal. A few people (instead of the normal dozen) were gathered on a corner, with the usual animated talk with background sounds of a guitar. Liberty was in the air. There were even a couple of dogs. I started to feel at home. I ached to join them but couldn't find parking. 🎼🚶🎸🐕🎼

What was left of the community had gravitated toward the east end of Haight Street, where they hoped there might be less police action. This was not always the case. This park is at the other end of the Haight business district from Golden Gate Park and the old McDonald's, about a half a mile away from them. It's named Buena Vista because it's on a small mountain, at the top of which are beautiful views. People camp on its slopes hoping to get way from the authorities. At least here there are no cameras yet. There are no bathrooms. The closest one is at the Chevron Station about five long blocks away.

🚫🚽 👣 → 👣 → ♿ → 👣 → 👣 → ⛽

At the corner entrance to this park is a beautiful façade flanked by two purple and turquoise pillars with curved stairs in between, each step a pastel color of the rainbow. All along the top there's an inviting-looking curved concrete bench where normally gypsies, vagabonds and holy men like to hold court. It's obvious that at some point these bright colors were painted by hippies. The stairs sparkle in the sun with some sort of glitter imbedded in the concrete. Bushes with purple flowers are in the two turquoise planters on either side. During the short time I was there, two groups of tourists stopped by to pose and take pictures there.

Strangely, there were no young people there either. At last I saw a group of people sitting on the grass on the side of the hill. By some miracle there was a parking space right in front. I almost ran up the rainbow steps.

NO LOITERING

This round of sparring with the Beast began just before I left San Francisco after New Years'. Officials told the longhairs they couldn't sit on the logs in the park because the logs were landscaping and not meant to be sat on, though people had been sitting on them for decades everywhere they lined the pathways. The kids got tickets for sitting on logs. One of the logs was actually removed where there had been a favorite gathering place.

Before that, there were all the new "NO TRESSPASSING" signs in all the shop doorways so that the poor couldn't sleep there when they needed to get out of the rain. And long ago there had been the time when they'd closed the bathroom on this side of the park, stopped "Food Not Bombs" from feeding the homeless, and had torn out some bushes there where youth used to camp in the years after the Summer of Love.

The nomads in the group on the hill were welcoming but none of them knew me from before. My brilliant pink and white flowing tie-dye was enough to make me welcome. They told me how the kids had been getting hassled, getting tickets for sitting, panhandling, camping, drinking, smoking. They said that some people they knew got two tickets the day before. They guessed that the crackdown was happening because somebody had been stabbed a year ago at the Horseshoe.

There was a pretty young woman named Brie sitting on the grass with her dog. She has a great dog, a white pit with velvety ears. When I read her something I wrote about the scene that used to be here and what it means, she cried. She told me that the reason nobody hangs out any more near the Horseshoe is because five security cameras are now installed where hippies used to congregate at the edge of the park.

She pointed to a new "NO LOITERING" sign attached to a lamppost directly above the rainbow stairs. The sign is meant only for street hippies. Most people don't even notice it as it's positioned high above eye level on the lamppost. But the hippies know it's there because they've gotten tickets for it. It's all right for tourists to rest on the bench so they can then go and spend more money in the pricey shops and restaurants, but not for young people to sit there and visit and make music, like they have in that spot for half a century since the Summer of Love.

The next day I ran into Brie on Haight Street. She was agitated and in a hurry. She said she'd gotten an "Order to Appear" about her dog, which wasn't licensed in San Francisco. She was surprised to get in trouble for this, because she and the dog came from an area where it's not required. She said this wouldn't have happened except for her big mouth. The police officers had come over because another dog was barking. She'd said something challenging one of them, and that's when he'd noticed that her dog had no tag.

He was mad that she'd talked back, and he'd retaliated. He told her that he would take her dog if he saw her or her dog again in the park or on the street. The white bulldog is a pet she brought from home and that she's had for years. She said it's really too bad that this has happened, because her boyfriend has just been offered a job and now, they can't stay.

MISSING MC DONALD'S

As I neared Stanyan I knew there would be something there that it would hurt me to see. I'd already known that the McDonalds would be closed-down but seeing it starkly behind a six-foot chain-link fence was shocking. The fence is the same clipped-together kind that they use to block off parts of the park, to fence off Paradise so hippies can't camp or sit there. The big windows are brown and dark without their lights and garish advertisements. Some are boarded up with plywood.

The fence goes all the way around the whole area, blocking off the whole parking lot, the back patio where homeless used to congregate, the front steps where hippies used to be on display for tourists. The loss of the parking lot alone is a huge issue in this place where finding parking is such a struggle. This used to be where you could park for a while and sit in the car or go get something to eat inside the restaurant if you couldn't find parking. It was where I'd been able to stay on Mondays between when the meters began on Haight at 9 am and when the street cleaning stopped on Oak at 10 am.

The loss of the toilets at McDonald's, and of a warm place to go at night and get cheap hot food, is catastrophic. ❌ 🚽 When it rains the street people will have no place to go. The sweet social scene that flourished there is gone. ❌ 🤝 I remember the time a man played beautiful guitar music in a corner after the restaurant had turned off the canned music for the night. ❌ 🎸   That was the night of last Christmas Day, a rainy night with lots of young people crowded into McDonald's and a couple of damp dogs hidden under the tables. It was the night when a homeless young woman had given away her only shoes to an old man who didn't have any, and then had gone out barefoot into the cold and rain. ❄ 👣 🌧   She'd reasoned, "They didn't fit me that well anyway."

So many things have changed. To make matters worse, after the closure of McDonald's, people can no longer use the toilets for free at Whole Foods. First, they have to buy something and get a receipt, and then they have to go to a separate desk to get a code. Then to enter they have to scan the receipt under a machine that doesn't always work. The special lights in the bathrooms that made the cobalt blue tiles and stainless-steel glow have been changed. There's no magic feeling in there anymore, even if you can get through the gauntlet of requirements to get in. Even the rainbow spirals that were painted on the wall of the entryway are gone.   The hot food counter has gone from a wildly expensive nine dollars a pound to an even more wildly expensive ten dollars a pound. My favorite dollar cookie is no longer being sold, the only affordable snack in the building. ❌ 🍪

Sometimes I walk sadly past the fenced-off McDonald's. It seems like an archeological site with its "NO TRESPASSING" signs and plywood barricades. You can try to imagine the people who used to be there, how they looked and what they said, the way you would imagine some culture in the mythic past by looking at their traces. But this was all here just a few months ago in all its glory. These are people I knew, not from long ago or far away. I loved them, was loved by them. I had painted a literary portrait of them which they seemed to feel showed who they were. The affection they gave me for it was something I fed on. It was a moment in time... How grateful I am to have preserved it and documented it in this book. ≷ 📖 ≶

281

But I want to make an important point: The Haight scene may be waning *for the moment* but what it represents remains as strong as ever.

Things that are natural and full of life have a way of surviving obstacles. The idea that people can live in peace and be happy is no small notion. A less brutish planet, where people don't starve or get put in cages, is mankind's dream. That millions of us still hold that dream is something of great value.

THE EYE

It clicks your picture if you roll through stop signs

      but that's not all that it can do.

With biometrics it could recognize, potentially, every person on Earth.

      Our body shapes are like a fingerprint that cameras can pick up.

Added to this, computer info can tell everything we've ever done,

      from health and work records to what we buy with grocery cards.

Software devices in our cars and phones

      can track our every move from outer space.

Camera-seller lobbyists want to install in alleys cameras that shout at you

      to make sure no-one dumps a bag of trash or an old couch.

It yells at you with a loud voice when an illegal act is seen, startling people out of their wits.

It warns suspects to get away but films them and their license plate

      so they can later confiscate their car or charge them with a crime.

The victims of this scam, always the poor,

      have a much better chance where muggers roam the streets.

The people see it on the news and they whisper among themselves.

      They are afraid the thing might hear inside their homes.

What if it sees into their yards, adjacent to where alleys are?

      What if it gets a new technology that sees through walls?

Behind what walls they find the people talk about the change.

      A year ago, they never feared to walk outside like they do now.

Since time began, we could find privacy in wilderness or in our homes

      but this is being thrown away so camera-makers can make bucks.

Now we'll have even more reason to stay inside, unseen,

      or is it true computers look at you, not only you at them?

Folks exchange rumors and half-truths,

      confused as to which are real news items and which are not.

Between saving the children and insurance law, there's not one inch

      of earth that shouldn't be beneath the camera's gaze.

That's surely what Spycams R'Us believes,

    and several thousand well-paid lawmakers do too.

Even in bathrooms we don't know if high-tech moralists

    might spy to save the kids from pervs.

At work of course the monitoring is just routine,

    to make sure we don't tell a joke or sneak a smoke.

It is a mandate of the insurers,

    who want to record everything in case sexual harassment suits are filed.

Recordings are not there to see if anyone gets hurt,

    but to help underwriters wiggle out of any claims.

For this we have to live in goldfish bowls,

    an easy prey for corporate predators trying to lock us up.

We know it's not the violent criminals they want,

    but normal people doing normal things.   🏚 = $

It's so much easier to prove a urine test than to solve violent crimes,

    with spy cameras to catch smokers and drinkers in their yards.

The prison-builders and surveillance-sellers go together to the bank,

while people learn to stay indoors, away from the gaze of the eye.

HISTORY'S WONDERS

How quickly something we value can vanish when the corporate Beast sets its sights on it. A sort of cultural genocide is taking place here and in other places because of real estate deals and goals. The highlights of communities and cultures are being shaved off in favor of "cookie cutter," profit-driven gentrification. Our liberties are leaking through a sieve of legalities.

If totalitarianism takes hold, what will the people of the future think of us if their freedoms are gone and their planet's a mess? Will they even believe that the Summer of Love and the Bill of Rights were real? How will history explain to them that yes, those wonders did exist right here, but that business entities put a stop to them for financial self-interest. For me, the hippies' being kicked off of Haight Street makes all of humanity less free.

With a heavy heart I look down the almost-empty streets, scouring them for groups of youth. It reminds me of something. It makes me think about other people through all time who've lost their homes or communities. Maybe it's a stretch to compare this to farmers losing their farms, or indigenous people their ancestral lands, or foreclosures, but this sadness has some similar elements. We lose the familiar, connections with people, connections with the past.

The way of life that people come to the Haight to see is at the moment no longer much on display. Those making a pilgrimage here find mostly expensive shops and restaurants and the big wall murals of rock stars. There are seldom colorful characters in top hats asking them how their day was. There are few dogs wearing clever outfits with spiritual or political emblems. Life pulsated through this place and now sometimes it seems cold and lifeless.

On Haight Street at night there remained two guys playing music as they sat in their van with the side door open. This must be one of the few things not targeted by the new policies, as long as there's no panhandling. When they stopped playing, we discussed the situation.

One of them said that maybe part of the reason the kids left was because the guy who'd run the homeless job program had been replaced.

The other one shook his head. He told me that there had been raids and undercover sting operations at the park, on the Panhandle and on the Haight. People had been arrested for things they did under the new cameras. Three dogs had been shot. He said, "It'll take years for the kids to return. You know how fast something like that spreads across the country through their grapevine."

The vibrant community that was here is *at the moment* dispersed. However, these people are like the birds, ready to take flight at signs of hazard but also able to fly back in an instant. Like the plants and other living things, free-thinkers keep coming back no matter what kind of corporate weedkillers the powers that be apply to them. They return with power as if the very forces of life are within them.

A DREAM-LIKE FEELING

It was a beautiful day. I was happy to see that there were people at both logs and on the ledge. Just a couple, not nearly as many as before, but it was still a welcome sight. The few who were still there smoked boldly right in front of the new surveillance cameras. The cameras set up at the Horseshoe and the five around the pond were keeping the rest of the people away.

I met "Uncle" Justin, who spoke like an angel about having to hold onto what all this means. He finds things for free, like snacks and toiletries, and goes around giving them away. He said he was organizing a gathering of all of us here at the pond two Sundays from now, a kind of protest about how they've been treating the house-free. He claimed that six hundred people would show up. I told him I would be there. I went but there was no one there, not even him.

Shawna Lou (she's in "When God Is in the Picture") has dyed her hair purple and has started a serious art business. On Haight Street she sells canvasses to tourists of a kind of psychedelic art of flowing colors, made with some special technique that makes the colors appear in layers. She sets up a table on the sidewalk next to her parked van, on which her pictures are hung on display, most about a foot square. Her silky, medium-sized golden dog sits calmly under the table.

I bought one of her paintings for only twenty dollars, the one with sky blue and turquoise and silver and green swirls that gave me a good feeling and would match my room. I'd much rather have this from Haight Street for twenty bucks than some exotic trinket. She took a long time autographing the back and leaving a special message for me. After she leaves town, maybe to hop trains again, the painting will be a treasure in my life because of who and what she is.

The JanisTree is a tree near Hippie Hill where Janis Joplin used to like to play her guitar. During part of the year, it's bare of leaves and I used to wonder if it was still alive. But in the correct season it forcefully revives with an outburst of wide dark green leaves. I hope the movement for peace can do the same. As I walked by, I was motioned to join a group of regulars of the house-free sitting under it. They were discussing religion.

A cool guy with tiny braids in his beard claimed he was not a hippie. We discussed any differences between hippies and street people. I'm trying to blend the two: the virility and vitality of street kids with the mysticism and powerful Pacifism of hippies.

The Ice Cream kid (Tom) was there, "a Deadhead Jesus Freak." He was dressed beautifully, like a sleek bicycle rider in the latest catalogue gear. He'd been giving things away to people like he often did, toiletries and protein bars. Some Christian girls from the pancake breakfast came along, also giving things away with love.

Tony, who used to wear a hat with a patch of a sword crossed with a long-stemmed rose, was there on his spot under the Janis Tree painting and drawing. He sits there almost every day with his beautiful Husky-dog Abby, busy creating colorful patterns and symbols deep with meaning. It occurs to me that although some people would tag his lifestyle as unemployed and homeless, others might view it as a vision of what Paradise would look like. He's spending his time making art in gorgeous natural places, surrounded by friends and free from rent and debt. He's living like Jesus suggested, like the birds of the air and the lilies of the field, not worried about tomorrow.

He said he can't handle the way churches push the Jesus thing, because of the terrible things which churches have done. He said that he's all right with God even though he doesn't go to church. He said that he's righteous, and he quoted a Bible verse: "God takes care of a righteous man." He said, "We're all in this together. I'm thankful to be on this side of the ground."

As evening approached, I came to the pond and stood near it, as if to gain some comfort from it. It was deserted under the cameras. I tried to imagine that the people were still there. Traffic hurried by above on the stone bridge over the tunnel. I tried to get closer to the pond, become a part of it, by going out and sitting on an outcropping of land with water on three sides, where I could smell the water and feel the breezes moving over it. The rippling of the water sounded like drumbeats from the drum circle, as if from another dimension.

A dream-like feeling filled my brain as I gazed at the silver reflections on the water against the golden glow of the setting sun that landed on the banks of the pond that look like miniature cliffs. Two ducks travelled together around the pond happily. The tree on the little island with the fountain was all lit up golden with sunlight. I breathed in the scent of the water deeply, as if having to keep it in memory in case they ever change the pond.

BULLDOG AND SHORTSTACK

His smile is like the sunshine as he stands on the corner of Haight and Ashbury, greeting passerby and the people driving by. A real live hippie, on the hoof, untamed. Maybe it's because I was so glad to see him that he looked so wonderful, like a vision. There's something about him that's life-filled. The graceful reddish curls of his hair and beard catch the sun and seem to radiate under his rainbow-swirled top hat.

 He was not panhandling. He wears a rainbow tie-dyed eighteenth-century coat with no sleeves.  Under that is the usual tie-dyed t-shirt and some tie-dyed balloon pants from India. The long coat (or vest) has black velvet lapels with gorgeous antique-looking buttons. Each button has a green glass four-leaf-clover embedded in a metal Celtic border. To complete the outfit, he wears bright red tennis shoes. "Look up and down and all around!" he shouts to passerby with a laugh as he bounces around.

With him is a very strange-looking dog, a "Rhinoceros/Weiner," really a Lab/Weiner. The dog, named "Shortstack" and the color of pancakes, looked up at me with his weirdly large head, his thick body on short legs. The man, named "Bulldog," told me about how his $800. coat had been a gift from Sunny Powers who owns the Love on Haight tie-dye store. Someone had stolen the coat and he and a friend had tracked it down and brought it back. She'd given them the coat as a reward but said they had to share it. He'd bought the other guy out. He wore a heavy chain draped across his chest. I asked if it was a statement about the condition of mankind. He said yeah, but it's also for protection.

About four other people stood there with him, including a tall young man with a black top hat covered with concert pins. These few people and a mandolin, on the corner of Haight and Ashbury, were some of the precious holdouts in this latest round of battling with the Beast. In my mind a mythic fight is taking place between liberty and slavery, good and evil, the forces of life versus the forces of death. The dragon of corporate totalitarianism is being fought by these young "travelers" with their code of honor. They risk arrest daily for **REFUSING TO BOW DOWN TO UNFAIR POLICIES THAT TAKE AWAY THE HIGHLIGHTS OF OUR LIVES.**

I've heard that developers want to actually tear out and replace the sidewalks on Haight Street, where giants have walked and so many hopes and dreams still live. They might even mess up the pond with their plans to cover the area near it with concessions and concrete. I've been told that there used to be benches for people to sit on near the Horseshoe, but that they were taken out a few years back. The closest bathroom had been closed, and Food Not Bombs had been stopped from feeding the homeless.

Now people are saying they're going to actually take out the logs. What fine energy those logs must have absorbed, from all those people sitting on them all those years discussing how to fix the world. In another insult I learned that they plan to re-paint the Rainbow Stairs, the purple and turquoise pillars, brown.

We're holding onto this place with our fingernails. We need the hope that's still in the Sixties vision, the enthusiasm to find solutions, the undiluted teachings of the Prince of Peace about better ways to live with one another. We need Rainbow Stairs where tourists come and take pictures because it means something to them.

Someone said, "There's no way for us to survive here anymore."

The guy in the other top hat said, "We can't let it go!"

Bulldog said, "This has been going on for years. If some people leave, others will come. They can't keep us away."

The brotherly love and peace thing of the hippie movement is **A DREAM THAT WON'T DIE**. It's the Golden Rule that Jesus taught. It's the pursuit of happiness that Jefferson, Madison and others tried to put into the Constitution, trying to free mankind from bullies at last. That's why **WE CAN'T LET IT GO !**

THE RAINBOW WAY

As the beautiful October summer comes and the damp places dry out and the cold winds stop, a few more street kids are showing up. Again, little groups congregate on Haight Street. How grateful I am to see them, to hear their laughter and music. In the park there are a few people at the log, and also next to the bridge and across the pond. There are even a couple on the steps going up to Stanyan, where before there have always been about a dozen people. ☼

It's not the boisterous crowd that was there before, but maybe it'll build up again. The people smoke pot openly in front of the cameras. Maybe some of them are new and don't know about them yet, but I think most just don't care. They deeply resent being told they can't do this, which most of them consider to be a religious and political act. These cameras in the hippie capital of the world fly in the face of anything that could be called liberty.

I ran into Scott, who had again lost all his stuff. His face was dirty, and his grey curls matted, and he wore an ordinary windbreaker instead of his usual gorgeous eighteenth-century coat. The brocade pants and vest were still there, though rumpled and dark. Gone was the amazing leather top hat with two live red roses on it. He told me the story of how he'd lost it all this time, including a tent.

I didn't get whether he left his stuff somewhere and it was gone, or if the rangers or someone else took it. He told me that the bush he used to sleep under for years has been cut down. That's another way they try to keep people from camping in the park, by clearing away brush and also by installing or turning on sprinklers at odd hours. A couple of weeks later I saw him looking gorgeous like before, after he got his check. He was all showered and groomed from a stay in a motel, dressed again like a high-class gentleman from another time. Now he'd have to eat out of trash cans for a month, but he sure looked happy.

I met Sweet Pea, a nymph-like beautiful girl who was wearing a fluorescent orange and green long skirt. I saw the skirt glowing and her smiling at me from fifty yards away where she stood across the pond with a group near the tunnel. She gave me a tremendous hug and she talked like an angel. I had some ladies' clothes and other things to give away in my truck, so we walked over there to see if there was anything she could use.

The beaded and fur hat I gave her matched her golden-brown curls perfectly. There was a satchel she needed and a lightweight blanket, and a small bag of clothes. She took everything, saying "some of the other girls might want something." I said she could trade the clothes. She said "No, I'm not that kind." She insisted on giving the things away. She said, "It's the Rainbow Way."

FRESH AND NEW

That warm evening, I was happy to see several groups of young people on the Haight sidewalks. A girl and her boyfriend gave me some tremendous news which I totally didn't expect. They said the "No Sit and Lie law" had been repealed, that soon they could start sitting on the sidewalk during the day without getting tickets. Had the war on hippies really scored a point for our side?

On a corner of Cole and Haight a group of seven young people with four dogs invited me to hang out with them. I told them what the girl had said. It was exciting and could mean that the scene could return, even bigger than before. Could things really turn around that fast? I asked if the police had stopped ticketing them for sitting down. They said no, people had gotten tickets that morning.

Chance googled the law on his phone.  After a while he said the legislation hadn't passed yet, but that they were only trying to pass it. He said that even some police are in favor of repealing the No Sit an8d Lie Law because they feel that enforcing it is a waste of resources. I was shocked when Chance said he'd been getting two or three tickets a week for sitting down. It would be great if it was really repealed, though they could probably pass another one whenever they wanted.

There's another thing on the horizon that could potentially disturb the magic feeling that can happen here. One of the shopkeepers told me that they plan to tear up the sidewalks and the street for sure very soon, and that the project will take two years. The hippies might be allowed to sit on the sidewalks but there might be no sidewalks to sit on.

A girl said that there's another reason why she's sad the sidewalks are going to be torn out. They contain painted messages and artwork, and things like handprints or thumbprints or initials in the concrete, made by "family" who have passed away. They will be broken up under the giant machines. Huge bulldozers are already parked along the side streets, as monstrous as dinosaurs, ready to deliver a blow to things we hold holy.

Nevertheless we celebrated, if not the uncertain political situation then the sweet warm evening, enveloped again in that special vibration. Someone down the street played a guitar. A man with one leg danced on crutches. Green and pink and purple colored lights glowed from the trees. We talked about God and Man. One guy said, "That's a beautiful thing, love and compassion and our people to be one truth, one heart."

As I walked down Haight Street, I saw that the big red hearts on the sidewalk are so faded that they're barely visible. I thought it would be good if someone came along at night and re-painted them fresh and new. A few weeks later I met a young man who is actually doing that. He believes he's on a sacred mission.

PAINTED BROWN

The first thing I noticed as I walked toward the beautiful rainbow steps at the entrance to Buena Vista Park was that there were no people there. Absolutely no-one sat on the concrete bench or the grass under the new "NO LOITERING" sign. There were no dogs, no backpacks, no sound of guitars.

This is the second time I've come here and found no-one here. It has to be because the powers that be and liability laws are compelling authorities to chase the young people away, maybe threatening to take their dogs. They might be willing to lose their stuff or even go to jail, but not to let anything happen to their dogs.

These kids are not faint-hearted and are willing to risk tickets and fines, or even having their stuff confiscated, in order to exercise their precious LIBERTY to sit and gather here in this special spot on the rainbow stairs, in the hippie capital of the world. One girl traveler, Frankie, had said to me, "This is the only place I feel comfortable." When I'd told her they were planning to paint the structure brown, I noticed tears in her eyes.

As I stood there staring at the empty steps and bench, I felt like I was in a kind of time warp. It seemed like an energy had shifted. It took me a couple of minutes to understand what had changed. Looking down I realized with horror that there were no rainbow colors under my feet, no sparkles. They had been removed by the city with power hoses. The purple and turquoise pillars, the bench and curved concrete planters, had all been painted diarrhea brown. Seeing that the three red hearts on the sidewalk at the base of the stairs were also gone, I cried.

AN OUTPOURING OF THE SPIRIT

Tourists often came here to take pictures of themselves in front of the beautiful colors, which seemed to express for them some of the spiritual things this place represents. Some showed up with cameras, a man and his wife.    I was in an emotional state. I said to them, "Do you know what's missing here? HIPPIES!"

I told them the sad story of what's been happening here, how the young pacifists are being chased away from Haight Street, away from something that many people hold holy. I told them what a precious resource this movement for peace is, how valuable its values are to the world. I said that the country should be proud to have produced these young people who believe so deeply in liberty and universal brotherly love.

I've started attending city meetings to try to find out whose idea it was to paint the stairway brown and if there's any chance that the powers that be might let us re-paint it in rainbow colors again.

We could probably get the same artist who did the gorgeous artwork on the storefront of "Love on Haight." It would be a tourist attraction. We could also lobby the city to replace the sidewalk hearts with permanent hearts of the same size and shape, imbedded in the concrete in the new sidewalks they plan to install. It would be "The Haight Street Walk of Love." Could a miraculous movement like the 60's, an outpouring of the spirit for peace and to reform the laws, start again if we re-paint the stairway and replace the sidewalk hearts? I'd like to try to find out.

LOVE ON OUR SIDE

The rainbow stairs at the entrance to Buena Vista Park have been stripped of color and painted an ugly shade of brown. Though this happened only a few weeks ago, the icon already seems like a far-off dream. Somehow the sparkles, the bright colors, had made "the Sixties" still be with us. A few years back a tree in the planter above the bench was cut down so groups of youth wouldn't gather there. It had shaded and sheltered generations of hippies talking about how to fix the world.

People gathering there could potentially create risk for insurers, whose goal is to have zero risk in our lives and zero payouts. I'd like to see the liability compliance agreements of cities and businesses to see what they demand. That would probably be like getting to look at the Vatican's secret underground libraries.

I'm guessing that there must be some sort of confidentiality clause in the policies, because nobody seems willing to talk about the million restrictions put on us by overreaching liability laws. They just call it something else like "legal issues" or "safety" or "equality." Constitutional rights and basic common sense are put through the shredder when it comes to the Liability God.

I'm not blaming the police or even some of the lawmakers for the procedures and policies they're mandated to enforce. I'm blaming the liability laws themselves, most of them enacted before we were born. I'm blaming gentrification for profit, a lot of it by foreign investors, and generations of bad lawmaking tainted with the self-interest of big corporations.

In my mind the hippies' being chased away from their longtime spiritual home is part of a struggle between the forces of life in the people and the forces of death in mindless, heartless business interests. After the Beast gets done snacking on our liberties, I think it plans to herd us into slave-like encampments and cities while it continues to devastate the Earth. Corporate personhood creates a super-citizen with more power than any of us. Even the people who run it have little control over it. Legislating that a dead entity on paper is a human being, is a dangerous lie for all Americans.

It's hard not to think that cutting down trees, and painting the rainbow stairs brown, is a deliberate effort to get rid of the longhairs. At one time, back in the day, there were lots of bushes at the entrance to Golden Gate Park that were cut down when the area was "renovated" years ago. Hippies used to hollow out grottos in the bushes and camp there in what must've been a very magical space. A while back, authorities also removed picnic tables from an area next to the pond, which had been another gathering place for young travelers and pilgrims who come to see what this place is all about.

Now no-one sits on the brown-painted bench, even though there are no cameras (yet). At Golden Gate Park, as soon as liability mandated that the cameras be installed around the pond and the Horseshoe, the whole community that used to gather there instantly disappeared. Some of them came here. Now there are no people on this desecrated ground. The Rainbow Stairs feel like a church building that's been bought and turned into a business. Tourists don't come to take pictures of it anymore.

So many things changed while I went away for a few months and then returned. The tunnel was closed, and the pond was drained. I walked out onto its concrete bottom to the island where the frog fountain is.  People had stacked stones to make rock towers there in a wordless expression. I picked up a white stone and put it on top of one of the towers. Were they planning to tear out the pond to build a concession stand, as had been rumored?

On the other side of the tunnel, they dumped a pile of what looks like fertilizer on some logs where people used to sit. It all seems so deliberate. Now the tunnel is sometimes open again, but there's a big empty spot where trees and bushes had stood next to it.

I was happy when I saw that there was water in the pond. I wondered why the pond looked so different, not all sparkly like it usually did. The surface of the water was very still and rancid looking. It was because the frog fountain hadn't been turned on to make ripples in the water. They had not re-filled the pond and might not be planning to do it. The water was there only because it had rained. ✖ ⛲ ? It turns out that later they did re-fill the pond and turn on the frog fountain, and also removed the pile of dirt from the log people like to sit on. But we never know what's going to happen next. ✖ 🐸 ?

Along with the much-missed McDonald's, Tibetan City Gift has closed. Now it looks so small on the corner with its empty windows, without the packed array of antique-looking treasures that used to be displayed there. I'm very sad to hear that the renown Haight-Ashbury Free Clinic is closing. I so enjoyed the one time I went there, climbed the steep indoor stairway to the upper floors of the pretty Victorian house. The ancient rooms have domed ceilings and beautiful windows. The doctor and staff there made me so comfortable that I planned to change my residency to San Francisco so I could have this as my doctor's office.

Their web site says that the examination rooms used to be painted in Day-Glo colors. The founder, Doctor David Smith, started the clinic's motto: "Health care is a right, not a privilege." He said, "I had an LSD spiritual experience and a vision that denial of healthcare to one segment of the population is a denial to all. So, there was a transformation of me in that period, like what happened to so many young people."

It would've been gratifying and organic to me to have my doctor's office locally, right in the heart of where I like to be so I can walk there. People have walked up and down that old wooden stairway during and ever since the Summer of Love. Now this chance to touch history will be wiped out, possibly turned into investment property. One of the few things to remind us of the clinic's existence will be the little dog at the tie-dye store named "Dr. Dave" after the sainted founder.

Its small-town feel is something I've especially loved about Haight Street. This old-fashioned tree-lined street with its gorgeous Victorian buildings has been the stuff dreams are made of in more ways than one, in addition to being the hippie capital of the world. It's been still like the communities of old with everything close together. Like I said before, the Haight has grocery stores, a hardware store, a post office, a doctor's office, an art store that includes a fabric store, bookstores, a music store, a printer, and plenty of coffee houses, taverns, and restaurants.

Now the landmark Haight-Ashbury Free Clinic will be gone. The world-famous Haight-Ashbury Music Center, where rock star icons hung out, is closing. Will that mean less music on Haight? Will street musicians still get to gather under the awning there?

Scott now wears a thin windbreaker instead of a splendid period costume. Cosmic Charlie, who toured with the Grateful Dead, has died. His painted heart on the sidewalk, one of the few remaining hearts next to "Love on Haight" on the Masonic side, will be what we have left to remember him by if the city lets it stay. He'd asked me to tour with him, with the Grateful Dead, as his driver. I regretfully declined, scared to drive.

Developers also plan to tear out the historic sidewalks where giants have walked. Pilgrims who come here enjoy the fact that these are the same sidewalks. This is where the biggest peace movement the world has ever seen exploded onto the world stage. Before the media got hold of it, the "Love Generation" was about peace on earth, respect for all, and fair laws. It was about the liberty this country honors. It was about the Golden Rule.

It's another heartbreak that the big red hearts painted on the sidewalks will be gone. About two feet across and placed about every thirty feet on several blocks leading up to Haight and Ashbury, they are periodically re-painted in the dead of night by various unknown persons. Removing the hearts might seem like a small thing, but for a nomadic people with only a tenuous hold on their favorite sacred gathering place, it cuts deep.

It's hoped that when they tear out the sidewalks, that over a dozen hearts on the Masonic side of "Love on Haight" will be undisturbed. But the remnants of the hearts on Haight Street will be destroyed, and things like where Hightower, an artist named Lacie, wrote in beautiful script, "Dance Like No One's Watching," and "Expect Miracles Every Day!" The miraculous gum hearts on the sidewalk that Bear and I marveled about will also be gone. We thought the stains of old gum on the sidewalk were shaped like hearts and that it was a message from God.

I found Frankie, the girl who'd said the only place she felt comfortable was on the Rainbow Stairs. She was sitting on the sidewalk (risking a ticket) on the corner of Haight and Ashbury, leaning against the iconic street sign. She admitted that she'd teared up over the stairs being painted brown. The back of her sweatshirt said, "IT TAKES THE HAIGHT TO STOP THE HATE."

A young man named Zombie with a zombie tattoo on his arm said, like they all said with incredible spiritual understanding, "We're all the same." He said, "We'll last because we have love on our side."

SOMETHING DIFFERENT

At Haight and Ashbury I ran into Bear, the one who'd seen his friend die after trying to jump from one balcony to another. He'd been jailed after being arrested at Haight and Ashbury for warrants for unpaid tickets for sitting on the sidewalk. They cost up to five hundred dollars each for repeat offenders. I guess his ambition to turn his life around and become a paramedic is seriously delayed. While he was in that place someone tried to cheer him up. He told me they'd said to him, "Your goodness is incorruptible." It sounds to me like an angel was talking to him.

It really seems like something's trying to corrupt the goodness that's on Haight Street. With all the cameras and crackdowns, and letting bullies and thieves run wild among us, 👊 🏃 it can seem like a negative death force is trying to stop the life force that's in this place. It's not the fault of the police, who don't make the laws they have to enforce. I've heard so many stories about our brothers in blue helping people in spectacular ways, risking their jobs to bend the rules. 👮 ♡

Is it the fault of legislators and businesses who push for these "Quality of Life Crime" policies that make the homeless suffer so much? To a point. Most of the laws making possible or even mandating these policies, were put in place before they were born. We have to stop letting dead lawyers decide how we live, and ancient theologians with agendas,

and global corporations who want to rule the world.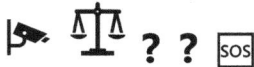

I feel that dark forces ♆ are trying to get rid of the hippies on Haight Street. Cameras were put up in the park, McDonald's was closed, the Rainbow Stairs were painted brown. A few people still hang out near the intersection of Haight and Ashbury, like survivors clinging to a raft. How hard would it be for the powers that be to send or bring the violent and the addicted here to make trouble? Call me paranoid if you like but could there be actual saboteurs commissioned to make the hippies look violent and dangerous? It's certainly happened before.

There was a discarded red vinyl armchair on one corner of Haight and Ashbury. It was late and the only person left there was BamBam, enthroned in the comfortable-looking chair, overlooking our spiritual domain. He looked happy and satisfied. 🪑 He always gives me a big hug. He has a surprisingly sweet smile for his fierce appearance and rustic costume. He invited me to sit in the chair. It was past midnight and there weren't many people left on the street, which seemed to have a special vibration. The famous intersection where we were, Haight and Ashbury, felt sacred. It felt like the center of the world.

We discussed some violence in the movement, how some people are kind of rough these days and don't call themselves hippies. I told him how I thought fighting weakens us, that the main thing we have that the world wants is peace. I told him I think we need both the virility and power of the nomads, combined with the pacifism of the hippies. We need all of us.

For a long time we sat silently, now almost the only ones out there as nighttime mists rolled in. BamBam wrote in a small leather book he had, an archaic-looking little volume with thick hemp pages sewn in, the kind of thing someone might've had and used hundreds of years ago. I still wonder what he was writing in that book that night, so carefully with such even lines.

At one point he wrote in my notebook a quote from his father: "If you always do what you have always done, then you will always get what you have always got. If you want something different, YOU MUST DO SOMETHING DIFFERENT."

LOVE WITHOUT LIMITS

I met Sassy and her little chihuahua dog sitting on the sidewalk on Haight Street (illegally), a container of colored chalks beside them. I found out that she also writes messages on the pavements, helping Hightower in this spiritual work inspiring the public. She'd just gotten done drawing a big lotus in pastels with a heart in the middle and the words PEACE, LOVE, JOY, and GRACE.

On the pavement in front of Frank's Liquor, Hightower wrote, "Don't Talk About It; Be About It. Do Something Today that Your Future Self Will Thank You For." I met Salvia, an intelligent and dynamic young woman whose other name is "Basket Case." I think the first name describes her better. The Bubble Man was there with his big bubble machine, filling Haight Street with thousands of luminescent bubbles that shone with rainbow lights.

Half Pint is a small elfin woman who looks like she's been on the street a long time. She has a boyfriend named Stumbles but he's as poor as she is. She used to be one of the most destitute on the street, but then something changed. One day I saw her with new clothes, jacket, new backpack and boots, which maybe some kindly housie had bought for her. Everything matched in army green and camouflage. I almost didn't recognize her. She looked like a picture in a fancy camping catalogue.

At the Haight Grocery Store I met Dallas, (not the one with the dog) a young man who gives his affection to strangers where he works at the hot food counter. He was so nice to me, treated me like an old friend. When I walked out of there, I felt energized. Even with the trees cut down, **THE LOVE ON HAIGHT IS STILL THERE.**
THEY CAN'T PAINT A GREEN X ON THAT. (See page 330.)

At the Club Deluxe jazz bar there is often live music. The managers there are so kind that they sometimes let Scott in his wheelchair panhandle in front of their store, even though he hassles customers. The band was playing a spirited old rock song and I couldn't resist going in there to dance. The place came alive as my tambourine ribbons were flung all around the room. Customers cheered and took pictures. These days I like to just make myself at home and start dancing anywhere there's live music. Even Mr. Brandy's piano in the van, or a street musician with an electric guitar and an amp, are enough to inspire a performance. I admit that I'm living a charmed life.

Heaven is so easy for me to find among the homeless on Haight Street. I keep hearing on the media about how dangerous street people are, disease-ridden, dirty. In fact, I feel the safest with these youth, who seem to be never sick and seldom dirty. The unsavory things they tell us about must be happening in other homeless communities, but not so much here on the Haight, a special place.

Most of the stories on the Internet about homeless camps are about people working together, forming instant communities. They quickly become friends and form alliances the way people have worked together since the beginning of time. We are a tribal animal. Getting along with those around us enhances our survival and may actually be wired into us. Could it be that this feeling of Heaven, of connection with others, happens among many of the homeless everywhere, not only on the Haight?

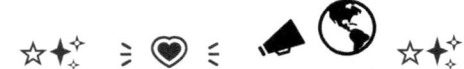

At the base of the Rainbow Stairs Hightower wrote in pastel chalks:

SEE MIRACLES EVERY DAY   KINDNESS   LOVE WITHOUT LIMITS

"THEY'RE NOT LETTING US BE GOOD"

The way a tree that has an illness can be attacked by insects, the Haight is experiencing some uncharacteristic events. Trees have natural protections to resist parasites and alien species, when they are healthy. But under abnormal conditions, when foreign matter runs through their branches or nourishment is depleted, trees can become helpless in the face of invasion. At the Haight we don't feel completely helpless yet from all the changes and the bad vibes that came with them, but we are baffled.

Bulldog "lost" his beautiful coat and his amazing top hat. He claims that he just spaced them somewhere, but in light of what happened later, I don't believe him. I think that some bullies took them away from him by force and threatened him not to tell anyone. I also learned later what threat they used. They threatened to hurt others if he didn't do what they wanted.

I was heavily invested in having him continue his performance at Haight and Ashbury. He was one of the main attractions tourists took pictures of. I happened to have a gorgeous blue tie-dyed top hat that I never wore because, though expensive, I didn't like the way it looked on me. I brought it to the Haight and gave it to him so he could do his job.

It fit him perfectly and he looked absolutely gorgeous in it with his red curls against the blue tie-dye.

At first, I saw him in it every time I passed the corner of Haight and Ashbury, but then one day the hat wasn't there. He told me he'd left it indoors because it looked like rain. But then the next time I saw him without it I assumed he'd either spaced it or been robbed of it. I tried to be polite and not ask what had happened to it. When I finally did find out the true story of why he wasn't wearing the hat, it completely blew my mind. Someone who knows him told me that he was threatened that if he wore that hat, "the whole community would pay."

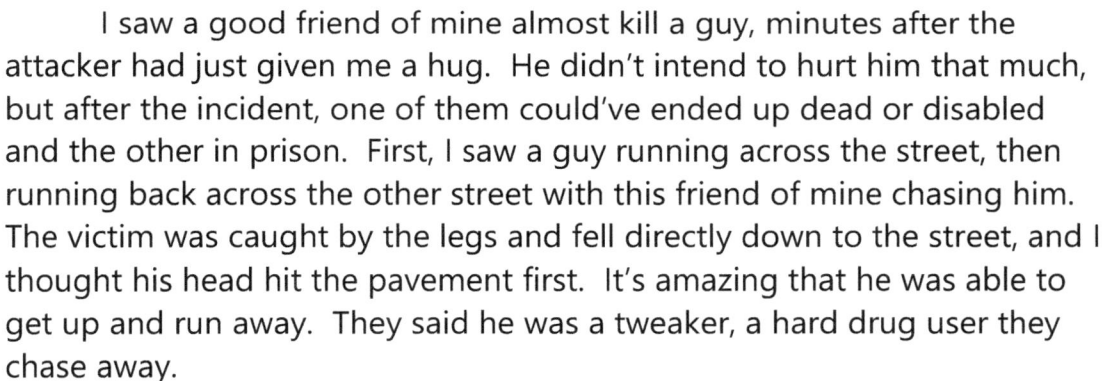

I saw a good friend of mine almost kill a guy, minutes after the attacker had just given me a hug. He didn't intend to hurt him that much, but after the incident, one of them could've ended up dead or disabled and the other in prison. First, I saw a guy running across the street, then running back across the other street with this friend of mine chasing him. The victim was caught by the legs and fell directly down to the street, and I thought his head hit the pavement first. It's amazing that he was able to get up and run away. They said he was a tweaker, a hard drug user they chase away.

In the confusion, Kage's white Pitbull was hit by a car and was stunned. Kage is a friend of Orange and Izzy. He folded his beautiful jacket of many colors to make a soft pillow for the dog while we all stood around them. The dog just lay on his side in a kind of stupor. After a while he was all right.

Then BamBam was arrested on that same intersection of Haight and Ashbury. He got into a fight after a housie, someone who lives in the apartments up above, shoved him and threw water on him. They've got him locked up for the duration because of past warrants for other things.

🏛 I wonder what happened to his dog Titus, strong as a lion, who'd served up a ram for his crew's dinner. I wonder if BamBam will ever get his little leather book back, and what was written in it.

I ran into Bulldog. He was upset because he just saw his friend put in handcuffs *for smoking pot on the corner of Haight and Ashbury!*

🚬 → ⛓ It was right under the big antique clock whose hands are always at four-twenty, which tradition says is the time to smoke pot. As I leaned on a trash can, I read to him what I'd written about how they'd painted the stairway brown and cut off the bench. (See page 321.)

It seems strange that all these incidents are happening at this same important intersection within so short a time. A guy was attacked and almost got his head cracked open, then BamBam was provoked and got himself in big trouble, and Bulldog's friend was arrested for something they normally do all the time.

A couple of blocks away is where the guy attacked thugs with a rock because they'd stolen his backpack with his brother's ashes in it. There had been blood on the sidewalk, so I knew he wasn't kidding when he'd told me. With his trembling hand he'd showed me the rock. He'd kept saying he was not a violent man.

If there is a center for the hippie nation, it's right here. The authorities have chased the young people out of the parks with cameras and tickets, and made laws saying that they can't sit down and have to stand up all day. They took away McDonald's at one end of Haight Street, and destroyed the Rainbow Stairs at the other end. Now the totalitarian Beast has its eye on the corner of Haight and Ashbury, our remaining stronghold. The people are bitter. They've lost their stuff too many times. One of them said, "They're not letting us be good."

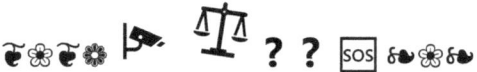

A TERRIBLE LOSS

In my late-night wanderings among the house-free I met a young man who'd gotten his backpack stolen the night before while he slept. His cell phone was in it with all his contacts, and much worse, an urn with his brother's ashes was in it. He was very upset, said he really needed a hug, which I gave him. He said that he and his buddy were sleeping about a block away, with his backpack placed carefully between them with his shoes on top. He woke up to see one shoe six feet away, his backpack gone.

He was furious, though he kept saying that he was ordinarily a peaceful man. He said his mother would be mad at him for losing his brother's ashes. His brother must've been young like him when he died, a terrible loss. I guessed that the container of ashes, which he'd brought with him on his dangerous and lonely journey, was all he had left of his brother. He'd risked bringing it probably because it made him feel closer to him.

He was outraged that someone could be looking at his family pictures on his cell phone, his young nieces and nephews. That's not where the story ends. He said he had tracked down the tweakers who'd taken it, finding one wearing the scarf he'd bought for his girlfriend. They had a large carrying case on rollers containing several other people's backpacks. Now he reached into his pocket and pulled out a round white rock about the size of a fist. Repeating that he wasn't a violent man, he said he'd hit one of the thieves on the head with it and had drawn blood and had gotten some of the things back but not the ashes.

Now he was guarding the other people's backpacks, asking people if they knew whose they were and if they'd seen a guy with blood all over his face. I looked at the carrying case on the sidewalk and a white plastic bag of stuff. They looked like someone had spilled red jelly on them. It didn't look like blood, more of a pinkish color against the white plastic bag. But he assured me it was blood. I realized that these events had happened more recently than I'd thought.

Later at home I thought about him. How sad for someone to come here, full of hope and dreams, to have their only possessions stolen while they slept. He felt so bad about having turned violent, kept saying he'd done it to protect the community from the thieves. I wanted to tell him that I thought what he'd done didn't make him into a bad person or "not a hippie." I wanted to tell him I didn't think God would be mad at him for fighting back when provoked to that extent, having lost his brother's ashes. I wished I'd given him another hug, which I'm sure he could've used.

MICROAGGRESSIONS

I hardly recognized him. Scott broke his leg and spent weeks in the hospital and is now in a wheelchair. He's not wearing a beautiful period costume and magnificent top hat with roses like before.  Most horrible, his long grey curls have been shaved off. He looked so wonderful before, the stuff that dreams are made of. Now he looks somewhat like an inmate at a concentration camp. Some kind souls at Club Deluxe let him park his wheelchair in front, even though he intimidates some of the customers.

He has no blanket. When I complained that his amazing hair was gone, he kept saying several times that cutting it had been necessary at the hospital. I don't see why that would've been the case for a leg injury. To make matters much worse, his backpack was stolen while he slept. I can't imagine what anyone could hope to gain by stealing a backpack from a penniless old man in a wheelchair, unless someone is being paid to steal backpacks in order to chase the house-free out. Then big investors can get control of the area and make money rebuilding everything. That's my private conspiracy theory. Later, Scott got his wheelchair stolen.

People are systematically getting their backpacks stolen while they sleep. This is devastating and destroys the trust in the community. Remember: each stolen backpack contains everything that person owns. Lost with it are treasures like family photos, diaries, cell phones with all their contacts, and in the case of the one young man, his brother's ashes.

Stealing a person's backpack while they sleep is a cowardly and easy crime to commit, with serious consequences for the victim. I wondered if someone could be sending thieves out here, as part of how the powers that be are trying to disrupt us. By the way, I've noticed that people with dogs don't get their backpacks stolen while they sleep.

I ran into Ryan, "the Professor" who'd discovered a new species of scorpion that scientists had named after him. At some point on some dangerous adventure, he'd lost everything. Gone are all his state-of-the-art equipment, his amazing tiny stove that could fit in your pocket, his super-comfortable incredibly light camp chair, his folding bicycle. In addition, he'd also been robbed of his backpack while sleeping. I found him quite upset but with a surprisingly resilient attitude. With his usual vitality, he seemed confident that he could replace these items very soon.

I saw Dragon, her leather jackets and violin long gone. The hair she'd dyed bright pink is growing out. For months she and her husband and their two dogs made their home on the sidewalk at this one spot on Masonic just off Haight. She was very uncomfortable and depressed. They tried desperately to find money to get to Colorado, where she said they had a trailer they could live in.

One weekend I was glad to see that they were gone, hoping that she was now finally warm and safe. She is not young or in perfect shape, though with tremendous stamina. A short while later I saw that they'd returned from Colorado and were back on Haight Street, staying on the Burger Urge corner of Clayton. "Why are you still here?" I asked her, knowing the hardships she'd gone through.

She said, "The same reason you're still here. It's my home." I am not a San Francisco native, and I don't know if she is or not. I understood that she meant the Haight is our spiritual home.

I was happy to see BamBam free again. He'd gotten locked up after a fight with a housie who threw water on him. His lion-like dog Titus, whose head is bigger than mine, was at his feet. (That guy who threw water on him is lucky to be still alive and not in the same condition as the ram Bambam's dog attacked previously in the woods.) Again, I got big welcoming hugs from someone who looks like he just stepped out of a time machine from the Bronze Age.

Conversations continued on Haight Street, in the usual forum of suggestions and enthusiasms about how to fix the world. A Native American young man told us about the sacred land where they used to gather pipestone to make peace pipes. He said that war was banned there, and that it was open to all tribes.

CAGES

Thousand-year prison sentences with ten life terms,
  and huge probations and million-dollar bails,
hair and saliva drug testing, cameras that know who you are,
 wait to entrap the inadvertent who don't even know they broke the law.
They are the easiest to catch and the least able to defend,
  as they commit under the camera's gaze
things normal people do, or that were not a crime a year ago,
  or that have never been a crime before.

People who wouldn't hurt a fly are just as valuable in prison gold
  as dangerous felons whose capture might involve risk,
or those guilty of violent crimes who might get off and sue the state,
  or whose conviction could be overturned on technicality.
"Drug crimes" are so easy to prove, or statutory crimes,
  in which the letter of the law not only kills but bludgeons Liberty.
Folks get life sentences for merely being where there was a crime,
  or for an accident they didn't intend.

To spy on people in their privacy the corporations have devised
    "smart dust," tiny machines smaller than coins that look like bugs.
They are designed to fly or crawl upon demand.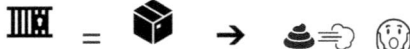
    They have computers, sensors, and microphones to report all.
So who needs horror flicks when surveillance-sellers make the laws?
    Supermax cages yawn to get us all and drive us mad with mind control.
Will we be inmates screaming and throwing feces at the wall?
    Could cops break down our door because some neighbor told a lie?

Built to Last

Weird legal terms that entrap the innocent,
    like "Implied Malice" or "Impaired Consent,"
"Indirect Criminal Contempt" and "Risk of Injury,"
    have turned to felons normal people doing their best.
Huge punishments are handed out, mostly to poor,
    for things that didn't hurt anyone or things that others did.
We're put in cages for our life for accidents that couldn't be helped,
    so insurers can shift the blame and not pay claims.

Backbreaking fines the Bill of Rights strictly forbade enslave the poor
    but not the rich, fined a much smaller portion of their goods.
To pay a fine, parents give up school clothes for kids and Christmas too.

In this harsh race, you can lose everything for one wrong move.
Cities "get tough" on peeing in public, sleeping on library steps.
  Without public toilets or shelters, homeless are inmates in a flash.
As lobbyists haggle to enrich the builders of cameras and jails
  our Liberty is bought and sold.

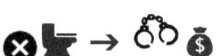      

Orwellian horrors that would make the Founders run
  have become part of daily life.
In the weird maze of lonely rooms where employees rest between jobs,
  then go outside again and shuffle on beneath the cameras' gaze,
we have no time for family life or to read books or make a friend.

  The tripled price of everything makes sure we don't look right or left.
We don't have time to cook and so submit to poison in fast food,
  no time to marry so instead we adopt pets.

The cry for brotherhood is seldom heard,
  unless you count the sound of the same sports from everywhere.
Instead of smiling at each other we've been taught to look away,
  in case our neighbor is a psychokiller or3 a pervert of some sort.

So then we sit between four walls and wonder why we feel alone.

The advertisers fill the gap with poisonous goods and thoughts.

Each pillow is wet with its separate tears in each small cell,

not different really from the cages in some prison blocks nearby.

LET'S TAKE ONE STEP TOGETHER: At the giant Rainbow Gatherings in the wilderness people yell "WE LOVE YOU!" repeatedly on one side of the camp and others answer back, "WE LOVE YOU TOO!" Let's do the same thing out our windows at sunset on Saturdays, so that the Voice of the People can be heard! We could also play drums for half an hour at sunset on Saturdays at a window. Visit with or meet neighbors!   WE NEED ALL OF US! (right + left)

Poems may be reprinted and shared by homeless for donations they can keep.
TELL TEN TO TELL TEN TO VOTE DEMOCRAT!   REGISTER 100 DEMOCRATS!
(https://www.usa.gov/register-to-vote)   (vote.gov) (rockthevote.org)
Democrats against forced mandates and other oppressive liability laws.
BILL OF RIGHTS   GOLDEN RULE   peacedrums.org   UNITE!

Democrat

LIABILITY GODS

Bulldog told me they want to cut down the beautiful tree on the clock corner of Haight and Ashbury. He asked me to try to save it with whatever influence I could get with the city. It's a very attractive tree, symmetrical and vibrantly healthy, without a thing wrong with it. The sidewalk around it is not buckling either. The tree isn't very close to where the new sidewalk will be. We've heard that they need to cut it down to accommodate the big machines that will be parked there.

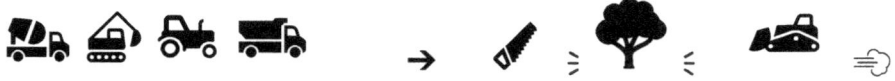

Even though there's not much need of shade in this cloudy city, the groups of youth who like to gather in that special spot, feel sheltered in the presence of that tree. Its trunk may not hide them much from the busy traffic a few feet away, but somehow they feel a little more private because of it. For people who live on the street, places like this are their living room. This is where they meet with their friends, have deep conversations, standing up of course, because of the "No Sit and Lie Law."

This makes me wonder: how many other trees are they planning to cut down? A fine tree in front of the bicycle shop was cut down recently. Walking by I noticed the starkly cut-off trunk. The flat top surface of it is a light color, not darkened by time, still oozing resin. I touched it and said, "I'm so sorry."

I asked the people who ran the bike shop about it, and they told me how unhappy they are that the tree's been cut down. They were told it had something to do with the power lines. Again, I wonder how many trees they're planning to cut down when the new sidewalks are put in. Is it possible that they could actually *remove the trees*?

What if liability issues require that they cut them down in case their roots eventually cause the new sidewalks to buckle and pose a risk of injury? I have to shut my mind off to the vision of Haight Street with no trees, with gentrified sidewalks like a mall. The night wouldn't be the same without the magenta and green and orange lights on the trees. The skateboarders wouldn't look as magical sailing down the street.

This is one of the finest-looking trees on the Haight, bigger and fuller than some of the ones with the lights on them that line the street. It's actually on Ashbury, about ten or more feet from the intersection. In that holy place where a peace movement was born, the nomads and pilgrims find shelter under its branches. For people who really care about trees, this is a very special tree.

The rootless young people so enjoy congregating under the graceful branches of the tree, where they feel a kind of home or comfort, or the achievement of a destination. They play music there, tell each other stories about their amazing and dangerous travels. Now chain saws are scheduled to slice the noble trunk against which so many have leaned. It's another assault on the holy things that this place, this intersection, stand for.

I called the Department of Urban Forestry and asked an official to save the tree. She said she'd see what she could do but didn't sound too hopeful. It was then that I learned the awful truth: *liability is causing Public Works to cut down almost every tree on Haight Street.* It's allegedly because they were planted forty years ago and that's their official lifespan. If the city knows that the trees are past their official lifespan and a branch falls on somebody, they could be faced with a lawsuit. For this reason, and not because there's really anything wrong with the trees, the magic and small-town feel of Haight Street is scheduled to be yet another idolatrous sacrifice on the altar of Liability Gods.

🌱✿🌱❀ 👯‍♀️😱👯‍♀️?? 🌷✿🌷

OLD SIDEWALKS

Cutting down the trees is supposed to be so they can install the gentrified new sidewalks that will stick out with "bulb-outs" into the street at every corner, taking away four precious parking spaces from each block. Losing all those spaces will hurt the shopkeepers, who will also have to deal with two years of construction. Where will their customers park and how will they get past the big machines and barricades? Will nomads and street musicians get to even stand on the new treeless sidewalks?

 = 🌸🌸🌸🌸

The very concrete of these sidewalks seems infused with special energy for us, where rock stars and political and spiritual greats have strolled. 🎩 🤸 It's cool to think that they stepped over the same curbs, and also to remember that huge crowds surged here, a representation of the whole world, during the Summer of Love. Somehow these old sidewalks, stained and bent as they might be, make us feel like the magic time of "the Sixties" is still with us. Walking there you can feel a connection to the high vibration of the Way of Peace and the Golden Rule. ⋛ 📏 ⋚

The idea that people are basically good is the meaning of the dozens of red painted hearts on Haight Street. They have been worn off and scrubbed off, but their message is still clear. Love is the answer, the simplest and only answer. If they rip out the sidewalks like they're planning to, those red hearts will be destroyed. So will dozens of mementos engraved there to remember friends who have passed away. Of course, the gum stains shaped like hearts, over which Bear and I pranced around and thought it was a miracle, will fall into powder under the jackhammers.

It's the kind of thing that big business has no understanding of. Like it says in the Old Testament, "My ways are not your ways and your ways are not my ways." The depth of meaning that's on this street and these old sidewalks, is something that big business entities have no time to notice in their mad rush for profit and power. The spiritual awakening on Haight Street is a gem so rare that it's hard for some to recognize its value. 💎

JACKHAMMERS

I couldn't believe it. I think my jaw literally dropped when they told me. The beautiful curved concrete bench at the top of the Rainbow Stairs at Buena Vista Park is no more. It got hacked off with jackhammers and other heavy machinery. The city workers came early in the morning, about 6:30 am, when there wouldn't be many people around. They must've been pretty quick about it, because I think that if word had spread through the community of the house-free, dozens of people would've shown up to express outrage.

There's a reason why people come here to Haight Street, why so many feel that they have a kind of center here, even if they've never even been here. This place stands for something all humanity has longed for. The Way of Peace is the miraculous key that can make us survive. It can rescue the animals, the trees, the oceans, and our liberties. The Rainbow Stairs express mankind's desire to be free.

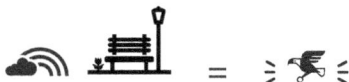

It's amazing that a concrete bench, something so heavy and permanent, can be gone so abruptly. People have been sitting on that bench almost since the park was built in 1867, the oldest park in San Francisco, then called Hill Park. This park is the highest point in the city and still has an ancient oak woodland on its slopes. Oak groves like this one have been held sacred by Native Americans and Europeans alike. The beautiful art deco curved façade and bench have been there until steel-jawed real estate or liability interests violated them. It's another example of how our lives are cut off, sandblasted and jackhammered, by corporate policies. Every pretty thing, every human thing, is despised by the forces that want to enslave mankind.

Even though it was late and dark I walked all the way down past Masonic to Buena Vista to take a look. The wall where the bench used to be is flat and ground smooth. On the front of the façade there's like a scar, with grey concrete where the bench was attached, and the ugly brown paint around it. Several people stood there complaining about what had happened. They said they would get milk crates to sit on and still stay here, where they feel they have a right because of what this place represents. ☮

Since it was kind of a warm evening, there were actually a few people sitting on the grass on the hillside. They called my name. They too were discussing what had happened, how everything seemed to be conspiring to get the hippies off of Haight Street. There in the night sitting on the grass on the side of the hill, staring at the desecrated shrine, we talked about liberty and how easy it is to lose it.

Later I called the city to ask why the bench had been removed without any public input. They had no real explanation and claimed vaguely that they did it in order to repair the concrete retaining wall which the bench had been attached to. I went there and carefully inspected the wall and found no cracks in it. Three big portable concrete planters had been placed where the bench had been, with some tall spindly vegetation that defeated the idea of putting a mural on the wall behind them. I suppose the planters were put there to prevent the young people from sitting there and leaning on the wall.

Stripped of the rainbow colors, the stairs look dirty and stained. The pastels formerly masked the many blotches on the stairs where alcohol, food and other substances had been spilled over the years. Every crumb of glitter is now gone. That's how big business interests treat humanity, removing from us anything too shiny or bright that doesn't fit into their single-minded pursuit of profit. On the brown-painted wall I noticed the word "PHOENIX" still on the wall. Instead of being just painted, it had been etched into the concrete so that it was still there even after the wall was scraped and painted. A Phoenix is a bird that rises from the ashes. It's the San Francisco emblem.

What happened at the Rainbow Stairs cut to the heart. It's the vision of brotherly love that was struck by the jackhammers, that was violently eradicated from this monument. It's what Jesus taught that was assaulted when the beautiful colors were shorn off. The powers that be can remove a concrete bench so people can't gather on it, but they can't get rid of the high concepts it stood for, which are written in people's hearts.

NO MCDONALD'S

Even though people warned each other: "Don't say the "R" word," it rained. Now there's no more McDonald's to stay dry or get warm in, no more hot coffee for a dollar. The only other place somewhat friendly to nomads is Coffee to the People, half a dozen blocks away from the park. There are couches there where people can sit and stay a while, with three-dollar coffee and expensive pastries. 🥐 There are no "Pick 2 for $2.50" deals like at McDonald's.

For decades, McDonald's was a place where the community found refuge and gathered in happy camaraderie instead of shivering outside when it was cold or wet. Under the rough conditions they live with, even a half hour of being warm and drinking a hot liquid can make a huge difference. Now there are no cheap restaurants, and a shortage of accessible bathrooms. ⊗🚽

It's even hard for people to get water to drink and for their dogs to drink. It was easy to fill water bottles in the privacy of the McDonalds bathrooms, or even to take a rudimentary quick sponge bath. The water in the bathroom pod on Stanyan has a sign on it saying not to drink it.

There's no toilet seat on the stainless-steel or porcelain toilet, which is always cold and wet. Not very comfortable on a freezing cold morning.

The whole interior of the metal pod gets washed down and disinfected between each use. 🚿 After you leave, an automatic door closes and the next person has to wait several minutes while the whole place gets wet. What a contrast to the luxurious accommodations that used to be at McDonald's, which now sits fenced off and boarded up right across the street. When I think of old folks in poor health who sleep on the sidewalk or in the park, and who desperately need a decent bathroom in the morning or a hot cup of coffee, my heart aches.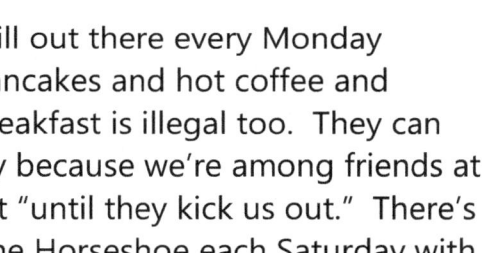

At least our Christian friends are still out there every Monday morning, rain or shine, feeding people pancakes and hot coffee and oatmeal. It turns out that the pancake breakfast is illegal too. They can get away with feeding the homeless "only because we're among friends at the park." They said that they would do it "until they kick us out." There's another church group that shows up at the Horseshoe each Saturday with big stacks of boxed pizzas for everyone. Unlike the others, they preach with a microphone to those waiting in line. I wonder if they too are skirting the law by feeding the homeless, which is illegal.

The bus stop benches at Haight and Stanyan used to be the green metal kind with walls that protected people from the elements. Then about ten years ago they took those out and put in the wavy top awnings that are open on three sides. They removed the domed bus shelters so homeless people couldn't go there to get out of the wind and rain. They fixed the benches, put dividers so nobody could sleep there. In Colorado, being in a sleeping bag gets a camping ticket.

A guy told me how the powers that be try to designate the young people as 5150's: mentally ill. Any street fight and lots of "quality of life" crimes can put someone into that category. A record of broadly defined 5150's could make it hard for millions of young people to later get a job or rent a place. A new California law allows involuntary commitment for a year after a certain number of 5150's or emergency room visits. 𝍤

The homeless can already be locked up for seventy-two hours if in any way anything they do can be seen as having a potential to be "a danger to themselves or others." The new "conservatorships" only require a certain number of 5150 police holds to get locked up for a year. Doctors and family members don't get to make the decision like before. Hospital administrators can decide to recommend that someone should be "conserved." They have a financial incentive to limit costly emergency room visits from the homeless. 💰

The law is vague about the living conditions of inmates in the proposed tax-funded privatized building projects and prison industries. It does specify that the incarcerated may be placed somewhere in the state that's not close to home or family. Some people and I went to Board of Supervisor meetings to try to stop California Senate Bill 1045 from being implemented in San Francisco, but with no luck. At the podium dozens of outraged citizens voiced their concerns about the Orwellian features of this legislation. 😱 Their outcries were drowned out by the arguments of experts whose bosses salivated for the potential profits of another blow in the death by a thousand cuts to our liberty.

THE ONLY ELEGANT SOLUTION

A man named Dylan told me that a hummingbird comes to visit him each morning even though there are no flowers around his tent. 🐦 He said "I'm here for a reason. I know it." He said, "The vision here is more beautiful than people can imagine. Haight is like nowhere else in the world." ✌🎩☮ He's been banned from the area by authorities for thirty days, taking a risk just being here. A guy came by and asked him if he could trade a cigarette for some vodka. Dylan handed him a bottle he had and wouldn't take the cigarette. He said, "I share everything I have."

 The Pacifist movement, vibrant for half a century, is not the way the media has portrayed it. It shouldn't be defined by things that have been overly associated with it, like sleaze or weirdness or addiction or exotic religions. In all these months I haven't heard any riskee banter, no gay banter, no hard drug banter. I don't remember hearing put-down humor about others. I've heard no hate toward the gentrifiers or the police.

 Pacifists respect and love people with other religions or lifestyles, like they would anyone else. **They defend their right to be treated fairly, but <u>not</u> at the expense of restrictive liability laws that prevent everyone else from being treated fairly.** Their strategy is simple: they try to do unto others as they would have them do unto them.

 At Haight and Ashbury, I met Albert Owlbird. He told me about guerilla gardens, seeds planted anonymously anywhere they will grow. There was a woman sitting on the sidewalk who used to be a manager at Wallmart. She said she was much happier now. She quoted, "We are the ones we have been waiting for." I saw Amal pouring out love at the Cedar Deli. Street kids and housies in turn lined up to sit on the bench near the soup counter to get her motherly attentions. She now has her own sidewalk heart with her name on it, near those of Jerry and Janis. ♥ Amal

 I ran into Rainbow, sitting on the benches of the "parklet" across from the Haight Grocery Store, where some of us like to gather in the evening. He gifted me a painting he'd made of Jesus calming the waves and saying, "Cool it!" He was waxing poetic and mystical. He said, "All art is from God. I'm just playing a part in the play of life. You're the energy, the consciousness, that's what everybody is. The transformation has happened." With psychedelic music from a headshop in the background, he went on. He said, "It's about human beings versus inhuman beings.

My parents and society taught me hate. Then the Beatles came along nd told me all you need is love. Whatever God is, it's coursing through my veins!"

What a treat it was to find Wendy Whimsey again, returned at last from parts unknown. At first, I didn't recognize her as I saw her looking at me from across the sidewalk, but when I saw the tattoos, I knew exactly who it was. We hugged, each recognizing a kindred spirit. She was wearing a beautiful gown, made of silver and cobalt blue silk from India that seemed to shimmer in reddish tones. There were rows of narrow ruffles along the edges, and a fitted bodice with lacing.

As we walked together, it felt like we were sisters or twins, the only two on the street dressed in gorgeous flowing clothes. Though I'd only run into her a few brief times before, we shared thoughts as if we understood each other. There's something radiant and deep about her, something mother-like and at the same time goddess-like. A purple glow seems to surround her. Her charisma is so strong.

It was a homecoming and a crowd of people gathered to greet her wherever we went. She told breathlessly about her adventures on the road, how some kind cops changed her oil for her somewhere in the Midwest. She said that she could handle most situations except that "I can't fight the man," meaning the powers that be. She said,

"Consciousness is the only elegant solution."

Those few moments with her were more fleeting and rare than I realized at the time. While waiting for her to visit with a group of people I went into the store "Love of Ganesha." When I came out a short time later, she had walked on, probably looking for me in the wrong direction. I chose a direction and looked for her and asked if anyone had seen her, but I never found her and now I'm sure she has left the area. She appeared like a vision and then vanished again.

SAINT PATRICK'S DAY 🍀

Saint Patrick's Day was a big deal with so many Irish-style taverns on Haight Street. The Michael Collins Irish Bar had a live Irish band and people were dancing on the sidewalk. The Magnolia and Victorian Punch House and The Milk Bar were packed. The street was dotted with bright green top hats and other sparkly tokens to the Emerald Isle. I had forgotten to wear green but was saved by the green ribbon on my tambourine. Someone put a shiny green plastic necklace on me that said, "Kiss me I'm Irish."

It was a beautiful day, the first warm weekend after a long cold spell. People were in good spirits and not as drunk as what I'd thought they'd be. I learned more about Saint Patrick. It turns out he didn't exactly drive the snakes out of Ireland, which has a cold climate unlikely to attract the reptiles. By "snakes" the chronicler seems to have meant that they were the healers and leaders of the old religions of Europe, Pagans and Celts, hunted as wizards and witches.

The Michael Collins Irish Bar was filled to capacity. I entered it and started dancing with my tambourine. Even though it was standing room only people quickly cleared a space and started clapping to the music as I swung the ribbons around the room. A man borrowed my tambourine and put it on his head and danced on a table.

Out on the street with the homeless I ate like royalty, as often happens. First some nice Chinese people rolled down the window of their expensive car and gave us a take-out box full of delicious steak and shrimp. The others were vegetarians, so a homeless man and I shared it. We ate with our fingers, he preferring the steak and I the shrimp. A few minutes later a restaurant worker came by and gave us a whole taco salad that had been used for a display that day.

Later while walking to my car I also found two untouched pieces of fancy pizza in a box that had been carefully placed on top of a trash can so that someone could find and eat them. I've sometimes found a good unopened loaf of expensive "sprouted" bread on top of trash cans, where grocery workers surreptitiously place them when they're expired instead of throwing them away as demanded by liability rules.

One time I found a big box of old-fashioned rock candy on strings, in the original box from the candy factory, just sitting on the sidewalk after dark. Everyone got lots of candy that night. I was curious as to why items like this are sometimes found abandoned on the sidewalk, like the time I found a very large unopened expensive bottle of rum just sitting on the curb with cars whizzing by. I've been told that some cultures give away items that might have "bad juju" attached to them. For instance, if they came from someone or from a situation with negative energy. The street youth and I were happy to dissipate the bad vibes by eating the pretty candy.

Scott was there celebrating Saint Patty's Day, looking almost like his old self. Though in a wheelchair he looked sharp in a beautiful blue and black brocade period coat. His hair had grown out and now there were again salt and pepper curls around the brim of his new high-class leather top hat.

On a corner of Haight and Ashbury I met a real saint, not the kind that hunts down infidels or idolaters. A street kid called "Simber" told a story about two guys who tried to stay at a shelter in cold weather, but there was only room at the shelter for one of them. Neither of them would go in if the other couldn't. He said that when he became homeless it took some getting used to. He said, "But then I got humble. It was better."

CHAIN SAWS IN THE MORNING

It was shocking the first time I saw a big green X painted on one of the trees on Haight Street, which meant that it was going to be cut down. This "renovation" is happening too fast to lobby the city to try to put some brakes on it. Some of us from the Haight-Ashbury Neighborhood Council tried to get a hearing about the trees but were told it was too late.

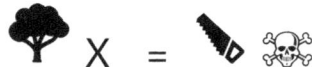

I pestered the Department of Urban Forestry, the area supervisor's office, and even tried to make an appointment with the Director of Public Works, without results. I was told that signs had been posted on each tree telling people of the plans to cut it down, and that a hearing had already been held the previous year. Despite protests, the decision had already been made. It had all happened while I was in Joshua Tree, away from San Francisco. If the signs were posted, it's strange that nobody told me about them. I wonder how long the signs were up.

Now there's a big green X on fifteen trees on Haight Street. That's not counting the ones that have already been cut recently. I didn't see a green X on them before they were cut. Maybe they were cut on other pretexts. At the bicycle shop they thought theirs had been cut because of branches touching the electric wires. Another shopkeeper thought theirs had been cut because a branch had hit the top of a truck.

An aide at the Supervisor's office said it was because branches could fall on people's heads. Sixty-five thousand trees in San Francisco have been designated as "dangerous" after a branch in another park fell on a lady and she was awarded fourteen million dollars. Of course, there's also the liability involved if roots buckle the new sidewalks.

Like many of the horrible restrictions in our lives, it's a liability issue. Cutting the concrete bench off the wall so people wouldn't sit and gather there was a liability issue. Putting up cameras in the park was a liability issue. Closing the McDonald's because the homeless gathered there was probably a liability issue.

Possible alternatives could include reforming liability laws, limiting payouts, or reinstating the municipal immunity against lawsuits that cities used to have. Instead of limiting the reach of liability laws, some profit-seekers have chosen to limit risk by controlling and surveilling everything we do. Living things like trees and people get in their way.

Twenty-two-thousand Ficus trees in San Francisco have been identified as dangerous and are set to be cut down. I was told that they haven't been properly pruned and maintained, that their roots grow upward and damage the sidewalks, that they're past their official lifespan, and that they shouldn't have been planted in the first place. Liability laws always have "safety" reasons to destroy beautiful things.

It's believed that Buddha was enlightened under a "Ficus Religiosa," recognizable by its heart-shaped leaves. "Bodhi" means "enlightenment." December 8th, supposedly when Buddha was enlightened, is a religious holiday celebrated with heart-shaped cookies. It's believed that the tree can make rain and heal the sick. They make prayer beads out of it.

As they Liability Gods cut down the trees to reduce risk, are the trying to chop off the enlightenment that happened on Haight Street?   The young people say they wake up to the sound of chain saws in the morning.

DREAM ON

    Two big trees have been cut on the ridge of Hippie Hill, right where sunbeams used to shine through onto the drummers so beautifully at the end of the day. From the drum circle I saw their giant trunks in pieces on the ground. Some tree-cutting company that lobbied for this has changed the look and feel of the drum circle at Hippie Hill.

    Scientific tests have shown that when the sounds trees make are slowed down, an actual drumming emerges that sounds a lot like the drum circle. It's called "synchronization." A new sign that's hung on the gate of the tunnel says that Alvord Lake, the pond, is also going to be "renovated." What in the world are they planning to do?

    The pond is already perfect. Does this mean that the whole area that was our special gathering place will be fenced off for years?   For half a century the Way of Peace has been heavily discussed and debated right on this spot. Now they're going to tear it apart and turn it into some gentrified tourist area. The bathroom building that's been shut down for years will be turned into a snack bar.

    There were a couple of twin redwood trees near the pond which I hadn't noticed until now. What caught my eye was that one twin, attached to the other at the base, had been cut cleanly off. Though the cut was fresh the debris had been completely cleared away, maybe so people wouldn't notice as much. I walked over and touched the damp cut surface.

I told the tree how sorry I was and didn't even care if people walking by heard me. I took a loose piece of the soft redwood and kept it.

  A sign on the fenced-off area that looks like Paradise says it's also being "improved." Already several big trees have been brought down, the heavy pieces of their huge trunks lying askew in a pile on the hill. Some other trees, tall Eucalyptus, have the dreaded notices stapled to them saying that they too will fall. There are liability issues at play. Trees and branches have been falling on people since the beginning of time. It used to be called an accident before it became a reason to bankrupt cities. Getting rid of trees and bushes also makes it hard for the homeless to hide and camp in the park, another ugly liability issue.

  "Pipe Dreams," on the block east of Masonic, is called the oldest head shop on Haight Street. It's a "Legacy Business," along with Amoeba Records and Distractions and some others I don't know about, because they "contribute to the spirit of the neighborhood." It has the most amazing collection of glass pot pipes I've ever seen. Owners Cassie and Josh and I lamented all the changes. We stared at the stump of the fine old tree that had stood in front of their shop.

  The cut was fresh and there were big nails driven into it where orange cones had been attached. They'd removed the cones and pried out most of the nails but had been unable to wrench out these last few. The beautiful tree had given their business an old-world feel. Now the place looks like any storefront in any inner city. In a detail that seems symbolic, the new sidewalks are going to be black.

  Next to the stump there's a big pit, a hole that goes to a tunnel under the street. It's covered with a piece of plywood and surrounded with big orange plastic barricades. A young man, in an act of civil disobedience, got spray paint and wrote on the barricades in big letters:
DREAM ON MUCH LOVE.

Note: All these things were said by Jesus (from KJV), though not in the same order. A few words in parentheses were added.

God's Message to Treehuggers and Peacemakers:

THE SPIRIT IS WILLING

The spirit indeed is willing, but the flesh is weak. (Matthew 26:41)

    In the world ye shall have tribulation. (debt, illness, legal problems)

But be of good cheer; I have overcome the world. (John 16:33)

    And I say unto you **my friends, be not afraid** of them that kill the body, and after that have no more that they can do. (Luke 12:4)

    Fear not them which kill the body but are not able to kill the soul.

Unto whom much is given, of him shall be much required;

    and to whom men have committed much, of him they will ask the more.

                                      (Matt. 10:28)(Lk. 12:48)

Verily I say unto you, except a corn of wheat fall into the ground and die,

    it abideth alone: but if it die, it bringeth forth much fruit. (John 12:24)

I say unto you, that ye shall weep and lament, but the world shall rejoice:

    and ye shall be sorrowful, but **your sorrow shall be turned into joy.**

A woman when she is in travail hath sorrow, because her hour is come:

    but as soon as she is delivered of the child, she remembereth no more

the anguish, for joy that a man is born into the world.

Your heart shall rejoice, and your joy no man taketh from you.

 (John 16:20-22)

In your patience possess ye your souls. (Luke 21:19)
    If any man serve me, let him follow me; and

where I am, there shall also my servant be:

    if any man serve me, him will my Father honour. (John 12:26)

Whosoever shall confess me (or his advice to love) before me

    him will I confess also before my Father which is in heaven.
                                                (Matt. 10:32)

Built to Last

Lo, **I AM WITH YOU ALWAYS**, even unto the end of the world.

   HAVE PEACE WITH ONE ANOTHER. (Mark 9:50)(Matt. 28:20)

Writer's definition: There are many ways to "kill the body:" fine, incarcerate, confiscate, induct, litigate, indebt, impoverish, enslave, brainwash, leverage, downsize, buy out, outsource, foreclose, bankrupt, plan obsolescence on, lay off, furlough, de-industrialize, appropriate, legislate, etc., etc.

JESUS DIDN'T TEACH: that all are born in sin, the Inquisition, excommunication (shunning,) slaves and women "obey in all things," Adam and Eve, idolaters and gays are "worthy of death," antisemitism, shame of the body, hell, tithing, having to go to church, the Divine Right of Kings, that the Bible was perfect, or that he created the world. Paul the Apostle and OTHERS ADDED those, plus "obey every ordinance of man," "let the unjust be unjust still," that you have to believe or be damned (right before it says that you can "take up serpents" and drink poison,) and that it's not what you do that counts, but what you believe in. Dangerous red letters in the book of Revelation are the writer's vision or dream and don't teach what Jesus taught. The Prince of Peace taught kindness, brotherly love, and Heaven on Earth.

LET'S TAKE ONE STEP TOGETHER: At the giant Rainbow Gatherings in the wilderness people yell "WE LOVE YOU!" repeatedly on one side of the camp and others answer back, "WE LOVE YOU TOO!" Let's do the same thing out our windows at sunset on Saturdays, so that the Voice of the People can be heard! We could also play drums for half an hour at sunset on Saturdays at a window. We could visit with or meet neighbors the first Saturday of the month.   WE NEED ALL OF US! (right + left)

Poems may be reprinted and shared by homeless for donations they can keep.
TELL TEN TO TELL TEN TO VOTE!   REGISTER 100 VOTERS!
(https://www.usa.gov/register-to-vote)   (vote.gov) (rockthevote.org)
Democrats against forced mandates and other oppressive liability laws.
BILL OF RIGHTS   GOLDEN RULE   peacedrums.org   UNITE!

 BILL OF RIGHTS DAY

The young house-free decided to have a sit-in to protest the No Sit and Lie Law. A pretty girl named Izzy, in an elaborate braided hairstyle and a pink tule skirt, wrote this poem about the Rainbow Stairs and bench and the No Sit and Lie Law:

"As we stand we complain.

As we walk we see no shame.

A wall always filled with friendship and compassion

now returned to hate and human frustration.

Concrete, a simple element creating happiness

removed to abide by your rules of corruptness.

Now you may not sit and with that wall you cannot lie.

A colorblind fool removing happiness from each passerby

because of your messed-up law of "do not sit and do not lie." 💔
Izzy

I didn't start or organize this demonstration and couldn't even be there until late in the day because of a prior commitment. When I arrived, there were still about a dozen youth sitting down in civil disobedience on the sidewalk in front of Love of Ganesha, which was conveniently closed. The colorful murals painted on the store's sliding metal security doors made a nice backdrop.

It had been going on all day, without any trouble from the police. Even though sitting down on the sidewalk between 7 AM and 11 PM is illegal, it's a constitutional right when part of a political protest. There didn't seem to be any police around as people and their dogs sat and lounged on both sides of the sidewalk with ragged signs they'd made from discarded cardboard. 🚶🐕

I then suggested that we could do this again on Bill of Rights Day, December fifteenth, and on the birthdays of the founding fathers and other patriotic holidays. Instead of dark banners with angry slogans, we could have signs about the Golden Rule and the Bill of Rights. We could have the nicest and biggest American flags. We could have beautiful signs with sparkles and tinsel on them telling people how to register millions of new Democrats. We could have an actual birthday cake with candles and birthday streamers, and paper horns and multicolored party hats, and singing "Happy Birthday." For presents we could wrap up drafts of better laws.

We would make the protest last only an hour, so as not to take up police resources and antagonize the police. But we would take videos and try to make them go viral and would encourage other people nation-wide to do the same thing locally in small groups on the birthdays and patriotic holidays. It could be part of a movement to unite the Democrats and to reform the laws to make them more fair.

An upcoming event could be May 29th, Patrick Henry's birthday. I bought fluorescent felt pens, poster board, and beautiful metallic stencil letters in different bright colors. I bought a large new American flag and also some little flags the people could hold. I think an American flag is a good protection a hippie can have in a protest, a likely symbol to allow dialogue between the two sides.

There's one more. On the prettiest sign, the one with gold glitter borders and "The Golden Rule" in large gold letters, I mounted a picture of Jesus. It wasn't huge or overpowering but it was big enough to recognize from a distance. Its unspoken message was, "He's with us!" The street kids were not embarrassed to hold it.

The protest was incredibly spontaneous, as none of my friends had said for sure that they were going to be there. I just showed up with the posters where I saw a group of young people on Haight. Before I knew it, they each took a poster and sat down on the sidewalk. I had posters that said, "REPEAL THE NO SIT AND LIE LAW!" and one in green metallic letters saying, "DON'T CUT DOWN THESE TREES!" Three trees were marked to be cut down right where we were demonstrating.

It only took about ten minutes before four big police officers arrived. I was so busy I didn't even notice them at first where they stood lined up against the wall on one side of the sidewalk. They had asked us to please only sit on the street side of the sidewalk so as not to obstruct business. There had been no such request at the previous protest, though it was probably part of the safety guidelines. It meant that the protestors would be in the sun and would not be able to lean back against a wall. We also had no place to hang the big flag, which otherwise could've been attached to the iron gate of a store that was closed.

Nevertheless we got along fine, even when a couple police cars also pulled up and added the number of officers to eight.   I showed all of them the big flag we had, even though it couldn't be hung up. A police Sargent showed up and we had a nice conversation. He was a real human being, not some cardboard cutout.   He was sympathetic to our cause but wanted to know how long the event would last. After an hour he seemed hopeful that we would call it a day. In my mind it wasn't the sort of protest that's supposed to last a long time, but only long enough to make a statement and get it on film. It was political street theatre more than civil disobedience.

I had not gotten a birthday cake and candles. The Sargent was willing to wait while I went off trying to buy some nearby, but I thought it might take too long and it would be hard to light the candles in the breeze. The protestors were melting away in the heat.   I looked at the eight police officers standing in their hot uniforms and bulletproof vests and guns, and I have to admit it was kind of a scary thing to see. In the interest of making a good first impression on them I took the pictures I wanted and then decided an hour had been long enough. A police officer actually offered to hold the camera for me so that I could be in the picture.

We would re-group and do this again another day with better planning and more people, with props ready and a knowledge of what to expect. This was a good dry run and I hope it helped make for a good future rapport with the police. People had arrived saying that the police had actually told them to come to the protest if they wanted to sit on the sidewalk. I've been told that a lot of police don't like enforcing the No Sit and Lie Law. ☮ 🤝 👮

I am aware that even a small political act that seems insignificant at the time can be the start of something big. The big Hemp rallies my friends and I started at the Los Angeles Federal Building, held four times a year, are an example. We had rock bands and speakers and booths, and over a thousand people would come, including media and celebrities. The powerful rallies began with one tiny potluck on a rainy day with only about five people and an uneaten turkey. Two of those who were there, Jack Herer and Chris Conrad, can be seen by history as patriarchs of the Hemp movement. I am proud to have been the one to suggest that we have that first benefit potluck, and that we have one the first Saturday of every month. ☮

"The price of freedom is eternal vigilance." **Thomas Jefferson**

"I would rather die on my feet than live on my knees." **George Washington**

"We hold these truths to be self-evident, that all men are created equal, that they are endowed by their Creator with certain unalienable Rights, that among these are life, Liberty, and the pursuit of happiness. That to secure these rights, Governments are instituted among Men, deriving their just powers from the consent of the governed, that whenever any Form of Government becomes destructive to these ends, it is the Right of the People to alter or abolish it. Prudence, indeed, will dictate that Governments long established should not be changed for light and transient causes." "All experience hath shown, that mankind are more disposed to suffer, while evils are sufferable, than to right themselves by

abolishing the forms to which they are accustomed."
Declaration of Independence

Note: Author believes that the ideals in our carefully-made Constitution and Bill of Rights can be used to rescue our liberties from the tyranny of the rule of money over every single one of us, both rich and poor. WE NEED ALL OF US to stop the poisons, the oppressions, the spiritual molestations, the thousand assaults on out personal liberties, that out-of-control corporations have made.
Joan Rivard

"The truth is, all might be free if they valued freedom, and defended it as they ought. Our unalterable resolution should be to be free." **Sam Adams**

"Is life so dear, or peace so sweet, as to be purchased at the price of chains and slavery? God forbid! As for me, give me liberty or give me death!" **Patrick Henry**

"Our lives begin to end the day we become silent about things that matter." **Martin Luther King**

"I believe there are more instances of the abridgment of the freedom of the people by gradual and silent encroachments of those in power than by violent and sudden usurpations." **James Madison**

"Those who would give up essential liberty to purchase a little temporary safety deserve neither liberty nor safety." "Tis a common observation here that our Cause is the Cause of all Mankind; and that we are fighting for their liberty in defending our own." "Freedom is not a gift bestowed upon us by other men, but a right that belongs to us by the laws of God and nature." **Benjamin Franklin**

*"**I hope we shall crush** in its birth the aristocracy of our monied **corporations** which dare already to challenge our government to a trial by*

strength, and bid defiance to the laws of our country." **Thomas Jefferson**

THE BILL OF RIGHTS   Please print and distribute.

Amendment I: **Congress shall make no law** respecting an establishment of religion, or prohibiting the free exercise thereof; or **abridging the freedom of speech, or of the press; or the right of the people peaceably to assemble, and to petition the government for a redress of grievances**.

Amendment II: A well-regulated militia, being necessary to the security of a free state, the right of the people to keep and bear arms, shall not be infringed.

Amendment III: No soldier shall, in time of peace be quartered in any house, without the consent of the owner, nor in time of war, but in a manner to be prescribed by law.

Amendment IV: **The right of the people to be secure in their persons, houses, papers, and effects, against unreasonable searches and seizures, shall not be violated**, and no warrants shall issue, but upon probable cause, supported by oath or affirmation, and particularly describing the place to be searched, and the persons or things to be seized.

Amendment V: No person shall be held to answer for a capital, or otherwise infamous crime, unless on a presentment or indictment of a grand jury, except in cases arising in the land or naval forces, or in the militia, when in actual service in time of war or public danger; **nor shall any person be subject for the same offence to be twice put in jeopardy** of life or limb; nor shall be compelled in any criminal case **to be a witness against himself**, nor be deprived of life, liberty, or property, without due process of law; **nor shall private property be taken for public use, without just compensation.**

Amendment VI: In all criminal prosecutions, the accused shall enjoy the **right to a speedy and public trial**, by an impartial jury of the state and district wherein the crime shall have been committed, which district shall have been previously ascertained by law, and **to be informed of the nature and cause of the accusation; to be confronted with the witnesses against him; to have compulsory process for obtaining witnesses in his favor, and to have the assistance of counsel for his defense.**

Amendment VII: In suits at common law, where the value in controversy shall exceed twenty dollars, the right of trial by jury shall be preserved, and **no fact tried by a jury, shall be otherwise reexamined** in any court of the United States, than according to the rules of the common law.

Amendment VIII: **Excessive bail shall not be required, nor excessive fines imposed, nor cruel and unusual punishments inflicted.**

Amendment IX: The enumeration in the Constitution, of certain **rights**, shall not be construed to deny or disparage **others retained by the people.**

Amendment X: The powers not delegated to the United States by the Constitution, nor prohibited by it to the states, are reserved to the states respectively, or to the people. *"Love is all you need."* **The Beatles**

POLICE SWEEPS

I found out more about why not a single one of us is hanging out at the pond any more at all. It isn't only the cameras, but big police sweeps that took place several months ago. I knew that the police had been pressured to give the kids tickets, but I hadn't realized the extent. Orange told me what had happened.

He said that whenever any of them tried to sit on the logs or near the pond, and they did anything whatsoever against the rules, police or rangers on motorcycles or ATVs roared out of the forest and gave them tickets. He said that three dogs had been shot in the process of enforcing the new regimen. It's not hard to imagine that some of these Pitbulls might get aggressive toward someone arresting their owner.

The cameras, the jackhammers, the ticketing, all seem personal, like they're aimed specifically at getting the hippies off of Haight Street. But it's all a part of overall policies toward the homeless all over the city and the country, who are being increasingly criminalized. The big prison industries are the winners, and the surveillance state, and faceless global investors in gentrification.

After being harassed in Golden Gate Park and driven away by the offensive cameras, about a dozen of the few young people who remained would often gather at Buena Vista Park at the other end of the six or seven blocks I call Haight Street. By the way, my using that name isn't intended to refer to the whole length of that street, which continues on some distance toward the business district.

They usually sat on the grass on a favorite spot on the side of the hill, next to the oak forest where they sought refuge to sleep at night. They left few traces and weren't in anybody's way. Then I noticed that people no longer gathered there. Inquiring I was told that sprinklers had been installed there, and that even when they weren't turned on it took hours for the grass to dry out. Sprinklers would also randomly be turned on and drench the forests where they slept.

That's why they were sitting on the dry stairs and landing, right under the NO LOITERING sign. On the now bare steps of the former

Rainbow Stairs, a girl complained, "They took away my couch!" She'd arrived from her travels to find the graceful concrete bench hacked off the retaining wall, and all the rainbow colors painted brown. It didn't take long before the people were told they couldn't gather there at all.

Authorities also got rid of a popular program giving jobs to homeless youth keeping the streets clean. Now the community has no real center. Bulldog is still here, but not at his corner at Haight and Ashbury. He got a job at Frank's Liquor. Chelsea is no longer working at the Hattery but got a job at the Haight Street Grocery where her husband Hayden also works. Orange got a job at a Whole Foods across the bay.

Dragon and her three friends remain, often seated on a low retaining wall bordering Buena Vista Park along the sidewalk and the street. A few feet away is her little silver car where she now sleeps at night, a small sedan in which also live two dogs and nine puppies.

Since they can't hang out on the grass like before, all this has to be kept in the car all day. It's not just because of the sprinklers. They've been warned to stay out of both parks.

Tourists don't come and take pictures of themselves on the Rainbow Stairs anymore.

"The rights of every man are diminished when the rights of one man are threatened. **John F. Kennedy**

A VORTEX

On one corner of the intersection of Haight and Ashbury there's the "Four-Twenty Clock," always set at 4:20 as the official time to smoke pot. Next to it is the famous Haight and Ashbury street sign against which rock stars and tourists and pilgrims have leaned to take pictures for half a century. They came here because they hoped there was a way to make peace on Earth. Many came here hoping to find the Kingdom of Heaven within that Jesus talked about.

The negative forces trying to discourage us seem to be focused on this intersection, which many would say is a vortex of powerful life energy. At first, I thought that the fight over this spot was just a territorial thing between some new bullies. Bulldog had been threatened that if he wore his beautiful blue tie-dyed top hat, "the whole community would pay." Now the people who I thought bothered him are gone, but he still doesn't wear the hat. It makes me wonder if the spiritual vibe here is what the powers that be are trying to get rid of, the belief that people can be free. That's what this place stands for. That's what hippies stand for.

✌ 🎩 ☮ = FREE

There are problems not only with arrests and ticketing, but with thieves and fights. Within a short time over a dozen people have gotten their backpacks stolen while they slept. 🏃 Scott even got his wheelchair stolen while he slept. Kage's dog got hit by a car when a friend of mine attacked a guy right in the center of the intersection of Haight and Ashbury. A lot of people were showing up with black eyes, including my friend Orange. 👊 Had the citadel of brotherly love degenerated into this? Were thieves being brought here? One girl got hit in the face while giving an anti-drug lecture to a hard drug user. "Tweakers" are

not appreciated on Haight.

Adding insult to injury, the storefront on the southeast corner of Haight and Ashbury is displaying horrible weapons in its two giant corner windows. Baseball bats studded with huge screws that stick out several inches could do someone serious damage. These are more frightening in a way than some more complicated weapon they could display that we've seen before, because they would be easy for someone to make.

Displaying them is suggesting them. Someone who buys one because they think it's "cool" might later get drunk or angry and use it on their friend or wife.

These are the only things in the large display area, dozens of them hanging from the ceiling and strewn around on the floor. When I complained and asked when they would be taken down, I was told that it was an art exhibition and would be changed in two weeks. This assurance has been repeated every two weeks several times without any change. Now it turns out that they're selling this "art," and that the same artist who made this exhibit is going to make the next one. His last offering was a simulation of Jerry Garcia's finger in a jar. (Displays got better later.)

I saw a fight between two girls. 👭 One had hurled soup at our group while we sat on the sidewalk. I got a piece of noodle on my jacket. The other girl chased her, and several people followed to see what would happen. Someone said to someone else in a worried tone, "She's gonna get her ass kicked." Someone else said, "...as long as the dogs don't get involved..." 🍜 👋

The girl from our group beat her up with repeated swift punches to the face until two of her friends pulled her off, saying "that's enough!" ✋✋ Previously, the soup-throwing girl had been angrily shoving trash cans into the street. She was a pretty girl and didn't look crazy. She was just very upset about something. She was injured but not seriously hurt. She walked off crying. It was then that the same girl who'd beat her up sent one of her male friends to walk with her and make sure she was all right.

Cave Man got his dog taken away for it not being on a leash. He said it would cost $500. to get him back. Dylan was arrested for a warrant for unpaid tickets for sitting down. It happened because he left his dog in his car for two hours, when it was cool and comfortable, and he had water and was fine. Someone reported it and there's an ongoing investigation. The fine for sitting down is $50. to $500., depending on how many priors.

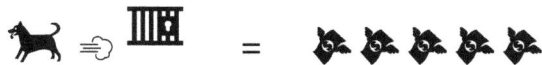

BUSINESS IMPROVEMENT DISTRICTS

I found out what might be destroying Haight Street and it's not exactly the residents and merchants there, or even the police. It turns out that big corporations are pushing for lucrative renovation programs, paid for with tax dollars, that end up privatizing public space. These programs are called BID's, "Business Improvement Districts, and GBD's, "Green Benefit Districts," and also CID's, "Community Improvement Districts."

Even when local merchants allegedly propose these programs, I doubt that they fully realize that big trees may be cut down, parking spaces lost, cameras put up, and the homeless treated badly. I'm sure that the companies who are going to profit from all these tax dollars sent out armies of consultants and advocates to paint a rosy picture of these programs to people who just wanted to do something good for their community. I'm guessing that these experts didn't highlight for them the lopsided approval process that would make it almost impossible for them to reverse these policies once they are put in place.

In the case of Haight Street, the "greening" process begins with cutting down the big healthy trees that are already here. One of these companies' stated goals is getting the homeless off the streets in any way possible. They are responsible for Proposition L, the No Sit and Lie Law, and things like spikes or planters on the sidewalks to keep people from sitting there, called "hostile architecture." They push to install cameras.

These financial entities use a powerful political machine to lobby for repressive policies that affect the whole city, not just their districts. They hire private security to monitor the homeless and report to the police. It wasn't your gentrified neighbor who called the police on you for sleeping in your car. It was SOMETHING ELSE. Benches on Masonic and also at Ben and Jerry's fold up and lock at night so people can't sleep there.

Everything on Haight Street is being eyed by developers. What they propose for the boarded-up McDonald's site is a five to seven-story stack'n pack apartment building of 120 units, with *absolutely no parking* provided. I think this could be harmful to the businesses who have hung on up to this point. Where will their customers park? (Later Covid 19 bankrupted many of the stores.)

I worry that recent changes, including the "traffic calming" bulb-outs and "pedestrian-friendly" wider sidewalks, the high-rise with no parking, could perhaps be part of "Agenda 21." Some say this is a scary United Nations plan to reduce the Earth's population, get rid of cars, and herd people into urban areas to live in tiny apartments where they can be controlled. I need to read the 300-pg. document to see what it really says.

It allegedly would involve tearing out roads, taking away lots of people's land with Eminent Domain, increasing restrictions on building or living on your own land, and monitoring everything we do and use, all under the pretext of saving the environment. I haven't heard of anything in there about stopping mountaintop removal or the making of plastic containers, or anything else the corporations could do to save the environment. Are the beautiful trees on Haight Street, with their colored lights, being sacrificed on the idolatrous altar of developers' agendas?

If some underground parking were provided in the plan, an influx of new residents could help the merchants. This would cost developers more and could result in fewer units, but it's possible and necessary. Having no parking could further damage the special businesses in this unique community. Positive things about this plan are that a modest percentage of the units are supposed to be for low-income people and seniors and that they might possibly include a new fast-food restaurant and also a center for "Transition-Aged Youth." I'm hoping that these last two things could help bring the young pilgrims back to Haight Street.

A customer at a bar went crazy and started attacking people with a broken cue stick, injuring several. Then before anyone could stop him he went out into the street, and he attacked a peaceful friend of ours for no reason. DeWitt has an open gash on his right cheek and a knot the size of a golf ball on his left temple under his blond curls. He's not pressing charges.

He said he feels sorry for the man who did it, who was taken away in a trail of emergency vehicles. He isn't even going to the doctor, though it's obvious that the deep cut could leave a scar on his young face if it's not sewn up. His friends are worried that he shouldn't go to sleep, in case it's a serious concussion. They're going to camp together tonight.

I ran into wonderful Ferox, a pretty girl who holds down the corner and sometimes sells healing stones and jewelry from a little stand she makes from an upside-down milk crate covered with a colorful shawl, giving away more than she sells. Her conversation has depth and wisdom. She gifted me a beautiful amethyst crystal set in intricate silver work.

Standing on the corner of Haight and Ashbury there's often an African American young man named Chris with a nice smile and neat dreadlocks. I was parked across the street when suddenly I noticed that there were ambulances and paramedics and the young man was lying on the sidewalk, not moving. A friend said Chris was "just tired," but he didn't look that good to me. I wondered if maybe it was a reaction to hard drugs, something I haven't seen on Haight Street. The friend said no, he knew Chris didn't do that. I think he'd just sort of fainted before their eyes. They said his backpack had been stolen the night before while he slept.

There's an enormous transmission tower with three prongs that people call the Trident, which can be seen all over the city and in Golden Gate Park. It's been called both "Neptune's Trident" and "The Devil's Pitchfork." A rumor circulates among the house-free of Haight Street that the Trident has sent a bad vibe. ⚓

APPROACHING GOD

I'm very sad about the trees, the cameras, the friends who have left. There are green exes on fifteen trees on Haight, including the two beautiful tall ones outside of Amal's with the lights on them. One of them has already been hacked, all its foliage gone, and all its branches cut except for two naked ones sticking up weirdly alone against the sky. The tall trunk still stands, scheduled to be chain sawed at a different time. There are barricades of orange plastic mesh around the small trees that are not going to be cut. On the street giant machines are parked, and there are metal plates covering big holes where the street is being torn up. Thugs hired to steal backpacks also urinate on people and their stuff.

Where a lively community used to gather outside of Amal's, now there are usually only a couple of real down-and-out bums. Officials don't seem to chase them away as much as they chase away the young nomads with their neat backpacks and well-behaved dogs. There's an unspoken understanding among the house-free that their freedom is a challenge to the forces that threaten our liberties. 🆓🚶🐕 🆚 ⛓️

I stood next to a young man who looked less bum-like. I expressed my anger and grief about what was going on here. I was sorry I did. With a haunted look he said it didn't matter because he was free and could "just choose to leave." I asked him what he meant, hoping that he was just planning to go to another city. He said matter-of-factly that he could kill himself. 😱💔

I recoiled, thinking it was because of something I'd said. Any negative attitude on my part can affect others. I felt really bad but a few moments later I got a chance to make a feeble effort to make it up to him. He thought he saw a cigarette on the street and chased after it in the wind. It turned out to be something else. When he came back, I asked him what kind of cigarettes he liked. He named his favorite brand. I went into

Amal's and bought him a whole pack, choosing the more expensive selection in an effort to lift his spirits.

He was surprised and grateful for the whole pack of high-class cigarettes. His whole demeanor changed. He carefully opened the package and took one out. The first thing he did next was think of someone else. Instead of lighting it for himself he said, "that guy over there would like one." He walked over to an older, more disheveled man who lay on the sidewalk with only a blanket and handed him the cigarette.

I met Rich, a professional chef who'd recently lost his job and had become homeless. Then his van with all his things in it had been stolen. He was dressed neatly and didn't look poor, but he was going to sleep outside on this cold night without even a blanket. He said his experience the night before had been brutal. I happened to have in the truck an extra sleeping bag which I gave him. It was the last one of five which I'd bought cheap at a garage sale and given the rest away. Even though it was a kid one it would make a big difference for him. At that garage sale I'd also gotten an excellent backpack for only seven dollars and had given it away to someone who it turned out had been praying for one.

I've occasionally included here some of the ways I get to help the house-free, to try to pay them back for the inspiration and strength and wisdom they give me. I believe and hope that mentioning this is not out of ego, but to show how to buy happiness and the love of others for very little money. It feels good to try to give a man self-worth and hope for just a thirteen-dollar pack of cigarettes instead of a ten-dollar pack. My helping others is partly motivated by self-interest: it gets me high. It buys me their love. I don't see anything wrong with that. Jesus taught us to give to each other and to love each other, because that's how we approach God.

A day later I got a voicemail from the man who'd wanted to kill himself the day before. He was breathlessly excited. He said, "Something happened last night after we talked. Something opened inside of me. I felt lovely... for the first time... I felt so close to God!" A few days later I saw him with a soft new beige puppy, his new best friend. He was holding the puppy very close inside his jacket, putting his face against the puppy's face.

Even though there aren't that many of us left, the evening Haight magic is still there. There are still a few green and magenta lights on some of the trees that haven't been cut down yet. Orange and his friends were making music with a variety of instruments, including a huge double bass, a giant violin as tall as Tad who was playing it. They looked so cool, and the music was great. I joined in with my tambourine and danced. Linda Kelly came by and took pictures for her magazine, The Haight Street Voice.

Tad, an intelligent-looking young man with wire- rimmed glasses, gave me a very nice hug, but I had to be careful to avoid the spikes on his leather jacket. He told me how he'd recently lost two RVs with everything he had. One was taken for unpaid tickets and the other for no registration. I wonder where he's keeping the double bass.

SHOT TWICE IN THE CHEST

I showed up as usual at Buena Vista Park at the stairway which used to be called the Rainbow Stairs, before the city used water cannons to blast the colors off. Before jackhammers hacked to pieces the beautiful concrete bench there where people used to sit and gather. Before the cameras were installed.

Young people still congregate there, in fewer numbers, and much less comfortably. The big white bulbous cameras on the lamp posts are a constant presence. The people kind of ignore them, do what they normally would do, in defiance of police state legislation. The damp and muddy grass on the sloping hillside near the pond is not nearly as comfortable as the wonderful row of big logs we used to be able to sit on next to the beautiful pond, where hippies exercised their Constitutional right to gather for half a century. Until the cameras went up around the pond.

The big trees we loved on Haight are cut down. There are no more green and magenta colored lights at night. I'm bringing these things up

again not just in outrage at what's been done to this special place. I want to bring attention to the way it's being done the same way to all the holy places, the forests and the waters, and all living things. It's being done to the holy things inside of us.

The violence that the totalitarian Beast unleashes on us showed its true face on Saturday night. A friend of ours was shot twice in the chest by an off-duty FBI agent. I believe he could've been sent there to make trouble. It happened right on the corner of Haight and Ashbury.

I wasn't there, though I'd been standing right there with a group of people for hours the night before. When I arrived at the stairway on Sunday morning, I was surprised to see an unusually large group of young people gathered there. They told me what had happened.

The plainclothes FBI agent had arrived, evidently looking like any of the house-free. He started arguing with an African American man who he was taller than, and then shoved him violently against the wall. I was told that the guy who got shoved was saying, "I'll roll one for both of us and we can smoke it together." Our friend tried to stop the fight. The FBI agent, who they say was drunk, pointed a gun at him and shot him twice in the chest.

It was a shock that it happened right on the corner of Haight and Ashbury, our special citadel of the biggest peace movement the world has ever seen. It was jarring that I'd been standing right there the night before, dancing with Bulldog to street music. And despite the obvious danger I'll probably stand there again. We're holding onto that corner as if in a siege, keeping the dream alive. I was shaken about where it had happened, and that I could've caught a stray bullet in my favorite hang-out place. But I was about to have my mind completely blown.

The night it happened I was at home working on what I thought to be the very last procedure to finally complete this book, arranging the photographs on the back cover. I was finished and in a celebratory mood, pleased with the result of my work. Just a few days before, Linda Kelly of the Haight Street Voice had taken a video of some friends and I making music on the street, including a mandolin, a guitar, my tambourine, and Tad playing his giant double bass.

I asked her to email it to me and I took some stills from it to put on the back cover of the book. I put in a great picture of our impromptu little street band. The bass was so big that the top of it covered Tad's face in the picture, so I decided to add a different picture of just him with the double bass, at the top left of the back cover of the book.

When I found out who'd been shot, it made me dizzy. It was him. It happened at 11:34 PM, while I was working on that page with his picture on it. It was just minutes before the final moments of working on this book, its actual birth.

Something violent and horrible happened in a place considered sacred by many. However, God used it to show that the force is with us and with this book. I've seen so many times how the miraculous can take something awful like this and somehow use it to encourage or help us. In my experience it doesn't send us trouble but tries to turn it to our advantage when it happens. It turns out that Tad will survive, though I'm not sure in what condition. On the night when he almost lost his life, his picture was being placed on the back cover of this book, maybe in some way letting him live on. (I wasn't able to put these pictures in yet due to limits of Amazon cover formatting. Will fix back cover later.)

Injustice and violence are made by man, not God. I'm not blaming the local police or even the local officials who go along with unjust business policies to get the homeless off the streets. I blame their bosses' bosses' bosses, and whoever or whatever sends guys out there to make trouble on Haight Street. We know that clandestine operations to screw things up around here have historically happened before.

Following the money trail usually reveals that it's big investing corporations that want to get rid of the homeless everywhere, that want to rebuild everything and make tons of money and enslave mankind with cameras while they're at it. In my mind those hippies on that corner are facing off with a corporate plutocracy, like true Americans. It's good versus evil, liberty versus enslavement, humanity fighting the Beast.

As the day continued, I ran into people who'd been there when it happened, and others who'd shown up after they'd heard the gunshots. They said that Bulldog was holding him as he lay bleeding in the street. They said that Tad had said to Bulldog, "I think I'm dying. Will you grab my guitar?" Later Tad said he thought that Bulldog had saved his life by telling him that he wasn't going to die.

Bulldog had been in such high spirits the night before. He'd been going around telling everyone he loved them. He'd even said that he might again start wearing the beautiful blue tie-dyed top hat I'd given him, about which he'd been mysteriously threatened, that if he wore that hat here, "the whole community would pay." We'd talked about what this place represents, brotherly love and freedom. He'd said about the scene here, in a very serious attitude, "It's my *life*." What happened must've been a terrible trauma for him. His beautiful tie-dyes must've been soaked with blood. Nobody's seen him since the shooting.

It's said that 911 wasn't called for ten minutes, and that when the ambulance finally got there, they didn't do anything for him for a long time. Chelsea and Hayden got there soon after it happened. They told me that they saw a sheet covered with blood in the middle of the street (north side of Ashbury.) They said it was completely soaked, and that it was left there for over an hour. You can actually see the sheet in one of the news photos.

It shook me that I was putting his picture on the back cover of the book while he was getting shot, and that it happened in what I believed to be the last moments of completing my three-year project. Two amazing coincidences were enough to convince me that the miraculous was involved and was trying to encourage us. But God wasn't done blowing my mind.

I ran into another friend of mine, a Renaissance man with a white beard named Skywalker. He handed me a copy of this book. He said he'd found it just lying on the sidewalk on the corner of Haight and Ashbury the night of the shooting, twenty feet from where it happened. He'd thought he'd better pick it up before the police cordoned off the area. I'd only made ten advance copies bound with clips, and I thought they were all accounted for. Other people saw it, but nobody knows how it got there.

LIABILITY LAWS

I'd thought the book was finished but then had to add more. I went to visit Tad in the hospital. He's alive but in pain and hooked up to many tubes and wires. The wound down the whole front of his chest and torso had become infected. At one point he'd thrown up and the sutures had ripped apart, and that morning they'd had to do surgery over again. As soon as it was allowed, about a hundred of his "street family" had come to visit. Three were there when I arrived. He said that having these visitors made him feel better, instead of making him tired. His story hit the news wires and made it all the way to the New York Times.

Tad claims that he didn't touch the FBI guy, whom people say was drunk. The guy said he was FBI as he tried to rummage through the other man's pockets, but he didn't show a badge. The kids didn't believe him and thought he was just a tweaker (on hard drugs, unwelcome on Haight Street.) When they saw the gun, they didn't believe it was real. He waved the gun around and then pointed it at a dog, which is probably what prompted Tad to act. Right before it happened Tad was lifting up his shirt to show that he was unarmed, and he was telling the guy "Go home Bro!"

I went to a community meeting about the shooting. People seemed to be blaming the local police for the FBI incident, who probably had little to do with it since the FBI is not in their jurisdiction. I'm convinced that liability procedural laws mandated the actions of local police that night.

It was horrible that Tad had been handcuffed with his hands behind his back while he was bleeding to death in the street, and that he'd had a gun held against his head the whole time. He'd also been handcuffed to a bed at the hospital at first. Again I think this must've been due to insurance-mandated liaility procedures about "safety." If the officers don't comply with such horrors, I think they can lose their jobs even if nothing "unsafe" happens.

In the emergency room Tad had asked for his mother and they didn't contact her, probably an influence of "HIPPA" laws to "protect privacy," another liability law which makes those who love liberty throw up, and against which police and hospital staff have no defense. At first we could't contact him, because when there's been a violent crime, hospitals list patients with a false name. When his cousin drove up from Southern California to see him, he was turned away.

It amazes me that liability laws which impact almost everything we do, are rarely mentioned though they slaughter our liberty. Liability laws molest us financially, spiritually, and even sexually (getting felt up at airport gates.) I believe they are the reason Tad was handcuffed and why a gun was held to his head.

HIT AND RUN AT HAIGHT AND ASHBURY

They didn't just accidentally bump into somebody with their car. It was deliberate and it was vicious. They drove right up onto the sidewalk, pinning a friend of ours named Chris against the wall with their SUV. It was on the same part of the same wall, the same exact spot, where the altercation had begun about two weeks before that had ended up with Tad being shot twice in the chest for trying to stop a fight.

Again, somebody they'd never seen before showed up trying to start trouble on that iconic corner. I think it's more than a coincidence. Developers who invest in high-rises and who rebuild sidewalks and streets and cut down trees have a lot to gain from places being designated "high-injury corridors" under the "Vision Zero Plan" to eliminate traffic fatalities by 2024. I'm also often suspicious of windfall-generating entities like BID's, "Business Improvement Districts, and GBD's, "Green Benefit Districts," and also CID's, "Community Improvement Districts."

On a Monday night two people showed up, again trying to start trouble on that particular corner. The story is they argued with the people there because they wouldn't sell them drugs. Somebody told me you could smell alcohol on them twenty feet away. Then they got into their white SUV and drove around the block aggressively for a long time, over and over. Nobody could've imagined what happened next.

Suddenly the SUV made a U-turn on Haight, gunning the engine. Then it rushed over the curb and onto the sidewalk, pinning Chris against the wall and seriously injuring him with internal bleeding. Someone said he had a skull fracture. (Chris is mentioned in "Business Improvement Districts.") One person got their foot run over and a girl landed on the hood. The driver then backed up and continued the rampage down Ashbury, driving on the sidewalk all the way down the block to Page Street. On the way he hit a wall, some parked vehicles, several planters, and a metal fence railing. He drove away but police caught him near Twin Peaks, where he also rammed a police car. 🏁

We tried to see Chris in the hospital but couldn't find him because he wasn't listed there under his real name. When there's been a violent crime, they use pseudonyms to "protect privacy." His friends are eager to support him and find out how he's doing, but only immediate family are allowed to do that. Being a street kid, chances are he probably doesn't have any immediate family around here. He only has his "street family."

I found out about it a few days after it happened. I heard the story from several eyewitnesses, who claimed that the people in the car were "rich yuppies." I saw the chalk markings the police had made when gathering evidence. On the intersection of Haight and Ashbury you could see a white chalk circle where they made the U-turn. There were chalk marks on the wall where Chris had been pinned by the SUV. There were small chalk circles on the sidewalk where evidence had been gathered. White chalk lines were drawn all the way down the block where the vehicle had barreled down the sidewalk. I saw the broken wall and planters, and the broken fence railing lying on the ground. Even our favorite tree, one of the few left on Haight Street, has a gash in it. I hope they don't use this as an excuse to cut it down.

Two violent events attacking hippies within a little over two weeks, both on that same special corner, seems like more than a coincidence. Three months later again a car jumped the sidewalk, at Haight and Masonic, narrowly missing about a dozen people. If it's not the powers that be that are doing this, like developers and investors sending provocateurs, could it be the very powers of death trying to stop the powers of life? Is it despair trying to get rid of hope?

Soon afterward they put up two cameras at Haight and Ashbury, aimed at the spot near the 420 clock where young people like to sit when they arrive here on their pilgrimages. The powers that be also installed two blinding lights there. I cried.

Note: All these things were said by Jesus (from KJV), though not in the same order. A few words in parentheses were added.

God's Message to Treehuggers and Peacemakers:

IF THE WORLD HATE YOU

Blessed are they which are persecuted for righteousness' sake:

> **for theirs is the kingdom of heaven.**

Blessed are you when men shall revile you, and persecute you, and shall say

> all manner of evil against you falsely, for my sake. (for his peace teachings)

Rejoice, and be exceeding glad: for great is your reward in heaven (here, now):

> for so persecuted they the prophets which were before you.
> (Matthew 5:10-12)

Herein is my Father glorified, that **ye bear much (spiritual) fruit**;

> so shall ye be (already are) my disciples. **Continue ye in my love.** (Jn. 15:8-9)

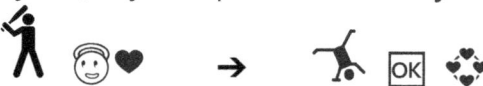

If the world hate you, ye know that

> **it hated me before it hated you.** If you were of the world,

the world would love his own: but because **ye are not of the world**, but

> I have chosen you out of the world, therefore the world hateth you.

If they have persecuted me, they will also persecute you.

if they have kept my saying, they will keep yours also.

This cometh to pass, that it might be fulfilled that is written in their law,

"**They hated me without a cause.**" (John 15:18-20, 25)

(could say that about the homeless)

Woe unto you when all men shall speak well of you!

For so did their fathers to the false prophets. (Luke 6:26)

Blessed are ye, when men shall hate you,

when they shall separate you from their company, and shall reproach you, and cast out your name as evil, for the Son of Man's sake. (teaching peace)

Rejoice ye in that day, and **leap for joy**: for your reward is great in heaven: for in the like manner did their fathers unto the prophets. (Luke 6:22-23)

But **there shall not an** (long) **hair of your head perish.** (Luke 21:18)

If men call the master of the household (Jesus) the "Prince of Evil,"

what sort of names will they give to his servants?

But **never let them frighten you**. (Matthew 10:25-26)(Phillips Bible)

Behold, **I give you power over**

all the power of the enemy (bad laws):

Built to Last

and **nothing shall by any means** (truly) **hurt you.** Notwithstanding in this rejoice not, that the spirits (of corporate greed) are subject unto you;

rather **rejoice, because your names are written in heaven.**

(Luke 10:19-20)

Woe unto the world because of offences! = 💩

All they that take the sword

shall perish with the sword. (Matthew 26:52)

Every one that doeth evil (economic exploitation)
hateth the light, neither cometh to the light,

lest his deeds should be reproved.

But he that doeth truth (you) **cometh to the light,**

that his deeds may be manifest, that they are wrought in God.

(John 3:20-21)

JESUS DIDN'T TEACH: that all are born in sin, the Inquisition, excommunication (shunning,) slaves and women "obey in all things," Adam and Eve, idolaters and gays are "worthy of death," anti-Semitism, shame of the body, hell, tithing, having to go to church, the Divine Right of Kings, that the Bible was perfect, or that he created the world. Paul the Apostle and OTHERS ADDED those, plus "obey every ordinance of man," "let the unjust be unjust still," that you have to believe or be damned (right before it says that you can "take up serpents" and drink poison,) and that it's not what you do that counts, but what you believe in. Dangerous red letters in the book of Revelation are the writer's vision or dream and don't teach what Jesus taught. The Prince of Peace taught kindness, brotherly love, and Heaven on Earth.

ORANGE PLASTIC BARRIERS

In Golden Gate Park there are now big swaths of bright orange plastic mesh fencing on both sides of the entrance. The intrusive orange penetrates the forest and continues on over the hills. Most of the spaces where hippies gathered (before the cameras) have been blocked off. There's a six-foot chain link fence all the way from the street to the bridge. For several hundred feet it covers the stairway and every single log the community used to sit on.

In the beautiful area that was already blocked off, which I wrote about in "Fencing Off Heaven," there's an empty spot of sky where a gorgeous, huge Eucalyptus tree used to be. Peering into a small opening in the green tarps covering the fencing, I saw that the whole place is churned up with bare dirt. They may even have removed some of the oaks. Attached to the chain link fencing there's a big green banner showing diagrams of the many planned changes. Across the bottom is written: "THIS SITE IS MONITORED FOR SECURITY PURPOSES. IF YOU WITNESS ACTS OF VANDALISM OR TRESPASSING, PLEASE CALL 311."

The magic of the pond is about to be desecrated with a dozen cheesy exhibits all around it telling people nature facts. The plan is to put an ugly wooden pier jutting out into the water, so that those in wheelchairs can have equal access to the edge, which is just a few feet from the flat road from which they can already comfortably enjoy the pond. I think many of our handicapped brothers and sisters might rather see the wonderful pond the way it is.

Looking at Haight Street without its trees is like looking at a beloved child whose beautiful curls have been cut off by a stepmother. The Hippie

Capital of the World is still beautiful, we don't love it any less, but seeing it that way brings up sorrow and rage. How much do we have to give up to the machines, the liability laws, the financial goals of banks and big companies? Must every pretty thing in our lives be swallowed up by the corporate Beast? Is debt slavery forcing people to worship a non-human entity, the corporation born on a piece of paper, instead of the living God?

The street is very dark at night without the green and pink colored lights that used to be on the trees. There are very few people. The new sidewalks are a dirty grey, though they do sparkle. There are big orange plastic barriers everywhere, or the orange plastic mesh around the remaining trees, plus large and small machines. Two years of street construction is putting many shops out of business, and the new "traffic-calming" "bulb-outs" of the new sidewalks are destroying precious parking.

On that dark street I met Colby, an appealing young man and former foster child with short blond hair. He told me a heavy story about a miraculous experience he'd had. He said he'd tried to kill himself by taking some pills. About a half an hour later, he said, "suddenly a gust of wind blew into the room and hit me in the chest and knocked me down and I started to throw up all the pills." Strangely the pills were still intact, though they should've been dissolved by then. An hour later he got a phone call saying his mom committed suicide at the same time he'd tried to. He feels that in some way his mom exchanged her life for his.

LOOKING FOR SOMETHING TO BELIEVE IN

It has become hard for the house-free to even survive. Train hopping is a criminal act called "Theft of Services." Squatting is "Adverse Possession." Urinating on a tree can get someone put on a sex offender watchlist. Vehicle Habitation can lead to huge fines or confiscation of the vehicle. Bus benches are designed so people can't sleep on them, and the bus shelters are now made open on the sides so that homeless can't be protected from the wind there, more "hostile architecture." Some sinks and water fountains are even designed to make it hard to fill water bottles. I tried to get water for someone's dog, managed to sneak into a bathroom at a bar, but couldn't get the bottle into the tiny sink to fill it.

    The young travelers are being treated with hate and fear, like other homeless people who are resented and despised. The new policies are being enforced with little regard for what this place stands for and why people come here. I believe that most of the business investors causing this situation don't even live or work here. I know that many of the people who live in houses or apartments here, and many of the shopkeepers, enjoy the young people. They seem to understand that many of them are foster kids who've never had a real home to go to, who've come to this place looking for something to believe in.

    Some shop owners, however, have had enough of a few street kids who hassle or scare away customers, who make it bad for everybody. There are those who stand near restaurants and ask departing patrons with take-out boxes, "Are you attached to those leftovers?" A few actually lay guilt trips on the customers, venting their anger about the way things are. During this challenging time of street construction and also greatly increased rents for their stores, who can blame business owners who worry that the presence of a pack of gypsies and Pitbulls near their door might discourage potential clientele?

    With the community dismembered and "the regulators" gone, the people who used to keep the other ones in line, violence and theft have increased. Shoplifting has become more of a problem. Previously, if someone saw something they knew to be stolen, they often might take it and bring it back. Nobody wanted the community to get a bad name. At that time business was better than it is now, and the vendors could absorb an occasional loss. That's no longer the case.

The closing of the McDonald's must've been a tremendous boost to Coffee to the People, now almost the only place the house-free can go in the morning to get indoors, get a warm drink, or maybe to try to use the restroom. There's a sign on the window that says, "Restrooms for Customers Only," but the restaurant cuts the young people some slack. It's possible to just wait until someone uses it and comes out, without having to ask to be let in. Most people just go ahead and buy the three-dollar coffee or four-dollar pastries, or even the seven-dollar lasagna or quiche. It's worth it if you can afford it to get to sit around for hours with Internet access, not only at tables but on cushy couches in a lounge area with bookshelves full of books you can read for free.

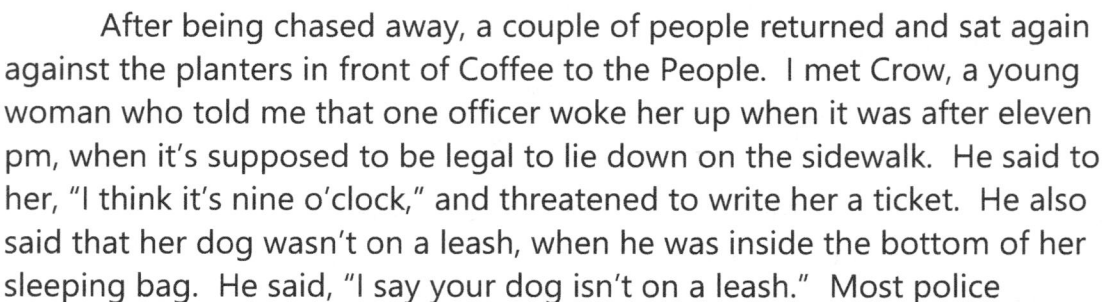

In front of Coffee to the People is one of the few places where a handful of youth can still gather. Though it was after eleven pm, when supposedly people are allowed to rest there near the closed restaurant, I saw three big police officers addressing about four people. A smiling Bam Bam was telling the police that they and he should understand each other because they're both peacekeepers.

After being chased away, a couple of people returned and sat again against the planters in front of Coffee to the People. I met Crow, a young woman who told me that one officer woke her up when it was after eleven pm, when it's supposed to be legal to lie down on the sidewalk. He said to her, "I think it's nine o'clock," and threatened to write her a ticket. He also said that her dog wasn't on a leash, when he was inside the bottom of her sleeping bag. He said, "I say your dog isn't on a leash." Most police officers we meet aren't like that at all and often do what they can to help the kids, despite strict official policies.

She told me about her horrible childhood, a violent father who beat up her mother in front of her, "beat a baby out of her." She said he also was a molester and tried to set her home on fire. She was extremely bitter and teared up when telling me the story. Maybe she tries to make up for the family she never had with her dog and two cats, at last something warm she can love and trust. I was so glad that the officer decided not to take her dog. She seemed to get a lot of comfort out of her animals, petting them one after the other.

I saw her a few days later and she told me about a frightening experience. She was sitting on the sidewalk in daytime eating a cup-a-noodle when two police officers asked her to stand up. She told them that she had a medical exemption to sit down because she might have seizures, and that the information was in their system, and that they'd already seen her paperwork. She didn't stand up. They told her that if she didn't stand up, they would take her dog. She said, "You're not taking my dog!" She admits that she was rude to the cops.

Two other officers showed up. Though she was by then standing up she was slammed to the ground. She started having a seizure. A female cop pulled a male cop off of her. One officer tied her feet, and another handcuffed her. Luckily, the police let a friend be put in charge of her pets. She was taken away in an ambulance. She was released the next day but has an order to appear in court. She's charged with two serious misdemeanors, Resisting Arrest and Battery on a Police Officer.

I met Mitch, who has a van and a huge black Lab called Bear, with big paws though still a pup. He said he'd met a guy who'd told him he'd been working eight-hour shifts for four months putting shackles in train cars. I asked another man, an electrician, what he knew about the surveillance projects he'd been hired to work on. I asked him if FEMA camps were real. He claimed that across the country there are three thousand of them.

BOLD OUTLINES

    My heart aches when I look at Haight Street without its beautiful trees. How dark the street is without the green and magenta lights wound around the trunks of those big trees, lighting up the night and the graceful skateboarders sailing past. Sometimes the area is strangely silent. With the trees cut down, the birds have also gone. There are still just a few young people playing guitars and talking about how to save the world. When the place is turned into a mall, will there be any real community left, any human interaction besides that of business?

    Our end of Golden Gate Park is completely crisscrossed with bright orange construction barriers. The pond has been drained, the edges stripped of vegetation, and an ugly pier is being built that juts out into the middle of it. The logs we used to sit on are now behind a chain link fence. The concrete horseshoe area has been completely demolished. The stairway near Stanyan where we used to gather no longer exists. The parklet benches in front of the grocery store have also been removed.

    Some bizarre circular benches have been installed around some of the park's big trees. They feature "hostile architecture," special "armrests" designed to prevent the homeless from sleeping on the benches. The strange awkwardly angled armrests look like they should be backrests, but they are placed in the opposite direction. The benches are inscribed with weird cryptic sayings that don't always make sense. I guess we're supposed to focus on that instead of on nature. You can't lean back or rest your arm on these benches. They look like something in a surreal, dystopian painting.

Somewhere in this city and maybe in foreign countries, investors and contractors are celebrating. I can't believe that all that life is gone, and all this deadness has arrived. The corporate regime seems to be all about **TAKING THE HIGHLIGHTS OUT OF OUR LIVES!** The tall trees, the colorful youth, don't fit into its plan. What Jesus said about brotherly love and the Heaven within us doesn't fit into what most churches tell people about mankind being cursed and born in sin, which Jesus didn't teach.

The bold outlines of nature and of love, and of our real interactions with God, must be curtailed in order for the totalitarian Beast to have power over us. Anything that's real, anything that's good and normal, must be bought and sold. Whatever deters from the Beast's single-minded profit-seeking and lust for power is discouraged. Anything that increases its sway over us, like divisive issues, is encouraged either by brainwashing or legislation.

Later **THEY REMOVED ALL THE LOGS** along the pond where the community used to sit and visit. They replaced them with these weird phallic-looking black metal pillars, about six inches thick and round on top. These fenceposts with chains in between line the walkway and discourage people from ever sitting there again. Just in case anyone should decide to step over the barricade and try to sit there anyway, the ground where the logs used to be is lined with big sharp rocks. 😱

The ledge across the pond where we used to sit has been bulldozed. Anywhere people can gather has been eradicated. Nitrogen-leaching wood chips, put there to keep plants from growing, cover the ground. They look uncomfortable to sit on.

I looked up San Francisco's history of trying to chase the hippies out of Haight Street. In 1992 a large encampment near the Horseshoe was bulldozed. This must've been the bushes with tunnels and grottos carved out which people have told me about. From what I hear it was an amazing magical space, a little hippie village. At that time there was a mean-spirited program against the homeless called, tellingly, "the Matrix." I need to look it up to see if it's still in force. The 1992 article that I read about it portrayed all the homeless as mentally ill or dope addicts. Some legislators wanted to put people "in camps," and some still do.

One day there was a big white police van parked for hours right across from the clock corner of Haight and Ashbury, the kind they can lock people up in. It made the kids nervous, as it seemed to them that the two police officers inside must be watching them. As I walked by Ben and Jerry's where the van was, one of the cops said "Hi!" We started a conversation.

They seemed very friendly and extremely bored from sitting there for hours, as they were required to do. They didn't seem to be doing any surveillance. From our conversation I got the impression that they liked the kids. It even seemed to me that they would've liked to be a part of the magic of Haight Street. One of them said sadly, "There's hate on the Haight," maybe referring to how some of the house-free feel about police and the mandates they're hired to enforce. He seemed hurt by this.

The other cop said with a laugh, "If I had the money I've spent buying the kids meals I'd be rich."

A LIVING SAINT

Manfred arrived with a shopping bag packed with hot food for everyone. He makes this food for free at least every Sunday when I'm here, and maybe a lot more. I don't know how often he does this during the week. He usually has a little two-wheeled cart with the food in it and often some hot tea. This time he only had the big shopping bag, but it was fully loaded with stacked plastic containers full of delicious home-made food. The containers were not the small size you'd get with one serving of food. They were the kind that are taller, big enough maybe to hold two meals for that person. 🍜🍜 ☺

He's a tall middle-aged man who doesn't look rich. He has a very kind face and there's a glow about him as he goes around passing out gifts to the penniless who sleep on the sidewalk. His story is that years ago he ended up at the Haight to give away leftover Thanksgiving food and it completely transformed his life. He felt that he'd seen God among the homeless and decided to devote his life to the service of others. ☺

A Newsweek article about him on Google titled "Man Feeds Homeless in San Francisco" says that he's been doing this for eight years and feeds about two hundred people. At the time of the article, he'd made over 80,000 meals and spent about $150,000. He is now listed among "Heroes of the Pandemic." The street kids call his dinners "Manfred Food" and give him little gifts. When he arrives with his cart, he calls out to them with his German accent, "Hey angels!"

With his radiant smile I let him give me one of the white opaque plastic containers. Inside there was savory macaroni with some vegetables, with two big pieces of chicken breast on top. The container was so packed it was hard to close the lid. It reminds me of what Jesus said that God would fill our cup "packed down and running over." Manfred didn't just throw this food together with cheap ingredients. He made it as if he were preparing it for someone he truly loved, with utmost care. It was as if he were preparing it for God.

There is always the risk of people being stopped from feeding the homeless by red tape and liability laws. I'm told that in some parts of town businesses have to spray bleach on food in trash bins to keep the homeless away, a liberty-destroying policy mandated by insurance.

Big insurance companies find or create new "risks' for their profit, then make giant "compliance agreements" with lots of rules that must be obeyed, or they cancel the insurance or won't pay on claims. Their lawyers use mammoth lobbying resources to make the insurance mandatory for all businesses, homes, organizations, etc. Their complex compliance agreements make it unlikely that anyone will be able to sue for the "protection" they're supposed to get. The remedy offered when they cheat us is laughable. Who wants to sue a corporation when you'd have to pay their massive legal bills if you lose?

Somebody spills coffee on their lap, then every restaurant has to have insurance in case it ever happens again. It won't, because compliance agreements probably say that the coffee can't be above a certain temperature. The million-dollar initial award, the "test case," sets the price of the insurance. It threatens the businesses, homes, or organizations with the loss of everything if they make an honest mistake or if something happens on property they own.

I haven't been personally able to track down the details about this system, or whether I'm completely correct about all of it, because people are so hesitant to talk about it, possibly because of gag orders in the policies. Maybe they're just embarrassed to be so enslaved. This is why restaurant bathrooms are for customers only, though nobody ever says so. This is why the cameras are put up in the parks. Insurers make laws to "protect" us from sexual harassment in the workplace, then they tell us who we can date or marry, and make employers install cameras.

Manfred keeps doing what he does even though his car's been stolen twice, and his credit cards are maxed out. A friend started a GoFundMe page for him, but he's only received $500. By some miracle he continues on the beautiful spiritual path he's on.

LIVING THE DREAM

People still gather in front of the music store that's closing. The area under the awning has always been a safe zone for street musicians. Now against the garish yellow signs plastered to the windows announcing close-out sales, people congregate. There are more there than just musicians, as if the survivors of the Haight community have piled into a lifeboat. Without the trees they feel exposed at their usual spot a few doors down, in the glaring light with no shade or shelter.

Here in front of the music store there's some semblance of how things were before they cut the trees. Soon this too will be gone. Will it become yet another trendy restaurant? I met the owner, a man who was grieving and apologetic that he couldn't hold onto it any longer in these economic conditions. Massoud Badakhshan has owned the Haight Ashbury Music Center since 1980. He said he hasn't paid himself a salary in years. Rasputin Records, with its colorful mural, is also closing.

Along with a few musicians and some of the old crowd I saw beautiful Stella, lighting up the place in a gorgeous red long skirt and blouse. I'd met her on the Rainbow Stairs months ago when she'd looked like an ordinary college student, and I'd introduced her that day to some of my house-free friends as we'd walked down Haight Street. Now she's often here and always dresses artfully, and she dances in the drum circle. She wanted me to look up a Grateful Dead song called "Stella Blue." A line in the song goes, "...and nothing comes for free. There's nothing you can hold for very long."

Also sitting in front of the music store was a woman named Sister Nikki playing a small drum. She'd come to the Haight looking for something, some meaning or connection, after a personal tragedy. Though with a broken heart, she tried to absorb the magic of this place. I suggested that maybe it was her love of God had that brought her here, not just being homeless. Maybe she chose the right thing in coming here, looking for more than the mundane.

Three police officers came and stood on either side of our group in front of the music store. They asked one guy to move on. Then another man started yelling at the cops, about how people's belongings get confiscated because of minor infractions. With emotion he asked them how they thought it would feel to lose every single thing they have, to be out here with no blanket or sleeping bag. They didn't do anything to him and after a while they walked on.

Many of the police are surprisingly sympathetic to the kids. These usually get transferred to other locations. There was a blond policewoman that everybody liked. She's not there anymore. In another part of town, I talked to an officer who was in charge of "cleaning up" the messy camp of an old homeless guy. He told me he was sad to have to take his blankets. He said, "I don't like this part of my job." He let the guy grab back a lot of his stuff off the truck as it was pulling away.

Dragon got her wonderful little car taken by the city because it broke down and she couldn't move it. Again, she and her husband stay on Clayton Street with a cart piled high with their belongings, two dogs and a big dog crate for the puppies. When they have to move their stuff, they put the dog crate with the puppies on a skateboard. At first she was very upset, but now her tremendous fortitude seems to have kicked in again.

Surrounded by the community that gathers around her, I saw her laugh while winning at "Dogimos," which is played with dominos on top of her cloth dog crate, which is not level enough to play dominos the usual way. She has gotten art supplies and has started creating and selling miniature paintings to tourists, using the dog crate for an art table.

A police car pulled up to the clock corner of Haight and Ashbury. Bulldog was asked abruptly, "What are you doing?"

He replied, "I'm living the dream."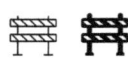

THEY CAN'T ERASE US

I hate to be the bearer of bad news, but here's a list of all the things that have disappeared in a few short months as the area was "cleaned up" to please developers. Our beautiful trees and lights are gone, the parklet where we used to gather in the evening, the McDonald's, the old sidewalks where giants walked, the big red hearts, the music store. Gypsy Men is gone where they sold period costumes and steampunk fashion. Where will I now find brass goggles or a top hat with gears on it?

Time-travelling at the gutted Magnolia brewery and the ancient Michael Collins pub, or the hattery, are all gone. The restaurant where you could smoke from a hookah is gone, and the Burger Urge with its giant plastic hamburger. "Taking It to the Streets," a non-profit that used to help the kids get jobs, is gone, and the Free Clinic. Bathrooms are gone, parking is gone, and some of the murals have been painted over. Love on Haight is repainted. The book store has been moved to a less visible location. The Red Victorian is empty and covered with graffiti.

The tie-dyed t-shirt shop on the corner of Haight and Ashbury that used to let the kids gather on that special corner under the clock, is gone. I hear that there are plans to put a flower stand on that spot to keep the kids away. Worst of all most of the kids are gone, their music, their smiles and hugs, their clever cardboard signs. Costumed icons like Wendy Whimsey and Scott have been chased away with threats.

I believe outside forces have been sending in thugs and hard drugs, like they did to destroy the movement in the 60's. There have been thefts, fights, stabbings, hit and runs, and a shooting. A dog was stabbed to death by a "tweaker" screaming that hippies ruined his mom's life. With so many of us gone, our Shanti Sena peacemakers are not here to stop trouble and keep out things like hard drugs, which are not welcome here.

At Buena Vista Park, the concrete bench is cut off. Day and night, the area around the "NO LOITERING" sign is under the eyes of two surveillance cameras. At Golden Gate Park about a dozen cameras destroy all privacy around the pond and what used to be the horseshoe. The logs are gone, replaced with a row of black metal pillars with chains between them so no-one can sit there, even on the embankment. Sharp boulders are lined up where the logs used to be under the chains, just in case someone tries to move a chain aside and sit there anyway.

At the pond, the frog fountain is gone. ✖ 🐸 💔 Most of the plants, the ferns and flowers, have been replaced with wood chips. The new big high jets of water with colored lights don't make the same gentle, sun-touched ripples that the little frog fountain made. Now the pond is just a hole with water in it. The ugly wooden pier jutting out into it makes it look so small.

There are empty spots of open sky where big trees used to be. Sometimes we're not sure if we remember if a tree was there, but it just feels different. Where the twin redwoods used to stand next to the pond it's pretty obvious: one trunk is abruptly cut off. There's another huge cut-off trunk like that in the oak grove I used to like to walk through on the way to the drum circle, and a gorgeous huge bush of blue flowers has been replaced with woodchips. Even the drum circle has been changed, big trees on the hill above it cut down so that the sunrays don't fall on the drummers the same way at sunset. 🪚 ☀️🌲🌲 → 💔

Some sort of lucrative urban renewal scheme started this process of destruction, then Covid came along and made the businesses fail. We can't even smile at each other any more behind those masks, or hug. 🦠 😷

Yet even all this isn't enough to wipe out the ideals and the hope that this place and these people stand for. Wherever they are opposed they will emerge stronger than before, because the heart of all humanity longs to free itself. THEY CAN ERASE THE PEACE SIGN BUT THEY CAN'T ERASE US!

SEEDS OF HOPE

I met Jimmy Flowers, surprised that I hadn't noticed him before in his nice suit jacket with flowers in the lapels, and with his charming demeanor. He's also called "The Flower Ninja" and "The Haight Street Gardener." He showed me a binder he has with big color photos of his beautiful creations. He finds a spot like a planter or the base of a tree, and plants flowers there with inspirational messages. Of the dozens he showed me I don't remember seeing any on Haight Street before. Could it be that the authorities take them down as soon as he puts them up?

The Bubble man was at his work with his big rolling bubble machine, filling the street with iridescent magic despite the absence of trees and people. The rainbow-colored bubbles popped against the cut-off trunks. Some amplified guitar music down the street seemed to express the wonder of this place, and the drama that's been taking place. I found out Dragon finally got a place in Public Housing after trying for years. I was told she showed up all dolled up, with her hair done and make-up.

On a weekday evening I felt drawn to the Haight, a time when I don't usually go. The streets were practically empty and dark. The only person I could find to talk to was John, a good-looking very clean young man with blue eyes and hair neatly tied back. It turned out he was very upset because he'd just broken up with his girlfriend. He said that he was glad to have found someone to talk to. ☾ 💔

He'd spent all his money on the extravagant girlfriend and wanted to find a way to earn at least enough to go back home in another state, although he didn't really want to leave. As we considered his predicament, something happened. Hayden and Chelsea were walking by and stopped to chat. They both work at Gus's Haight Street Grocery, and they said the store was hiring like mad. They were sure he'd get a job and Hayden said he could use him as a reference (even though he'd just met him.) It turns out he and John are both photographers and have a lot in common.

John applied the next morning and got the job. Now suddenly he has a good job and a new friend. The coincidences that had to occur to make this happen amount to what could be a miracle: I happened to go there when I usually don't, he was the only person around and happened to need a friend, Hayden and Chelsea happened to walk by, the store happened to be hiring, and he and Hayden both happened to be photographers. 📷 🤝 📷

My friend Johnathan was the first person to read this book, sitting on the sidewalk with his dog. He gave me a good review. When he's not reading it, he keeps his copy on the counter at Pipe Dreams so that other people can come and look at it. Cassie and Josh of Pipe Dreams bought the very first advance copy. 📖

I saw the couple Matt ("Everyman") and Grey, whom I'd met on the hill, who'd borrowed a manuscript of loose pages of this book. Grey had taken it away from Matt after he'd only got to read three pages. Then they'd split the pages into sections and secured them with metal clips and shared them with others. Kerry and Justin also got pieces of the manuscript. They all plan to switch sections when each person is finished reading. 📖 → 📖 → 📖

Matthew, a tall young man in a beautiful tie dye and long hair neatly tied back, was so passionate about finding solutions. He asked to meet with me over a meal to share ideas. A wonderful girl named Sophia did even more to give me confidence. She said she believed the "street kids" would all share my book on social media and make it go viral.

The area under the awning of the old music store is cordoned off with yellow tape so musicians can't gather there. My heart aches when I see and admit how much has changed. How glad I am to have made a record of what was here, and what might be again. I hope that what's in these pages will be like seeds of hope.

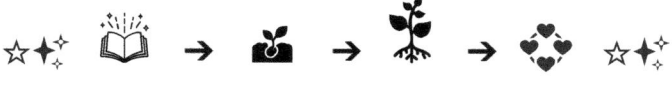

"WE LOVE YOU!"

On Haight toward Golden Gate Park there were a few people in a group. I met a graceful young woman, her blond hair shaved on one side. She wore a heavy chain as a necklace. ○○○○○○ = ⌒ I asked her about the sprinklers that had been installed in Buena Vista Park, which were turned on early in the mornings at random times to keep people from camping in the oak woods there. She said she didn't mind them, that she found it enjoyable to wake up refreshed in that way. She said that living out here had transformed her life for the better. ☼ 🚿 ▲ OK

Liking the sprinklers is an example of how the youth adapt and survive by making the best of things. It's like when we were told we couldn't sit on the logs and one kid said he preferred to sit on the ground because there he could feel the Earth's energy. It cheers me up just a little that cutting down trees might have made the place look more like it did in its heyday, when there were no big trees, as you could see in the big framed photo of the Grateful Dead playing there.

The hardy nomads said, "They can't keep us away." They will still gather on the gentrified sparkly sidewalks, even if they aren't allowed to sit

or lie down on them. They will still make music and get together in communities, like people have always done. They'll still talk about ways to3 save the world and ways to find God.

Everyman said, "I don't want to have security day to day from material things, but security in spiritual things. That's why I give things away, so I can be close to God. I have the strongest thing in the world. I have God. 😊 Because I want to rely on God, I'm the most bare-bones minimalist. Life is sufficient. Everything here is a blessing." Just then some well-off looking people in an SUV rolled down their window and gave us two containers of nice leftover food. 😊 🍲

A surveillance camera is pointed at what used to be the Rainbow Stairs, where people still like to sit even though the concrete bench has been hacked off. The other camera is aimed at the side of the hill against the trees, another favorite gathering place. Walking near there one night, I saw an official-looking vehicle and a man in a uniform get out, with what looked like a flashlight in his hand.

I stayed across the street in the dark behind a tree and watched to see what would happen. From where I was, I couldn't see if there were any young people sleeping on the landing at the top of the stairs, like they often did. If there were, was he going to chase them off or get them in trouble? From this distance I couldn't tell whether he was a police officer or a security guard. It looked like he was writing on a ticket book in his hand.

I got up my nerve and walked up to him and saw that nobody was trying to sleep there and that it was his cell phone in his hand, not a flashlight or a ticket book. Even in the dark I could sense that he was not aggressive or threatening. We started a conversation. It turns out he too was upset about the changes, would've liked for the stairway and the trees to stay the way they were. He said he'd made friends with a lot of the street kids. We both lamented the condition of the world.

      The Rainbow Gathering is a yearly peace celebration every July 1 – 7, with about twenty to forty thousand pacifists and hippies camped on federal land in different states. Everything is free and there are no leaders, as a functioning city is put up with string and branches and tarps in the wilderness and then seven days later is removed without a trace. There's a deeply spiritual feeling at the event, which is transformative for many. Strangers from all different economic and social backgrounds call each other "brother" and "sister." Occasionally some people shout, "WE LOVE YOU!" A loud voice calls out the words and is joined by others, until other people in a distant part of the camp shout back, "WE LOVE YOU TOO!" And so groups of people shout back and forth across the huge camp, sometimes for a long time.

      On Haight Street there are many people who've been to Rainbow Gatherings over the years. Recently someone stood on the corner of Haight and Ashbury and shouted at the top of their lungs, "WE LOVE YOU!" He kept repeating it, with different notes on the scale so that he was sort of singing it the way they do at the Gatherings. It didn't take long before someone recognized this and answered back, "WE LOVE YOU TOO!" Soon all of Haight echoed with a wonderful sound as dozens of people from Stanyan to Masonic joined in and made the call back and forth: "WE LOVE YOU!" ... "WE LOVE YOU TOOOO!"

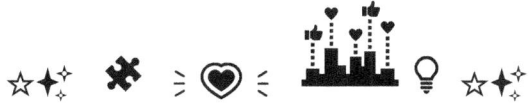

Note: The following things were all said by Jesus (from King James Version), though not in the same order. The few words in parentheses were added.

 God's Message to Treehuggers and Peacemakers:

GREATER WORKS

Blessed are your ears, for they hear: and your eyes, for they see. (Matt. 13:16)

Ye have not chosen me, but **I have chosen you**, and ordained you, ☮

that ye should go and bring forth fruit, and that your fruit should remain:

that what ye ask of the Father in my name he may give it you. (Jn. 15:16) 🎁

If ye have faith as a grain of mustard seed, **ye shall say unto this mountain**

(or bad law) **"remove hence," and it shall remove;**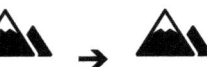

and **nothing shall be impossible unto you.** (Matthew 17:20)

Things which are impossible with men are possible with God. (Lk. 18:27)

Ye might say unto this sycamore tree, "Be thou plucked up by the root,

and be thou planted in the sea;" and it should obey you. (Luke 17:6)

Whosoever shall not doubt in his heart,

but shall believe that what he saith shall come to pass;

he **shall have whatsoever he saith.** (to heal the world) (Mark 11:23)

With God all things are possible. (Mark 10;27) ⛓ → 🗑

Built to Last

Hitherto have ye asked nothing in my name (to help reform the laws):

ask and ye shall receive, that your joy may be full.

I say unto you, **what things soever ye desire, when ye pray,**

believe that ye receive them, and ye shall have them. (Mk. 11:24)

What ye ask the Father in my name (healing laws), he will give you. (Jn.162:24)

If ye abide in me, and my words abide in you (Golden Rule) (Jn. 15:7),

verily, verily I say unto you, **he that believeth on me** (accepts his advice),

the works that I do, shall he do also:

and greater works than these shall he do; because I go to my Father.

If thou canst believe, all things are possible

to him that believeth. (John14:12) (Mark 9:23)

Be not afraid, only believe. (Mark 5:36)

JESUS DIDN'T TEACH: that all are born in sin, the Inquisition, excommunication (shunning,) slaves and women "obey in all things," Adam and Eve, idolaters and gays are "worthy of death," antisemitism, shame of the body, hell, tithing, having to go to church, the Divine Right of Kings, that the Bible was perfect, or that he created the world. Paul the Apostle and OTHERS ADDED those, plus "obey every ordinance of man," "let the unjust be unjust still," that you have to believe or be damned (right before it says that you can "take up serpents" and drink poison,) and that it's not what you do that counts, but what you believe in. Red letters in the book of Revelation are the writer's vision or dream and don't teach what Jesus taught.
The Prince of Peace taught kindness, brotherly love, and Heaven on Earth.

LET'S TAKE ONE STEP TOGETHER: At the giant Rainbow Gatherings in the wilderness people yell "WE LOVE YOU!" repeatedly on one side of the camp and others answer back, "WE LOVE YOU TOO!" Let's do the same thing out our windows at sunset on Saturdays, so that the Voice of the People can be heard! We could also play drums for half an hour at sunset on Saturdays at a window. Visit with or meet neighbors! WE NEED ALL OF US! (right + left)

Poems may be reprinted and shared by homeless for donations they can keep.
TELL TEN TO TELL TEN TO VOTE DEMOCRAT!   REGISTER 100 DEMOCRATS!
(https://www.usa.gov/register-to-vote)   (vote.gov) (rockthevote.org)
Democrats against forced mandates and other oppressive liability laws.
BILL OF RIGHTS   GOLDEN RULE   peacedrums.org   UNITE!

Democrat

Bill of Rights ≽ 📜 ≼ Use It or Lose It

A RENAISSANCE IS RUMBLING

    Johnathan now makes beautiful chalk pictures on the sidewalk. He uses art-grade oil pastels in brilliant rainbow colors. The wordless designs he draws are uplifting to passerby, who walk carefully around them in front of Pipe Dreams. He said to me, "I'm lucky I came to Haight Street, or I would've spent my life alone." Linda Kelly came by and took pictures of him making his art. She's re-starting her magazine, "The Haight Street Voice." The headline is, "A RENAISSANCE IS RUMBLING."

    Something is certainly percolating behind the scenes. We are more educated than past generations, more aware of things as they really are. Casting aside the dire predictions of prophets and seers, we can imagine a better future for mankind. We don't need to listen to experts trying to convince us that sensible laws are not possible.

    Linda and I went out to a seafood dinner at one of the newly reopened restaurants. I so enjoyed her conversation about trying to bring Haight Street back to life. We talked about getting the Merchants' Association to put back the lights on the trees, pink, green and orange like before. It had also been some local approval process that had painted the Rainbow Stairs in the first place, and so we hoped they might approve painting them again as a tourist attraction, this time by a professional artist. We talked about putting the red hearts back on the sidewalk.

We also talked about friends who have died recently, mostly of heart attacks and seizures: Bruce, with a big red and blue Grateful Dead logo knitted into his sweater, who always gave me a big welcome at the corner, is gone. Also passed away are Loki who had one leg, Troll, Greg at the drum circle, and Stumbles and Half-Pint, the tiny woman I wrote about when she got a new set of clothes and gear (in "Love Without Limits.")

Linda told me about when she had let Half-Pint and her boyfriend Stumbles into her apartment to take a bath. She said they were absolutely ecstatic and kept asking if they could stay in the tub longer. She'd let them stay there as long as they wanted.

HOLDING ON

The kids say they miss the way it was. It's heartbreaking to dwell on all that's been lost, and we try not to. But there are still live shoots of the Movement on our special corner and all around. Cool people still gather there and talk about wonderful things, even under the bright lights and cameras that have been installed. Our ideals about peace are like a powerful plant, from which even a single cutting can produce countless offspring.

Even in this war zone there are many spots of color and light. I was glad to see that Dragon had set up an oil painting easel on the corner of Haight and Ashbury, right next to the curb where tourists could see as they went by on tour buses. This is the picture of us that I want the world to see. She was making beautiful landscapes while others made music with a guitar and a mandolin. The colorful characters that still remain in the neighborhood made the place come alive.

Shawn in beautiful tie-dye was there, who'd fixed my truck ignition for free. "Danger," looks the part with his many tattoos and wearing train-rider overalls, but I found him to be surprisingly gentle and a deep thinker. He said, "Marijuana makes me a better person."

A man named Micheas, his flat-brimmed black hat offsetting his very blue eyes and red beard, said he was on the bus with the Merry Pranksters as a baby. There's a picture of his mom holding him on the cover of a 1972 Grateful Dead album called Oxamaxomoa. When he was twenty-one, Micheas was interviewed in front of Buckingham Palace, and he made the London Times and the BBC.

Across the street on the Haight-Ashbury corner next to Ben and Jerry's, T-shirt Mike sells beautiful t-shirts made with pastel spray paints, using crocheted doilies as stencils. The sight of his colorful t-shirts laid out on the sidewalk is uplifting. People stop to talk to him and admire his art. He tries his best to brighten their day, even if they don't buy anything. His beautiful friend Jessica, a street artist, painted this book's front cover.

Tank and his lovely and intelligent girlfriend Rayvan stood in our old spot where we had the demonstration against the No Sit and Lie Law, next to the grill of a closed business. They looked like the personification of freedom. He said, "I like to make people happy, make people smile. That makes me happy."

Lone Wolf and his partner of ten years, Tinkerbell, really like this book. When I walked up to them, she was actually hugging it. Lone Wolf, his Irish curls framing his cap adorned with colorful patches, spoke eloquently while petting his dog named Mamosa. "He's on YouTube under "Bum's Perspective." He said, "We're all doing the same thing. We all want to be loved, to be seen, to be heard, and we don't know how. Everyone's trying to be friends with everybody."

The kids told me that I should get a dog and a tattoo.

CONNECTION WITH GOD

A radiant woman named Goku played a Japanese flute called an ocarina, next to her caramel-colored dog named Goham. She said, "True knowledge is knowing you know nothing." She exclaimed, "People here are like real brothers and sisters!"

Wendy Whimsey showed up briefly, not in costume but in the disguise of ordinary clothes to shield her from attacks from whatever's trying to chase her away. She said, "When people are mean to me it's a challenge for me to be my best self."

At what used to be the Horseshoe, the elevated planter where people used to sit or lean is gone, where evangelists set up microphones and gave away pizza. Now there's a flat surface with a flat planter with desert plants, all lined with the hated black pillars and chains and in view of the despised cameras. An inscription of a quote by one of the park's founders, Andrew Jackson Downing, reads, "Plant spacious parks in your cities and loose their gates as wide as the morning to the whole people." I guess the proponents of hostile architecture didn't read that part. Hightower wrote on the new hexagonal tiles of the pavement in pink and white chalk: "Try to be a rainbow in someone's cloud."

At the drum circle I met Pineapple  and his two friends, who were on their way to Mount Shasta for a giant drum circle and to hear a friend's band called "Medicine Dogs." They were very excited about this book. Pineapple said, "I'm constantly trying to maintain my presence in the now, trying to honor the moment because that's my connection with God." At the corner ("the corner" always means Haight and Ashbury under the clock) Adon said, "We can do anything with nothing because we've had to do so much with so little."

A dynamic and intelligent woman named Ashel, a Rainbow Elder though young, sits on our corner almost day and night, as if holding down the fort. A girl named Lor wrote in my notebook, "You can wipe this street clean, you can get rid of everyone, paint it, change it, bulldoze it, but YOU WILL NEVER KILL THE LOVE AND HOPE OF THIS PLACE!"

WE'RE STILL HERE!

I sat with some people near the stairway at Buena Vista, on a ledge next to the sidewalk to avoid the wet grass and the NO LOITERING sign. Matt said, "I just want to be Everyman." He was carefully reading a book called "AMERICA." He said he wanted to start a blog called "Miracles, Mysteries and Mayhem, Stories from the Road." A guy with a cool felt hat with a feather in it said God had talked to him. A young man named Hermes said that he chose to take control of his mind so other men wouldn't take control of it.

A wealthy-looking man arrived in a nice car and said he had something for us. He brought out TEN PIZZAS, three cases of twenty-four beers each, and four boxes of a dozen soft drinks each. He said that his wife had died recently, and he was upset that everyone at his house was arguing, so he'd come here. He stayed and visited with us, and he gave and got a lot of love. By the time he left he was all smiles.

Haight Street is a special place where people gather not just because they're homeless but because it means something. Here I've seen Heaven happen, on the bulldozed ground of Golden Gate Park, on the violated rainbow stairs, on these old sidewalks.

Hippies are like the kind of plants that can break concrete so they can grow. Their spiritual force is like the roots of hardy life forms that can search out the tiniest crack in the hard surfaces man makes, and still find nourishment and life in the earth below. Heaven too, mankind's dream of a world without war and injustice, is something that won't be denied once it gets started. Maybe that's why the Beast has to work so hard to keep it from gaining a foothold.

Some of us here are trying to give Heaven a foothold, here in the hippie capital of the world. This is where the Way of Peace, that can save planets from economic violence, was so deeply embraced by so many from everywhere. That's why Bulldog returned, and he tells me he wore the blue tie-dyed hat again the other night at a concert. That's why I like to wear the brightest tie dyes I can find. That's why, when the double-decker tour buses go by, I like to wave my rainbow-ribboned tambourine at tourists and yell, "WE'RE STILL HERE!"

PEACE DRUMS

People have heard God speaking in the clouds,

    or in the rushing wind, or in bells.

I hear the same thing in the drums, the drums of all the nations together,

    struck with such power by the Pacifists.

Eyes closed and long hair waving free,

    the drummers seem transported on idealist dreams.

Their hopes fixed inwardly on the great world of the sublime,

    they reach for Heaven on Earth.

God says so much in the mighty pounding of the drums,
> which shakes the ground. What a great force
the hopes and dreams of those who wear the tie-dyed cloth,
> who lift the peace banners so high.
Isn't it they who represent some of the best man has achieved?
> Aren't their beliefs of brotherhood exactly those that Jesus preached?
"Brother" and "Sister" are the names we know each other by in Paradise,
> not by the titles and the ranks of the Machine.

The strong hands of the drummers never tire,
> pounding out the heartbeat of a great people.
The sound of swords turned into plowshares is their happy song.
> Gone are the slaughter and destruction when Christ in us is born.
Ages of ignorance and lies are soon dispelled
> when the Holy Word of "Love" is formed.
These people don't believe in war,
> and want to put the Golden Rule to strong political effect.

"Respect" is the sole dogma to which they cleave,
> and the co-operation of civilized folks with common sense.
Christ's Paradise is not so far when hearts embrace a love for all,
> and thoughts of hope and healing on the Earth.

Built to Last

Treating others the way they'd like to be treated

    is the litmus test of their religion, which has no walls

                      and doesn't fit in books.

God tells me in the drums that their gentle ways

    can move mountains of greed and hate,

                trying at last what Jesus really said.

They are the cornerstone which the builders cast off

    and what is written in their hearts

                is greater than the brute force of the world.

"...and they shall beat their swords into plowshares, and their spears into pruning hooks, nation shall not lift up a sword against nation, neither shall they learn war any more. But they shall sit every man under his vine and under his fig tree, and none shall make them afraid, for the mouth of the Lord of hosts hath spoken it."

                                                        Micah 4:3-4

LET'S TAKE ONE STEP TOGETHER: At the giant Rainbow Gatherings in the wilderness people yell "WE LOVE YOU!" repeatedly on one side of the camp and others answer back, "WE LOVE YOU TOO!" Let's do the same thing out our windows at sunset on Saturdays, so that the Voice of the People can be heard! We could also play drums for half an hour at sunset on Saturdays at a window. Visit with or meet neighbors! WE NEED ALL OF US! (right + left)

Poems may be reprinted and shared by homeless for donations they can keep.
TELL TEN TO TELL TEN TO VOTE DEMOCRAT!   REGISTER 100 DEMOCRATS!
(https://www.usa.gov/register-to-vote) (vote.gov) (rockthevote.org)
Democrats against forced mandates and other oppressive liability laws.
BILL OF RIGHTS   GOLDEN RULE   peacedrums.org   UNITE!

Democrat

WE WILL SURVIVE!

Though nobody has gotten sick that I know of, Covid restrictions have touched Haight Street in a big way. We can't see each other's smiles behind those masks. The blocks of closed shops behind black metal grates, the almost total absence of people, make the place so empty with the trees gone. Some of the shops might not come back. The ancient Magnolia pub has been gutted, with beige vinyl and bright lights.

Quite a few street kids are still here, many of them enjoying an unexpected bonus. The lot of the torn-down McDonald's has been turned into a sanctioned campground for homeless youth to shelter in place, with porta-potties and showers. Most of the Haight Street nomads are there, enjoying a respite from their usual fight for survival.

It has a high chain link fence all around it draped with black cloth, and a gate with a guard who won't let you in unless you live there. Others of the house-free have been allowed to pitch tents on side streets to shelter in place. Some are hesitant to stay in the enclosed compound because fences make them nervous. One boy said he's not going in there without bolt cutters.

Some people who chose not to go in there are camped on the Masonic side of Love on Haight, on top of the remaining red hearts. They have tents and furniture and everything. I met Shaggy and Panic and two dogs named Frenchie and Sadie. Shaggy made me feel welcome in their sidewalk camp, offering me the best chair.

The plywood barricading the windows of Love on Haight is spray painted, "WE WILL SURVIVE!"

THE PEACE SIGN

Just below Hippie Hill, near the drum circle, there's a giant peace sign painted on the pavement. Over ten feet across, they say it's been there since the Summer of Love. It doesn't get washed away like the pastel chalk drawings people leave there. Sometimes it gets faded and worn from so many feet walking on it on the way to the drum circle. Then in the dead of night various unknown persons come and make it new again. Painting on pavements can be prosecuted as a felony.

One day not very long ago on my way to the drum circle, I saw with horror that the peace sign was completely gone. The park service had either blasted it with water cannons like at the Rainbow Stairs, or painted over it with grey paint exactly matching the pavement. I couldn't tell which. At the drum circle I shouted to the people gathered on Hippie Hill, **"THEY CAN ERASE THE PEACE SIGN BUT THEY CAN'T ERASE US!"**

The following week a new, vibrant peace sign appeared. It had brilliant pink hearts in a ring all around the whole thing, each as big as the lost sidewalk hearts on Haight Street, bordered with fluorescent turquoise and yellow swirls. It was gorgeous. The following week it too was gone. There was a rumor that the employee commissioned with painting over the peace sign had expressed distress at having to do it. Officials tried to have it done early in the morning, hoping no-one would see.

Then someone painted another peace sign, smaller than the old one, and it was removed. Then for two weekends I actually drew the giant peace sign myself with some thick pieces of chalk. At my age it was hard to bend down all that time, trying to etch out a double line of the huge circle, over ten feet in diameter. The result had wobbly places and one of the lines of the "Arms Down" part was off-center, but I felt that it made a statement. The second weekend, two young passerby helped me.

Out on Haight Street, a Christ-like young man named Lee sails and swerves around gracefully on a skateboard, in brilliant tie-dyes from head to toe. He bought chalk and has been drawing lots of big hearts on the sidewalk, lining blocks on both sides. Passerby admire his work. Of course, both of our efforts won't last long. The chalk will be quickly worn away by so many people walking by in both places. But he just keeps drawing more and more hearts, dozens of them, all up and down Haight Street. Unknown persons supply him with chalk.

Last weekend the drum circle was in its power. About thirty drums worked together, making a kind of spiritual vortex of sound. Several didgeridoos made their ancient, echoing chants. An accordion added another timeless dimension. A drumstick clanging on a cowbell sounded like humanity's chains being broken on an anvil. The trees swayed in an evening wind, seeming to move to the rhythm of the drums.

The drums made a thundering heartbeat sound as I walked toward the big peace sign and saw with delight that it had again been repainted and looked magnificent. Interlocked purple and green swirls in different shades went around the circle, which was the full ten feet across, not small like the previous one that had been painted over. A painted white band under the colors made the big peace symbol seem to glow. It was more beautiful than ever before. It made me hope that the high concepts so many of us believe in can also be fresh and new.

LIST OF NAMES

Jimi Hendrix Red House   2

Haight Street Bazaar   9

Ducky   14, 59, 14

The Dog Whisperer   17

Avatar   19

Holiday Chris   19

Change   19, 93

Static (dog)   20

Empty   20

Wendy Whimsey   23, 24, 110, 244, 326, 375, 387

the hattery   23, 76, 344, 375

Love on Haight   22, 27, 77, 161, 290, 296, 301, 375, 392

Dr. Dave (dog)   22, 300

Doctor David Smith   22, 300

Haight-Ashbury Free Clinic   22, 299, 375

Sunny Powers   22, 161, 290

The Queen of Haight Street   22

Taking It to the Streets   22, 375

Rainbow   34, 38, 40, 154, 157, 207, 243, 325

Jubah   34, 207

Mr. Natural   35, 39

Bruce   37

Sacred Grounds Coffee House   40

Scott   40, 76, 184, 270, 292, 301, 305, 310, 311, 328, 345, 375

Dan in wheelchair   41

Darian and Adrian   42

Stella (dog)   61

Pan   62

Claire   63

Barney   63

John   63

Mud Angel   64

Apple   65

Apple Juice   66

Tramp (dog)   66

Orange   75, 120, 243, 307, 343, 345, 352

Yellow   74, 120

Grey   75, 120

Pink   74, 120

Blue (dog)   75, 120

Tibetan Gift Corner   2, 74, 121, 161

Cheola   74, 161

Decades of Fashion   76, 161

Cicely Hansen   76, 161

Distractions 76, 332

Jim Siegel 76

Michael Collins Irish Bar 77, 192, 327, 375

Victorian Punch House 77, 327

Magnolia Brewing Co. 78, 327, 375, 392

Bear 79, 301, 302, 319

Bushwacker (Cody) 80

Larken Rose 80

Kamrin 81

Soul Saver 86

God Finder 86

Old School 92

Mellow 93

Flag 99

Slinky 100, 192

Lasagna (dog) 105

Pikachu (dog) 15

Sonic (Adam) 107

Button (dog) 107

Rocky Raccoon 108

Ariel 108

Tater Tot 109

Pretty Tony 112, 201, 218, 264, 288

Aaron (4/20) 111

Aaron 112

Maybe (dog) 113

Prophet 118

Cherry 119

Side Show 119

Moonbeam 120

Gypsy Rose 126

Captain 138

Ground Squirrel 139

Love of Ganesha 2, 29, 146, 161, 326, 336

Noot 146, 161

Diamond Dave 35, 154, 156, 158, 162, 163, 207

Chris 154

Mutiny Radio 154, 156, 159, 161, 163, 207, 277

The Common Thread Collective 156, 159, 277

Coffee to the People 160, 322, 366

Dumpster 160

Jessy Kate Schlingler 161, 195

The Red Victorian 161, 194, 375

Amal 161, 193, 239, 325

Amal's Deli 161, 193, 239, 246, 350

Linda Kelly 161, 164, 352, 354, 384

"Deadheads" 161

The Haight Street Voice 161, 164, 352, 354, 384

396

Stanley Mouse 161

Mona Lisa 35, 161, 164, 166

Peace in the Park 161, 164

Global Val 35, 161, 164

Wavy Gravy 162

Barbara 163

Ryan 170, 311

Destany 173

ABlessin 173

ChaChaCha 174, 209

Shanti Sena 175, 376

Theo 176

Boogie (dog) 176

Dire Wolf 177

Ruby Lips 177

Richard the Third 178

Lisa 178

Mario 178

Justin 179

Dragon 179, 312, 344, 374, 377, 385

Daphne (dog) 180

Bear (dog) 180

Woody 183

Random 185

Earthsong (store) 191

Green Eyes 191

Jeryies 193

Sami Sunchild 195

Olive 195

David 195

Dinosaur (Trevor) 196

Shawna Lou 197, 287

Parking Lot 199, 200, 217

Shnookums Wookums (dog) 199

Lena 200, 264

Trey 205

Cosmo 205

Manfred 206, 370

Dago (Leather Man) 208, 242

Red 209

Kitty (dog) 210

Standing Rock Demos 156, 212

Cosmic Charlie 212, 301

The Ice Cream Kid (Tom) 215, 288

Buck Wild 215

Abbi 217

Kicking Raven (Atreyu) 220

Ashley 221, 223

Nightmare (dog) 224

Richie 224

Amber 224

Daydream (dog) 224

Elijah 230

Joshua 230

Dirtweasel 233

Pixie   233

Gus's Market   234, 378

Clutch   234

Matthew   239

Ron Greco   239

Bird   239

Mr. Brandy   239, 305

BamBam   240, 303, 307, 312

Titus (dog)   241, 312

Cave Man   241, 312

Davy Jones   242

Ginger (dog)   243

Panda   243

Scotty Don't   243

Dallas   245

Sugary (dog)   245

Josh   243

Balto (dog)   243

Chance   245, 294

The Burger Urge   3, 245, 312, 375

Kat   254

Swags   264

Toshi   264

Elecia   267, 270

The Stealie Cops   269

Al   269

Tia   271

Art Kunkin   272, 273

Free Press   272, 274

Sunny   272

Deborah   272

Beatnik Lounge   272

Mikey   272

Abbie   272

Danielle   272

Dee   273

Institute of Mental Physics   274

Brie   279

Uncle Justin   287

Shortstack (dog)   290

Bulldog   290, 306, 308, 316, 344, 345, 354, 374, 389

Sweet Pea   293

Frankie   295, 301

Haigh Ashbury Music Center   300, 373, 375, 379

Hightower (Lacie)   301, 304, 306, 387

Sassy   304

Salvia   304

Bubble Man   304, 377

Half Pint   304, 385

Stumbles   304, 385

Dallas   305

Club Deluxe   305, 310

Kage   307, 345

Izzy   307, 335

bike shop   317

Dylan   324, 346

The Milk Bar   327
Simber   328
Pipe Dreams   332, 378, 384
Cassie   332, 378
Josh   332, 378
Jack Herer   339
Chris Conrad   339
Chelsea   344, 356, 378
Hayden   344, 356, 378
DeWitt   349
Ferox   349
Rich   351
Tad   352, 354, 356, 358
Skywalker   356
Colby   364
Crow   366
Mitch   367

Massoud   373
Rasputin Records   373
Stella   373
Sister Nikki   373
Jimmy Flowers   377
John   377
Johnathan   378, 384
Grey   378
Matt (Everyman)   378, 380, 388
Kerry   378
Justin   378
Matthew   378
Sophia   379
Shawn   386
Danger   386
Micheas   386
T-Shirt Mike   386
Jessica   386

Tank   386
Rayvan   386
Mamosa   386
Lone Wolf   386
Tinkerbell   386
Goku   387
Goham (dog)   387
Pineapple   387
Medicine Dogs   387
Adon   388
Ashel   388
Lor   388
Hermes   388
Bruce (from the corner)   385
Shaggy   392
Panic   392
Frenchie (dog)   392
Sadie (dog)   392
Lee   393

Joan Rivard dancing at the drum circle at Hippie Hill in Golden Gate Park, from the San Francisco publication "Bay Area Voices for the Decriminalization of Cannabis"

Dancing on Haight Street

ABOUT THE AUTHOR

In brilliant tie-dyes Joan Rivard can often be found on famous Haight Street in San Francisco, often joining street musicians with her tambourine. She waves it at the tour buses and shouts, "WE'RE STILL HERE!" She believes that the mass movement we call "the Sixties" is still very much alive, and that its Way of Peace is the closest thing to what Jesus taught.

She finds the sublime in ordinary people, particularly the young "Travelers" who make pilgrimages to that historic place. She stayed among the "house-free," gathering their stories and insights.

Joan turning a giant upside-down American flag right-side-up at a Rainbow Gathering

    She has been to ten Rainbow Gatherings, yearly peace events in different states in the wilderness July 1-7. There are no leaders, it costs no money, and twenty thousand people sit down to eat together. She thinks the spiritual power felt there and everywhere shows that the country's solutions are found in the Golden Rule and the Bill of Rights. The poetry she includes about governments and religions is a roller coaster ride.

    A genuine heretic, she shows that Jesus didn't teach that people are cursed or born in sin, and that the Apostle Paul taught the opposite of what the Bible says Jesus said. Her book, The Liberal's Bible Guide: God's Message to Treehuggers, (480 pgs.) is an easy tool for anyone who wants to win arguments with those telling them they're cursed sinners.

Joan at her show at Mutiny Radio

With Stanley Mouse, who designed Grateful Dead logo

With Diamond Dave Whitaker, who gave Bob Dylan his first joint

She was an activist in the early days of the effort to legalize marijuana, working with Jack Herer and Chris Conrad. She helped start the big hemp rallies at the Los Angeles Federal Building, has attended dozens of environmental and anti-war demonstrations, and has helped put on free rock concerts and other events. She earned degrees in Journalism, Anthropology, and Criminal Justice.

Joan at L.A. Hemp Rally   at an anti-war demonstration   visiting the Great Peace March

She worked at the famous Los Angeles Free Press with founder and 60's icon Art Kunkin. She has sent her dynamic political poetry to legislators in what she calls "political art." In February 2003 her writing and activism swung a vote that passed a Los Angeles City Council resolution to oppose the Iraq war.

During the Sixties and Seventies, she lived in cabins in Alaska and also travelled throughout Europe and the U.S.

The Author   Author's Cabin in 1969   Joan was part of the swap meet community in Southern California for 23 years.

Recently, she has been privileged to be a part of the historic drum circle in Golden Gate Park in San Francisco, located in the same meadow that hosted the Summer of Love.   Contact: joanrivard1776@gmail.com

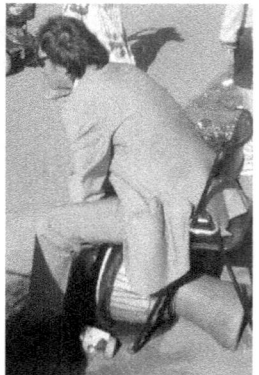

Linda Kelly, Dr. David Smith, Sunny Powers, and author

Newlyweds

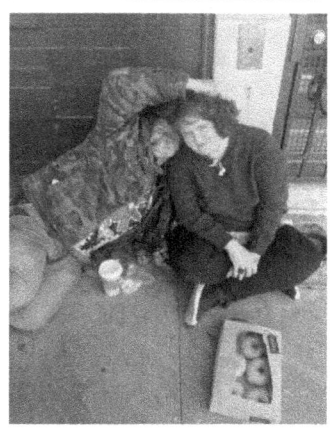

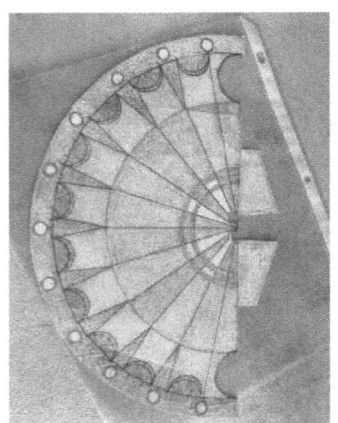

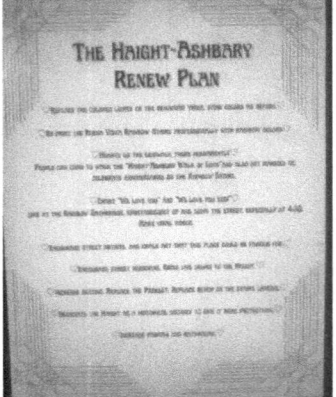

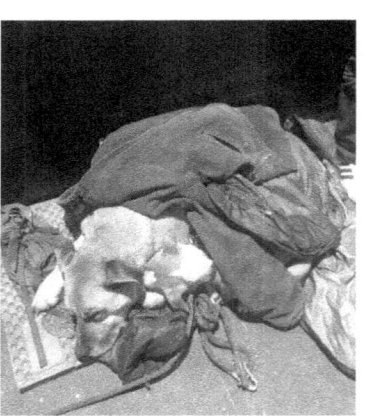

www.ingramcontent.com/pod-product-compliance
Lightning Source LLC
Chambersburg PA
CBHW081213170426
43198CB00017B/2606